Football FANATIC

FANATIC

A RECORD-BREAKING JOURNEY THROUGH ENGLISH FOOTBALL
Ken Ferris

TWO HEADS
PUBLISHING

First published in 1995
by Two Heads Publishing
London

ISBN 1 897850 66 2

Cover design by Lance Bellers
Cover photograph from Football Archive
Printed and bound by Caldra House, Sussex

For my father, Ken, and my son, Lyle

ACKNOWLEDGEMENTS

I thought it was all over – it is now. After being on the pitch at more League grounds than most players, I must admit I never realised how much time and effort was involved in writing a travelogue. My love of football kept me going on those long journeys and sustained me through the 0-0 draws that inevitably cropped up from time to time among 93 League matches. But I could always fall back on the many people who gave me encouragement when I was flagging, some of whom accompanied me to a game here and there. I would like to take this opportunity to thank them all.

There are four very special people who backed me all the way on my mad journey across the country. My girlfriend Nicky, my son Lyle and my parents, Ken and Sadie. I am grateful to: Lyle and Nicky for keeping me company at the Rochdales and Grimsbys as well as the Liverpools and Evertons; my dad who was always there to push me along when I was drowning in a sea of Premier and Endsleigh League fixtures and who worked out how many miles my journeys took, how many goals were scored and how many people watched all the games I saw; my mum who also helped to keep me going and patiently transcribed hours of taped reports and interviews.

Another group of people who supported my efforts (their football teams are in brackets) were members of the JAG (James Alexander Gordon) Society at Reuters, who also helped to raise money for charity by sponsoring my record attempt. Their line-up includes: Iain Rodger (Chelsea), Graham Jones (Manchester City), Steve Meadows (Crystal Palace), Simon Wright (Arsenal), Rob Simpson and Dave Pape (Newcastle), Tony McCormack (Celtic) and his brother John (Arsenal), David Nowell (Notts County), and Dean Ratcliffe (Everton).

Others who supported my endeavour and also came to one or two fixtures were: my old pal at Reuters Simon Denyer, now sadly missed in London but taking the Big Apple by storm (Portsmouth); his girlfriend

Sarah (Pompey too, I suppose); Dave Lewis (Barnet, sort of); Gareth Jones (Manchester City); Don Frier (Sunderland); and Richard Cheal (Norwich City). As you can see, I mostly travelled alone.

My thanks also go out to Douglas Cheal (also Norwich), who thought my journey was fascinating, partly because he's as eccentric as I am; and to his wife, Pauline, who probably thought I was completely mad but never said so. Thank you for that Pauline. Lou , Richie and Alfie also played their part, though I'm not exactly sure what it was!

Among those who provided information for the book I'd like to thank Alan Raybould and his mum Dorothy for their background on West Bromwich Albion; and Neil Winton for information about Brighton's latest ground sharing plans.

Mike Rich at Endsleigh supported my efforts all the way and probably opened more than a few doors with his backing for my record attempt. I hope it was worth it Mike. A special mention should also go to Vic Curtis (Arsenal) who always asked me how my record attempt was shaping up and showed a keen interest in my travels. Thanks Vic.

My colleagues on Reuters Financial Television were often bemused, and sometimes amazed, at the lengths I had to go to to visit 93 League grounds whilst working full-time. They are: Jon Engel, Mark Jones, Mike Lawrence, Steve Clarke, Ed Brunetti, Clar Ni-Chonghaile, Sofy Fearnley-Whittingstall and Gwen Dunne.

I couldn't blow the final whistle without mentioning: Dave Hefford, Barry Hughes and Paul Kemp – lifelong friends and still soccer mad even though they support West Ham; John Buckley, ditto, though he supports Manchester United and therefore knows what success is all about; the entire Ludlows football team from the Essex Independent Sunday League who badly missed my silky skills on Sunday mornings for a whole season; and finally, Johnny Allen, the manager, who had a hand, or should I say foot, in breaking my toe so that I did miss a whole season and thus had enough time to reach all 93 grounds. Thanks John.

All 93 League clubs welcomed me with open arms and gave me invaluable help throughout the season.

And there you have it; a group of individuals who in one way or another influenced my successful attempt to join the ranks of the immortal (or should that be insane) in The Guinness Book of Records. By the way, in case he thinks I've forgotten, I should also mention Brian Martin, the genial Irishman who is Jack Charlton's biggest fan!

INTRODUCTION

They said it was either a crazy idea or a brilliant idea. I guess most thought it was crazy but there were a few football fanatics who had sympathy with my eccentricity.

It first struck me during a series of trips I made to Stafford in north west England to visit a friend. As the train passed Wolverhampton and Birmingham, grounds you can see from the British Rail line, the first inklings of the idea began to take hold.

I can't remember exactly when I made my mind up to do it, but once I had decided there was no going back. I couldn't get it out of my head. I pondered the practicalities of doing it; I assessed the time and effort involved; I turned it over again and again in my mind rocking to and fro between what a stupid idea it was and what a great idea.

My weekends in the north west had also taken me past Stoke City's ground a number of times and within reach of Port Vale. I had already visited quite a few London grounds in my football supporting 'career' but my experience of away grounds was limited. (Away from White Hart Lane that is – so now you know I'm a Spurs fan. Above all, though, I'm a football fan and this book is for all fans and covers most clubs no matter how small.)

Then the idea grew. What would it be like to visit all the FA Premier and Football League grounds? What if I did that and wrote a book about my experiences, a sort of travelogue. But, wait a minute, hadn't I seen an entry in The Guinness Book of Records listing a supporter who'd visited all the League grounds in the fastest time. What about if I tried to break that record?

I checked an old copy of the Records book and found an entry for "Most peripatetic football supporters". Once I'd worked out how to say the word (not worth attempting if you're drunk!) I decided to look it up. The Collins dictionary defines it as "itinerant, walking, travelling about". The last definition was probably the most fitting for the Guinness entry since even the most ardent supporter would struggle walking to 92 League grounds (and Berwick Rangers of which more later).

The entry I found from the 1983 Records book listed a Michael Jones and Bob Wilson of Shrewsbury as having visited all 92 League grounds (and Berwick Rangers) in 264 days between 10 August 1968 and 30 April 1969. How come the record had stood for so long? Was nobody crazy enough to break it?

Next I looked up the most recent record. Sure enough, the latest edition showed a change. The new record holder was a guy called Edward Wood of Quarndon, Derby who had been everywhere from Arsenal to York in 243 days between 17 August 1991 and 15 April 1992. On four occasions he watched two matches in a day.

Could it be beaten? A quick back-of-the-envelope calculation told me that I would have to see three games a week for 25 weeks of the season and two games a week for the other nine weeks. A pretty tall order when you're working fulltime.

Again I turned the idea over in my mind. Some days I was convinced it was madness. Other days I felt I could do it. But throughout my assessment of the wisdom of attempting such a daunting project I knew it would be fun (and it was, most of the time).

In May and June 1993 I had travelled to see England play away in Poland and Norway during the World Cup qualifying rounds. The qualifiers eventually led to the showdown with Holland in Amsterdam and a 2-0 defeat which would see England blow their chance of going to America for USA '94 for a tournament Pete Davies called "The Greatest Show on Earth" in his book *All Played Out* about Italia '90. It was the first time I'd seen England away from Wembley but it whetted my appetite to become peripatetic.

I wanted to find out more about the previous record holders. Were they mad? Had their wife and kids walked out, leaving them with a burning desire to fulfil a mad ambition by default? Maybe they were poor lonely souls with nothing else to do in their lives but wander around the country from ground to ground seeking a modicum of fame, no matter how small, in what was otherwise an empty existence.

The people I told about my plans reacted in one of three ways: either it was a fantastic challenge (a few); downright stupid (some); or very sad (most). I wasn't the only fanatic though. Phil Ambler didn't attempt to break the record, but he did visit all 92 League grounds (he didn't go to Berwick Rangers but Darlington, by then out of the league, and Macclesfield, then the temporary home of Chester City, were in there to compensate).

Perhaps we needed therapy for the treatment of football fanatics. A specialised profession. "Sit down on the couch. How long have you been obsessed with football? Why do you feel it necessary to fill your life playing, watching or thinking about football?. What do you mean you considered suicide when your wife cancelled your subscription to Sky Sports?" The questions would be endless. The logic hard to justify.

I first came across Phil in a W.H. Smith sports books section. There on the shelf was a tome which immediately caught my eye: "Full colour views of the Football League Grounds. Photography by Phil Ambler." Inside the front cover it said, "After a lifelong obsession to see all 92 clubs in the Football League a dream has come true. Taking just over a year and using my holidays I managed to visit all the clubs, actually taking 16 days to do so plus travelling 6,000 miles."

That people like Phil Ambler existed intrigued me. Why would anyone travel 6,000 miles and spend all their annual holiday taking pictures of empty football stadiums? To pursue my interest I contacted the Ninety-Two Club.

Based in Whitchurch, Bristol, the club's members are people who have visited all 92 League grounds during their lifetime. It even has honorary members. The most famous are Alan Durban, who played for Cardiff, Derby and Shrewsbury, and Derby manager Jim Smith, former boss at Colchester, Blackburn, Birmingham, Oxford and Queen's Park Rangers. Another honorary member is the late Eric Northover, a Northampton director. To complete the list of personalities among the elite ranks of the Ninety-Two club are Gilbert Napthine (referee), Alan Smith (Physiotherapist) and Hal Mason (match programme editor).

By the end of my journey I hoped to have joined them and to have secured my place in history with an entry in The Guinness Book of Records. Along the way I discovered why former Soviet President Mikhail Gorbachov supports Wigan; how Huddersfield built the most futuristic stadium in Britain; whether Crewe's fans thought David Platt would become England captain; why Everton won the championship playing at Anfield; what Ken Bates thinks wealthy young managers should do with their money; the names of the two most powerful women in British soccer; and how Paul Gascoigne perfected his famous free-kick technique in his early days at Newcastle.

I also crossed the paths of players, managers and chairmen, past and present, including Denis Law, Frank McLintock, Stan Bowles, Sammy Lee, John Beck, John Jackson, Matt Le Tissier, Alan Ball, Alan Shearer, Tim Flowers, Chris Sutton, Joey Jones, Bruce Grobbelaar, Jimmy Neighbour, Peter Taylor, Mick McCarthy, Terry McDermott, Pavel Srnicek, Barry Fry, Ray Clemence, Norman Hunter, Trevor Brooking, Graham Taylor, Alan Mullery, Paul Allen, Kerry Dixon, John Sillett,

Alan Sugar, Mark Chamberlain, Frank Lampard, Harry Redknapp, Martin Allen, Don Hutchison, Joe Royle, Lou Macari, David Dein, Charlie George, Martin Peters, Les Sealey, Andy Townsend, Ronnie Whelan, Archie Gemmill, John McGovern, Jason McAteer, Alan Stubbs, Bernie Slaven, Gary Bennett, Phil Gray and Andy Sussex.

This book is certainly about football. But it's more than that. It's a personal account of what it's like to live and breath football for a season.

EARTH TO KNIGHTON
Carlisle United v Exeter City - Brunton Park
Saturday 10 September 1994

Ken Bates sat back in the departure lounge at London's Heathrow Airport looking relaxed and self assured. Chelsea's larger-than-life chairman, with his shock of white hair, had good reason to be pleased with life. His team were fifth in the Premiership after their best start for years - three wins in a row. Today they'd face their toughest test so far away to Newcastle. United, with the inspirational Kevin Keegan at the helm, were also unbeaten and heading for their best start since 1908.

As we waited to be called for our flight Bates' attention was drawn to an interview in the Daily Mirror with Chelsea manager Glenn Hoddle. The former Spurs and Monaco star claimed that a new breed of "rich kid" managers was driving the fear factor out of English football. "There are a new generation of financially independent young managers who don't have to live with the pressures of fear or failure and the negative football which that produces," said Hoddle. Bates smiled: "If they're that financially independent they should become chairmen and use their own money to buy players."

As we boarded the bus which would take us the short distance across the tarmac to the early morning British Airways flight to Newcastle I asked Bates to forecast the result of the match at St James's Park. "It's going to be tough up there," he said with a rueful expression. He had reason to be concerned.

The reason for his visit to Newcastle was clear. As for me, it was the first stop on a longer journey. I was headed for Brunton Park, home of Carlisle United and the remotest ground in the country. A local derby here was a visit from Newcastle 58 miles to the east. I'd decided that the best time to visit this outpost of league football was in the late summer, before the winter set in. Besides it was close enough for me to see the Middlesbrough Sunderland match at Ayresome Park the next day.

The train to Carlisle, the county town of Cumbria and its largest city, passed through breathtaking scenery. As I settled back to enjoy picture postcard views of rolling hills, fields enclosed by stone walls and sparkling rivers I got my first glimpse of a real Carlisle supporter at a place called Haltwhistle, just over halfway from Newcastle. Surprisingly, he was the only fan on the train.

The journey to Carlisle took longer than I expected. Making connections between the plane and the trains delayed my arrival. Luckily, my bed & breakfast was en route to Brunton Park. I followed the Carlisle fans walking to the match, stopping briefly to drop off my heavy bag. Carlisle is so close to the Scottish border that there was once speculation United would join the Scottish League, like Berwick Rangers who play in the Scottish Second Division even though their ground is in England.

Carlisle's links with Scotland crop up throughout its history. It's an ancient border fortress with a chequered past. The town was originally a Celtic settlement before becoming Roman during the building of Hadrian's Wall. The struggle with the Scots went on over centuries. In 1315 Robert the Bruce was repelled and Bonnie Prince Charlie's troops held the town for a few months before surrendering to the Duke of Cumberland. Today it's the region's centre for trade and commerce and, despite the history, Carlisle are still in the English Football League. The other Cumbrian teams with a League history, Barrow and Workington, both failed to secure re-election in the 1970's leaving Carlisle to fly the county flag alone.

I arrived at the main gates which said "Welcome to Carlisle United" and looked around the Main Stand. Simon Inglis in The Football Grounds of Great Britain was impressed when he visited the ground. "At the back of the Main Stand is an excellent new entrance hall, tastefully designed in almost high-tec decor, with rubberized floors, tinted glass and potted plants; a welcome and encouraging relief from all those football ground entrances decked in formica, garish carpets and simulated wood."

I approached the doorman, who looked like a redeployed bouncer, and asked if I could take a look at the club's new restaurant, Foxy's. The Cumberland fox, Carlisle's crest, had been discreetly used as a themed motif throughout the trendy eating spot. It had to be an improvement on the 'Brunton pasty' I'd picked up outside the ground before the match. "If you keep your match ticket you can come out for another one of those at half-time," said the elderly gateman. "Mind you, you'll have to make an appointment at the doctor's afterwards."

The restaurant is one of Carlisle's latest innovations. All chrome and gold plate on the outside, Edwardian splendour on the inside. The Cumberland Sausage fanzine described the place as "airy, spacious, bright, smelling of pine and monogrammed deep-pile carpets and high-backed padded chairs around polished tables, looking through the plate glass at the back of balding farmers in the paddock."

The Maitre de, dressed in pristine white suit with black bow-tie, told me business had been brisk since the place opened on the night of Mervyn Day's testimonial against Leeds before a crowd of about 8,000.

12

The former West Ham, Orient and Leeds goalkeeper had been forced to retire with a knee injury and was now assistant to Mick Wadsworth, Carlisle's Director of Coaching. "Does the level of business in the restaurant reflect the team's performance," I asked. "Probably," replied the Maitre de.

Carlisle's chairman Michael Knighton would have been interested to hear of a possible connection. "People don't stop eating good food because the team is losing," according to Knighton. The theory had yet to be put to the test since Carlisle were top of the Third Division after three wins and a draw.

Star of the show was striker David Reeves, the club's record buy and a snip at £121,000 from Notts County. 'Reevesy' scored 11 goals in 36 games during his first season and there was a sense of anticipation that he'd be even better this term. Reeves had already been picked for the PFA team of the season and couldn't stop scoring goals. "I went to see him in a reserve match for County and after 15 minutes I said to our coach: "We must have him no matter what it costs," said Knighton. "I did the deal that night and soon we will have big clubs trying to get him off us. But he is staying put. He is a First Division striker who has matured late."

Not unlike his chairman. Remember him? The ball-juggler from Old Trafford with the dodgy moustache whose "modest" millions weren't enough to secure a future at Manchester United. Knighton promised to lead the Reds to a new era of prosperity on and off the field with talk of trophies in the boardroom and a £100 million company. "The extraordinary thing was that I said at my first press conference there I am not a wealthy man, I'm a modest millionaire."

Knighton's bid to buy Manchester United for £10 million ended with a High Court injunction after the close friends he'd invited to participate in his project failed to deliver. He says he left United after achieving everything he set out to do and that he helped to transform a declining club into the force they are today.

It's hard to believe now that United were ever up for sale, never mind at a knockdown price. As Knighton acknowledges, Ryan Giggs must be worth more than that on his own. But when United's Chief Executive Martin Edwards put the club on the market in 1989 buyers weren't exactly queuing up outside Old Trafford. When Knighton showed up United rushed into a contract sparking off a period of uncertainty and, ultimately, embarrassment for all concerned.

"It's easy to forget that United had had a few bad years, that attendances were down to 23,000 and that Edwards was coming in for a lot of criticism," said Knighton. "I can't take credit for what has happened since, but there is no question I was a catalyst. I had a blueprint in 1989, and everything on it has come about.

"Prior to 1989 the club was losing money, but profits (in 1994/95 were) £10.8 million and overall turnover £44 million. In all modesty, and I am a modest man, you did not have to be an economic genius to predict that. It was staring you in the face. It's much more of a financial risk coming here (to Carlisle), believe me. With United you couldn't fail." When asked about the club now he replies, "Manchester who? There is only one United – Carlisle United."

Knighton's involvement with Carlisle began when he bought a majority share in the club who were then rooted at the bottom of the Third Division. They'd already been languishing in the basement division for more seasons than they cared to remember. Then-manager Aidan Macaffery talked about his players becoming part-timers as the club lost £6,000 a week.

Enter Knighton. He made it clear he didn't intend to spend anything on players. "The club must grow within its means." That meant any new signings were free transfers. Knighton was firm in his conviction that he'd not be waving a cheque book around like Jack Walker. Some of the supporters were upset by his tight hold on the purse strings, but Knighton knew he had to put the club on a sound financial footing. "The fans want me to be a rich benefactor, but I haven't got the money." He had learned his lesson.

Knighton's approach worked and within a couple of seasons he'd turned things around. The club was back in profit and the surplus was used to buy Reeves. "I shall be eternally grateful the fans gave me the benefit of the doubt," says Knighton. Tony Smith of the Carlisle Evening News and Star summed up the town's feelings about the chairman. "Everyone here thinks Michael Knighton walks on water. Eccentric or not, you can't knock his achievement."

The girl behind the bar in the new sponsors lounge testified to the change in atmosphere at Brunton Park since Knighton took over. "The club was going nowhere a few years ago and support was dwindling, but since Mr Knighton came in everything has begun to improve." Foxy's restaurant was only one small part of Knighton's redevelopment plans. "We've just finished the new restaurant and corporate facilities and my priority now is to create one of the greatest football clubs in the country."

Knighton had recently been profiled in The Times for a series called The Power Players. Simon Barnes had his own theory on Knighton's character. "Knighton's life has been marked out by pain. Two events shaped his life in football: the first was a knee injury, which scuppered his aspirations towards a career as a professional footballer; the second was the (Manchester) United affair, a period of sustained public ridicule that ended, three years on, with his departure from Old Trafford.

"His life has been carved out of frustration, bitterness and disappointment, but Knighton lacks the taste for dwelling on these things. Instead, he is gifted, or cursed, with a kind of idiot optimism. You don't normally find this trait among men of finance, but it is something you see all the time among professional athletes. This is a belief, one held with marrow-deep sincerity, that ultimate victory will be theirs."

Knighton had a 10-year plan for Carlisle but had also said that if the right offer came along he would sell tomorrow. He's full of contradictions. "One day I will pay myself a gargantuan salary," said the man whose efforts at Brunton Park had so far been modestly rewarded. So what exactly was his master plan for Carlisle, the team he expected to emulate the other United as future winners of the Premier League.

On the back of the programme was an artist's impression of the new all-seater East Stand which the club planned to have finished by Christmas 1995. Knighton said it would house a museum of British football. "We've got some marvellous stuff for a museum, lots of people will want to see it." Rob Pearson of The Cumberland Sausage takes up the story. "So there we all were, making our merry way along Warwick Road, full of expectancy for the season ahead. A new season – a new start. Not only that but the enticing prospect of seeing the fruits of a summer of hard work toward the construction of our glorious 6,000 all-seater stand.

"I had seen a vision of its towering splendour in my dreams two nights earlier. A monstrous, beautiful construction scraping the Cumbrian skyline, serving as a monument to the legend that is Carlisle United Football Club. Barely able to negotiate the Paddock turnstile in eager anticipation of the sight that lay before me, I took my first steps on Brunton Park terrace for the new season to find... the Scratchin' Shed (Popular Side) still there with its bloody roof off. Congratulations all round to those involved with such a fantastic feat of engineering."

The roof was removed from the Popular Side, also known as the Scratching Shed or Scratchers, "before it fell down" according to Carlisle's Commercial Manager Martin Hudson. Basically, it was the cheapest way of making it safe. The plan though was to build a new East Stand to replace the Scratchers by the end of 1995.

It was expected to cost £1.5–2.0 million. So where would the money come from? The club would get about £1 million from the Football Trust - and the rest? Rising attendances had contributed more than £200,000 to revenue in 1993/94 and Knighton had high hopes for the future of Carlisle United Football Club. "I predict that within 10 years, we will be among the 10 wealthiest clubs in this country. We will be competing in Europe and will have one of the finest stadiums." Really? Or, as Simon Barnes put it in The Times, "Earth to Knighton: hello? Hello?"

Some of the supporters had sort of latched onto Knighton's dream. The fanzine So, Jack Ashurst, Where's My Shirt?" (a reference to a shirt promised to one of the fanzine editor's after a crucial match) was taking a light-hearted view of his dreams. "Michael Knighton's 10 Year Plan hasn't allowed for more than three (years) in the Third (Division), and (coach Mick) Wadsworth is well aware that the European Champions League won't wait."

The comments were clearly tongue-in-cheek. Knighton's, on the other hand, had to be taken at face value. "Two years ago only 1,500 people were coming here. Now our average is 6,000 and that figure is going to grow. We have plans for a new stadium and we have already started some work. And I believe we will fill it when we reach the First Division and then the Premiership".

Carlisle have had one or two star players over the years, including Peter Beardsley. Cumbrians' fan Roger Robson remembered Beardsley "with the ball stuck to his foot, whether in a tackle or jinking into the box with panic all around". But the club has never won a major trophy. Not that failure has stopped them packing the trophy cabinet with priceless items like the vase inscribed with "Anglo-Italian Cup", recalling Carlisle's annihilation of Roma, or pennants from the club's Scottish cousins across the border like Alloa and St Mirren. The European Cup was strangely absent, as was the FA Cup, the League Championship and many other major trophies I could mention.

The only time Carlisle have graced the top division was in 1974 when they were in first place after three games but relegated at the end of the season. Former Carlisle manager Bill Shankly called their promotion to the First Division "the greatest achievement in the history of the game". When Shankly arrived in 1949 he was less enthusiastic. He called the stadium "a hencoop, a glorified hencoop. The stand and terraces and everything about the ground was in terrible condition, except for the pitch and that was always a good one".

The club's sports centre, a dark, windowless wooden building surrounded by barbed wire, was behind the Waterworks End. "That's

Auschwitz, our indoor sports centre. I know it looks terrible, but it pulls in 50k a year," said Knighton. Carlisle's Chairman hoped the brave new world he was planning for the club meant such eyesores would soon be a thing of the past. The aim was to raise the capacity to 28,000. "I think we shall command 18,000 home supporters once we are up with the glamour people."

The supporters certainly deserve success. Carlisle has a population of only 78,000 yet the club regularly topped the Third Division's home attendance figure. There was always plenty of support at away games, which was remarkable when you consider a 'local' derby involves a trip of about 80 miles. Record season ticket sales for the 1994/95 campaign showed the faith the supporters had in Knighton and his team.

The potential support was staggering and just needed a spark of success to be ignited. Apart from the odd cup run, the only real excitement in recent years had been local derby games with teams like Preston, variously described by The Cumberland Sausage as Carlisle's "loveable rivals from the deep south" and "the worst team in the world. Quite possibly". Preston were voted as "Most Disliked Opposing Team" in the fanzine's end of season poll, a quite staggering turnaround from almost every other year when Burnley topped this category.

So why are Carlisle fans so loyal? The club has had some great players over the years, but never a great team so the following can't be based on memories of a glorious past. They are, of course, the only team in Cumbria and that must surely help to attract local support. But the club is in one of the most sparsely populated parts of the country and their catchment is therefore tiny. Four Four Two magazine believed the support was partly because the Cumbrians are "a strange, hardy breed in themselves." The Cumberland Sausage had a different theory. "One can only suggest that some of us are simply born to be blue."

Forty-seven-year-old Geoff Tomlinson, a United fan for nearly 40 years, was certainly "born to be blue". A week or so before my visit to Brunton Park he set out for the Bescot Stadium in the supporters' club coach to see United play Walsall. It would have been his 1,900th consecutive Carlisle match. Unfortunately, the coach got stuck in a 27 mile traffic jam on the M6. After queuing for three-and-a-half hours the driver finally abandoned the journey, bringing to an end Tomlinson's extraordinary odyssey.

I settled into my seat in the Main Stand next to a little blondie, the mascot, and her mum. The view across the countryside on what was a sunny Saturday afternoon was breathtaking. Most people have seen it on Match of the Day since whenever Carlisle are featured (rarely) the coverage from Brunton Park invariably begins with the view over a pastoral scene once described by Brian James in his book Journey to Wembley as "a frontier post of football indeed, guarded only by sheep."

The teams ran onto the pitch to D-Ream's Things can only get better - a fitting theme tune for the new era being championed by Knighton. The 1-0 win over Exeter, thanks to a goal from livewire winger Rod Thomas, was one of many during the season that would see them streak away to a 20 point lead by the Spring. Thomas was a former England teenage sensation who burned out under the bright lights in London. He'd recaptured his form at Brunton Park.

I wandered into the sponsors lounge for a beer after the game. Knighton's personal assistant was at the bar. A tall blonde with gorgeous blue eyes, she was originally from Essex but had moved to Carlisle with her parents. What was Knighton like to work for? "He works hard," she told me. I made tentative plans to meet her for a drink later that night.

After the match, I went back to my B & B, Howard House. After a cup of tea and a short rest I went into town to find a restaurant called Zapotec: the Kitchens of Mexico and Spain. The food was hot and spicy, unlike the waitresses. I sat back to read the fanzines I'd bought outside the ground that afternoon. As I looked at The Cumberland Sausage I suddenly wondered what the hell I was doing hundreds of miles from home, on my own, on a Saturday night. Was I a sad bastard? Or had I embarked on a wonderful journey that would be the envy of football fans everywhere? I'm not sure I knew then, but I do now. I was definitely a sad bastard.

I then wandered the streets of Carlisle. Groups of youngsters dressed to kill were making their way to the pubs and clubs. I found the bar where Knighton's PA said she'd be going that night with a friend. She was supposed to be there at about 11 o'clock. It was 10.30, a little too early. I had a quick look around and then decided I couldn't stay awake much longer. I reluctantly gave up on the idea of a night on the town with a gorgeous blonde and wandered wearily back to my bed.

As I walked towards the market square a drunken Scotsman veered unsteadily along the street shouting abuse at the "Fucking English". I avoided him and weaved my way through the back streets to Howard House. So what's a guy to do on his own in a B & B after dark? Thank God for Match of the Day. More tea, a flick of the TV button and I was in my element. It didn't last long. I was knackered and even Blackburn Rovers couldn't keep me awake. Besides, a trip to Middlesbrough beckoned the next morning.

DIRTY NORTHERN BASTARDS
Middlesbrough v Sunderland – Ayresome Park
11 September 1994

I woke up just in time for breakfast in the quaint dining room of Howard House, the bed-and-breakfast down the road from Brunton Park. On my table sat a young couple from Brighton who worked in a religious bookshop (business was booming apparently) and an elderly couple born in Salford who were searching for their roots.

After half-an-hour I'd heard enough about great grandparents and long lost cousins to last me a lifetime, although the bigamist with nine children who lived for years at a time with each of his wives before returning to the other raised an eyebrow or two, including mine. There were two Swedish couples at breakfast who were also tracing their family trees. All roads lead to Carlisle it seems!

I thanked my hosts and hit the road to Middlesbrough. I was looking forward to my first Tees-Wear derby - the last at Ayresome Park before Boro moved to their new £25 million 32,000 all-seater 'Cellnet Riverside Stadium' in the docks area on the banks of the River Tees.

The journey would take me first to Newcastle, where I had to change. The train from Toon Town left Central Station and crossed the River Tyne. There were so many different bridges over the river it looked as if someone had been let loose with a Meccano set. I gazed back on the city with an air of satisfaction. I'd been to the first league ground of my record attempt. Only 92 to go!

The train went along the edge of the North Sea where I was treated to lovely views of the coastline. The terrain was quite flat, but with the sun sparkling on the water the morning promised a great day ahead. It didn't quite turn out that way!

There were two Sunderland supporters from Carlisle on the train who often travelled to Roker Park. They'd been at the Carlisle Exeter match the day before and had heard the half-time announcement over the tannoy welcoming me to Brunton Park and wishing me luck with my record attempt.

But why didn't they support their home town team Carlisle? "I don't know really," said the ginger one with the friendly face. "I just saw the name Sunderland in the paper one day when I was a kid and it stuck in my mind." The other lad with the crew cut and big smile said he was hooked from the moment he saw his first game at Roker as a boy. They made the 150 mile round trip as often as they could, going to Carlisle games only if Sunderland were away or playing on a Sunday, like today.

The train sped across the Tyne and Wear towards Sunderland. It passed alongside the city towards Seaham, a coal port with a badly polluted coastline, before going through Hartlepool. "The monkey-hangers," said the lad with the crew cut. I gave him a blank look. "Don't you know the story?" I again stared back blankly with a shake of the head. "During the Napoleonic wars a French galleon is supposed to have drifted into the harbour at Hartlepool. Nobody was on board except a monkey in Napoleonic battle dress. The people of Hartlepool thought he was a spy so they hung him."

On my flight to Newcastle from Heathrow was a middle-aged woman from Durham returning from a visit to her son's farm in Tasmania. She was originally from Hartlepool. "What's it like," I asked. "Pretty depressed," she replied. "Depressed or depressing?" I said, seeking clarification. "Both." I would find out for myself later in the season.

The Sunderland fans were telling me that Newcastle supporters were the 'hardest' when we were interrupted by half a dozen policemen boarding the train to keep an eye on the travelling away fans. The Sunderland lads were worried the police might check to make sure there were no troublemakers without tickets going to the match.

They decided it was time to get off and take a taxi. It was safer than being welcomed at the main station by the Middlesbrough fans. I decided to join them. They'd arranged to pick-up their tickets from a friend outside the ground – a Middlesbrough fan who had got them for the Holgate End amongst the home fans

I had a seat in the Main Stand as a guest of Boro's 100 club. The match was live on Tyne-Tees and the fans were watching the pre-match build-up in the bar, a sort of working man's club. Out on the pitch Middlesbrough were parading their new signing. The programme billed him as 'The Boy from Bolivia'. Name: Jaime Moreno, known to Bolivian fans as "Il Pichon", which roughly translated means 'Roadrunner'. Beep, beep. Club: FC Blooming, based thousands of feet above sea level at Santa Cruz de la Sierra, Bolivia's second city. What would he make of Middlesbrough?

The fanzine Bread 'N' Boro once listed the misconceptions 'outsiders' have about Middlesbrough picked up from a Boro exile. He'd had people tell him that it was near Newcastle and the locals are Geordies, or that it's near Birmingham; the blokes wear cloth caps and keep pigeons; they say "Why aye, man"; everyone works for ICI; it stinks of pollution; and that it's spelt Middlesborough.

Middlesbrough actually lies south of Hartlepool. It developed in the nineteenth century as a port and an iron and steel town. That explains why the industrial heart of the place is called the Ironmasters District, while the town was originally dubbed Ironopolis. ICI's Wilton petrochemical works are also nearby, though not everybody works there.

Boro were once sponsored by ICI but their shirt advertising had gone. Some visitors to Ayresome Park were glad. The Tranmere fanzine Give Us An R noted that the ICI logo had put a lot of teams off tackling. "It was a good idea really (that the ICI logo had gone) as everyone had been taking the piss out of this sponsorship deal for years due to all the chemical factories in the surrounding area. You always felt that when a Middlesbrough manager said he was experimenting with the defence it didn't just involve moving them about, but had more to do with a Mary Shelley novel."

Towards the coast, some three miles from Boro's new ground, is the Redcar British Steel Corporation works. British Steel had also been one of the club's sponsors. However, relations between them and Middlesbrough were now strained to say the least. British Steel were not amused when they found out that Boro's new stadium was being constructed with German steel and they promptly withdrew their £10,000 a year sponsorship. So much for community spirit!

Middlesbrough said the decision was made by Taylor Woodrow, the civil engineering firm in charge of building the stadium. And the Boro fans say they might have had more sympathy for British Steel if the company hadn't itself refurbished its Lackenby plate mill with... German steel! Nevertheless, the decision did upset families with a history of working in the Teeside steel industry and the ironstone mines.

Out on the Ayresome Park pitch Moreno was introduced to the crowd alongside the club mascot Roary the Lion. Bryan Robson had fought off top sides from Spain and Colombia in the race for his signature (Moreno's not Roary's!) The 20-year-old forward cost £250,000 plus a further £125,000 based on appearances. That was probably a lot of pesos, but in the world of multi-million pound British transfers it was peanuts.

Moreno was a product of the renowned Tahuici Football Academy (well that's what it said in the programme). He'd won the latest of his 30 international caps during the 1994 World Cup Finals in the United States when he came on as substitute against Germany and Spain. Apparently, his name is pronounced "High-me". In London, it would sound Jewish. But with a North-East accent...

Captain Marvel was well pleased with his new arrival. Moreno got a noisy welcoming reception from the crowd whilst Roary jumped around him. I guessed Robson was hoping Moreno would be soon be growling at opposing defences. He scored two goals on his debut in a 3-0 pre-season friendly win over Darlington, but was unable to take part in the serious business of league action until his work permit was approved.

Robson was angry at the delay. "I'm sure no Boro fans need reminding about the wait we have had in gaining Jaime's work permit. I just find it strange that some players wait only a week for a permit, while for others, like Jaime, it's more like five or six weeks. Surely there should be a set pattern and clear rules to adhere to so that gaining a work permit or not is a straight forward process, no matter who you are."

British clubs signing foreign players have to meet certain criteria. A permit is only issued to current internationals who've played for at least the previous two years in 75 percent or more of their country's competitive games. British clubs also have to show they've conducted a genuine and thorough resident labour search in the EC countries. But that search is often neither genuine nor thorough. Middlesbrough's consisted of an attempt to sign Darren Anderton. No wonder Moreno's permit was delayed.

Robbo had signed him to give Boro an extra attacking option, particularly when regular strikers Paul Wilkinson or John Hendrie were injured. They certainly could have used their Bolivian import against Sunderland as their North-East rivals took a commanding two goal lead.

I thought of the two Sunderland fans in the Holgate End celebrating among the home fans with a muted "yep" followed by "I could see that coming" or "bit exposed at the back weren't they". I guessed that inside they were jumping up and down with the rest of the Sunderland fans who were going barmy in the corner of the South Stand at the opposite end of Ayresome Park.

Their joy was premature. Boro staged an amazing comeback with just 12 minutes to go. Alan Moore pulled one back for the home side before captain Nigel Pearson headed the equaliser. Striker John Hendrie should have hit the winner for Boro but missed a sitter, firing into the side netting, in an incredible finale to a fine match.

Earlier, Robson suffered a kick in the balls from Shaun Cunnington. He was booked but could easily have been sent off. The crowd were incensed. "You dirty northern bastards," they shouted at Sunderland. I thought I was so far north already that shouting abuse at northerners wasn't kosher. But it seems anyone north of where you are is, er, north.

In Aberdeen there's probably only one choice. "You dirty southern bastards."

After the match a taxi ride to the metro and a train from there got me back to the airport but a mix-up over flight times meant I'd missed my plane to London. I then went on a wild-goose chase from the airport to the train station to the bus station but all in vain. There was no transport back to London. I got another taxi to the airport hotel and rang someone to cover me at work the next morning. That night I drifted off to sleep watching Woody Allen's Play It Again Sam. It had been a long weekend and I was shattered.

The next morning I bought a copy of The Journal to see how the local press viewed the match. The Robson incident had grabbed the headlines. "When Robbo got up, and it took a while, he fixed (Craig) Hignett with the same sort of death mask grin Joe Frazier used to reserve for Mohammed Ali."

I took the paper along to the dining room. It was like a throwback to the Sixties. Garish diamond-shaped mirrors and plastic chandeliers with a patterned carpet like a TV whose horizontal hold needed adjusting. The buffet included three jugs containing pink, yellow and brown liquid "What's in those?" I asked the waitress. "Milk shake, sir," she replied. Strange people these northerners.

INTO THE LIONS' DEN
Millwall v Burnley – The New Den
14 September 1994

Millwall's reputation leaves you wondering what the hell you'll be letting yourself in for when you visit their ground in South London. But my visit to the New Den, just off London's Old Kent Road, turned out to be a pleasant surprise. It's not just that I survived the experience without getting beaten up and dragged senseless into a back street. The new stadium is actually superb, the match was a five goal thriller and, although Millwall lost, everyone seemed to get home in one piece.

I have to admit I'd never been to the old Den in the aptly named Cold Blow Lane but, by all accounts, the former home of 'The Lions' was not the sort of place to be found on a cold, wet winter night. Eamon Dunphy, in his excellent book Only a Game?, described a visit to the Den as something most teams hated.

"I remember thinking 'Where is this?' Then you go and have a look at the pitch, which is bumpy, terrible. The away team dressing-room is a dungeon, no light, no window. The bathrooms are horrible. Then you get out there to face them – the Lions. And they come storming at you and most sides jack it in."

Simon Inglis in The Football Grounds of Great Britain, described Cold Blow Lane on a dark, wet night as "the perfect setting for a Jack the Ripper horror film; dry ice wafting about the cobbled streets and under the low tunnels. There are mysterious yards full of scrap, malodorous goings-on behind high fences, tower blocks looming in the distance, even old tram lines embedded in the roads. They knew what they were dealing with when they called it Cold Blow Lane."

The ground suffered bomb damage during the Second World War and was closed a record number of times because of crowd trouble in 1920, 1934, 1947, 1950 and 1978. The goal nets had a very close mesh to protect opposing goalkeepers from being hit by missiles thrown from the crowd. The last game there saw a pitch invasion, while balls and the goalposts were stolen. "No one likes us, we don't care," is the supporters' anthem.

So, would things be different at the new ground which is variously called The New Den, The New London Stadium or Senegal Fields – the name of the site of the ground from the days when London's Docklands area actually employed tough local dockers to unload bulging ships from around the world. Maybe Derby's players could provide the answer after the pitch invasion during the 1994 play-offs when their keeper was attacked. But if you ask most supporters they'll tell you the incident was caused by a senseless minority bent on destroying the club's image. Most fans are well behaved.

On the night of my visit, the Burnley fans in the North Stand upper tier were so far away from the Millwall supporters in the rest of the ground that only Peter Pan could have got within fighting distance. The atmosphere inside the ground was great. Both sets of supporters were chanting for their teams, the compact new stadium (capacity just over 20,000) providing an excellent environment for modern football.

Later in the season Port Vale's marvellous fanzine The Memoirs of Seth Bottomley prepared its readers for the trip to Millwall by organising an apocryphal 'Cockney Weekend'. "As soon as you reach London it's time for a 40-minute tube journey through some of London's most picturesque tunnels. You will spend the entire journey standing up in a crowded compartment with your face pressed against the armpit of someone who's just finished a 10 hour shift at Smithfield Market, while in your left ear you'll have to endure the buzzing of a crap INXS album from a personal stereo belonging to a hairy Australian tourist who hasn't washed for a week.

"Next is a traditional taxi ride with a cheeky Cockney chappie cab driver. You will sit for about half-an-hour in a traffic jam while the driver keeps looking over his shoulder at you and rabbiting on about the government or Terry Venables, calling you 'guv' and charging you about 20 quid for the privilege, and then calling you all the names under the sun if you don't give him a tip. Alternatively, you can travel in a vomit-ridden mini-cab driven by an illegal immigrant from Morocco with no insurance and bald tyres."

I decided to avoid public transport and drive west from the London suburb of Redbridge past the gleaming Canary Wharf tower – the tallest building in Europe – in the heart of London's Docklands. The name apparently comes from the canaries imported from the West Indies in the 19th century and brought into the docks to be unloaded and shipped to high class pet shops where they were sold to wealthy ladies who needed the company.

The regeneration of London's Docklands is amazing. Glass and steel constructions have replaced many of the old tenements, with the docks now surrounded by new homes and refurbished warehouses. The high ceilings and raw brick have been preserved to provide a luxurious setting for wealthy City traders, accountants, property developers and others on above-average salaries.

The less well-off are in places like Millwall's home at New Cross –

itself transformed by a rash of developments during the property boom of the 1980's. I drove to The New Den past some interesting pubs. There was The World Turned Upside Down, a suitable description for some of the turmoil caused by Millwall fans in the past, and the Thomas A Beckett on the Old Kent Road – famous because of the gym upstairs. Many a gritty London boxer, including Our 'Enry, cut his teeth (eyes, nose etc) training above the pub for a big fight. Opposite New Cross Gate station is The Rose, named after former Double Your Money star Monica.

Travelling fans are still wary of a trip to the Lions' Den. The Port Vale fanzine The Memoirs of Seth Bottomley gave Vale supporters this warning on using the local hostelries: "Remember where you are when using these pubs. Millwall supporters have a somewhat unsavoury reputation so it may be prudent not to steam into any of these houses shouting "Johnny Rudge's Black & White Army" or "Come and have a go if you think you're hard enough," as they're more than 'hard enough' and would probably jump at the chance of 'having a go'! A useful tip to blend into the surroundings, apart from shaving your head and tattooing "Kill the Bill" on your forehead, is to remember the local pronunciation of Millwall. The L's are silent."

I parked in a back street near the ground, carefully hiding the radio and ensuring the alarm was set before walking to the stadium. I sat in the comfortable padded seats reserved for match sponsors in the executive area of the stand. The view from just above the halfway line was perfect. The same couldn't be said for the weather as the rain began to drizzle down on a warm autumn night.

The game itself was a slow starter, goalless at halftime. I headed for the press room at the top of the main stand for some half-time refreshments. Tea and sandwiches were being served to reporters from the national papers, local radio and Clubcall line. Their main concern was to catch some of the Man United match against IFK Gothenburg in the Champions League. Millwall's first-half performance was hardly mentioned.

The reporter from the weekly Burnley Express had to write a match report plus a commentary and an interview with Burnley manager Jimmy Mullin. His deadline was three o'clock Friday afternoon, but he'd deliver his words of wisdom that night over the phone on his portable computer to avoid rushing back to Burnley in the morning. By the end of the second half he'd have much to write about.

I joined the press for the second half. There wasn't a single woman amongst them. It seemed that the advent of female television sports presenters on Sky and the BBC hadn't transferred itself to the printed press corp which was clearly still a bastion of male domination in a feminist world. Next to me in the press seats was a commentator from Radio Lancashire. Alongside him providing the expert analysis sat a Burnley player who'd been injured and was having trouble getting his place back after the record signing of Liam Robinson for £250,000 from Bristol City.

Former Spurs and Fulham star Alan Mullery was behind me providing the colour commentary for London's Capital Gold. There was plenty of colour to add in the second half when former Derby winger Ted McMinn collided with Millwall full-back Tony Cunningham in a clumsy attempt to play the ball. Referee. Mick Bailey pulled out the yellow card, then the red, implying that the unfortunate McMinn was being sent off for a second bookable offence. The problem was he hadn't committed the first one yet!

McMinn protested. He asked his manager what he should do. "I told him to stay on the pitch," Mullin explained after the match. The referee, realising his mistake, consulted his linesman. Not that either manager trusted his judgement. "How can you have much faith in a linesman who earlier gave offside from a throw-in," said Millwall manager Mick McCarthy.

There was only one possible outcome. The referee had to change his decision. At least he was brave enough to admit his mistake. And McCarthy, to his credit, said McMinn didn't deserve to get sent-off. Millwall's manager was just upset at the standard of officiating. Not that he or his team could blame the ref for their first home defeat in 20-odd matches at the New Den. When asked to pinpoint the reason for the defeat he just said: "Bad defending".

The winning goal in a 3-2 thriller had the Burnley fans on their feet. They'd already tried to build up the atmosphere with a Lancashire rendition of the Mexican wave in the first half. "It's called the Mexican wave because the fans first began to do it in Mexico at the World Cup in 1986," the man behind me explained to his female companion. She was obviously an expert on football!

After the match the journalists began to file their reports. One was shuffling pieces of yellow paper with scribbled notes all over them as if he couldn't make up his mind which bits to put where in his story. Another was giving his version of the McMinn mix-up. The Burnley Express reporter made his way downstairs to interview some of the players in their bar, while the rest of us waited for the managers to give us their words of wisdom at the post-match press conference.

Jimmy Mullin came into the press room first. A former Huddersfield star, he'd guided Burnley out of the Third Division and into the Second Division play-offs. A remarkable victory in front of 44,000 fans at Wembley had launched them into the First Division.

Mullin asked for a beer and then sat poker-faced waiting for questions. Anyone would have thought that Burnley had just been slaughtered given his sombre appearance. If this is what he's like when they've won a five-goal thriller away from home, how does he react when they lose? "Could you single out any of your players for praise tonight?" I asked. "They were all brilliant, just brilliant. I couldn't have asked for any more from them. It was a great team performance. Sometimes, I put my arm around them in the dressing room and they know they've played well."

His demeanour was a topic of conversation among the hacks as they waited for McCarthy to emerge from the dressing room. "Why did you take Mark Kennedy off and bring Dave Mitchell on? Weren't you removing the player who would have provided the crosses for him?" he was asked. "I don't know what game you were watching," McCarthy snapped back. "You tell me how many crosses he supplied while he was on the pitch." A fair point, but Kennedy had played well.

McCarthy was a reporter's dream. Controversial. Always ready to tell it like he sees it. A journalist from The Sun told me McCarthy had once brought his son into the press room and let him crawl around the floor with his toy car while he answered questions (McCarthy not the boy!). I was to meet the Millwall manager once again on my travels at White Hart Lane where he would be spying on FA Cup opponents Arsenal.

OLIVER HÄHNKE
Doncaster Rovers v Hereford United – Belle Vue
17 September 1994

My visit to Doncaster in South Yorkshire was dominated by one man: Oliver Hähnke. If someone had told me I'd be sitting in the Main Stand at the club's Belle Vue stadium talking to a football-mad ice cream salesman from Berlin and his Brazilian girlfriend from Rio de Janeiro I wouldn't have believed them. But that's exactly what happened.

I met Oliver at the refreshment bar before the match. I first noticed him because of the Brazilian baseball cap he was wearing. "Have you come all the way to Doncaster from Brazil?" I asked, half joking "No, I'm from Germany," he replied in a soft accent "What are you doing here," I asked, trying to work out why he had joined less than 2,000 die-hard Doncaster fans and 50-odd Hereford supporters on a cold Friday night.

The explanation was simple. Oliver was a football fanatic. Not just any football. He loved English football. He couldn't explain why, but he supported Everton, though he liked all English teams. Oliver's passion for the game was so strong that he spent a large part of his annual holidays travelling around England watching football. This year he'd hired a caravanette.

Oliver was one unique individual. If an English team was playing a German team he wanted the English team to win. He rooted for Norwich when they beat Bayern Munich in the UEFA Cup in 1994. He planned to watch 15 games in three weeks on this trip including Arsenal, Manchester United, Aston Villa, Ipswich, Everton, Wimbledon and any others he could fit into his schedule. (He ended up driving 11,000 kilometres and seeing 25 matches including England Romania at Wembley. On the way home from England they stopped at the Kaiserslautern Odense BK game. Why not?)

At the end of the Doncaster Hereford match he opened his wallet to show me all the tickets he'd already bought. He did have one slight problem. Arsenal's return Cup Winners' Cup tie against Omonia Nicosia and the Villa's UEFA Cup game against Inter Milan were on the same night. He had tickets for both matches, but not even football mad Oliver Hähnke could get to two games at the same time.

Oliver watched and played football all over the world. He was a regular visitor to the national Maracana stadium in Brazil, and often played football on the beaches of Rio. He was a goalkeeper, though at present he couldn't play because of a foot infection picked up on those Rio beaches. He'd be out of action for months.

Oliver was lucky because his girlfriend, Rosi, loved football too. Having said that, I'm not sure she enjoyed the Doncaster match. In her broken English she told me the weather was much warmer in Rio. I'm sure the football was better too, though, to their credit, Doncaster put on a show for her with some neat football and three goals.

Let's face it, how many men have a gorgeous Brazilian girlfriend who is happy to follow them all over England, come rain or shine, to watch Third Division Endsleigh League Football at places like Doncaster. Exactly. Oliver's last girlfriend, from Yugoslavia wasn't quite so keen. "She wasn't like Rosi," he told me. "Who is?"

Rosi's favourite player was Romario, though she didn't like the way he sometimes dived to get penalties. He should stay on his feet more. "Like Klinsmann," I said cheekily. "Even Germans hate the way Klinsmann dives all the time," said Oliver. "He's a good player, very quick, he should stay on his feet."

I'd arrived at Doncaster, a town of just under 300,000, well before kick-off for a tour of the ground. It didn't take long. After Wycombe and Millwall, with their brand new purpose-built stadiums, a visit to Doncaster was like going back in time. They were lucky to have a sponsor for tonight's match, but it looked as if times were hard for the second oldest League club in Yorkshire. The match sponsors received a football signed by the first team and a buffet was laid on for them in their own lounge which looked like someone's front room.

Rovers moved to Belle Vue in 1922 after the supporters moved a pile of ash from the nearby coal tips to build up the banking and lay the foundation for the pitch. The fans also jacked up the Main Stand from the club's previous ground at Bennetthorpe, wheeled it along the road and put it on the northern terrace. It looked as if little had changed since the 1920's. There was talk about building a new stadium with the town's rugby club but, so far, that was all it amounted to, talk.

The ground is opposite the town's famous racecourse. which lies on the east side of Belle Vue on Town Moor. Parts of its magnificent grandstand date back to the late 1700s and its oldest classic race, the St. Leger, was established in 1776. The St. Leger is run during the second week of September, while the William Hill Lincoln Handicap in March begins the flat-racing season in Britain. On race days the horse boxes are parked in the Belle Vue car park and traffic often comes to a standstill while horses are led across Bawtry Road.

The only other things Doncaster is famous for is railway engineering

– the Great Northern Railway established its workshops there in the 1800s - and Europe's largest indoor leisure complex, The Dome. The Railway Plant Works no longer play much part in the town's industry. But The Dome sure does. Touted as the "new heart of Doncaster" it completely overshadows the dilapidated Belle Vue stadium.

The football club had hoped the £22 million council-built sports and leisure complex would be part of a refurbished football ground. It wasn't and the club can only cast envious glances at its next door neighbour which comes complete with leisure pools (the lagoons), ice rinks, squash courts, sports hall, saunas, steambaths, indoor bowling green, multi-screen cinema and social club. The Dome hosts the Word Matchplay Snooker Championships plus international boxing and basketball.

Inside Belle Vue the referee had arrived and was inspecting the pitch. The game had been switched from Saturday to avoid clashing with the RAF Finningley international airshow. It was difficult enough to attract supporters without competing with one of the biggest airshows of the year. The organisers expected a record attendance of more than 150,000 because the impending closure of Doncaster's RAF base in 1996, after 60 years' service, meant this was the last show.

The referee was admiring the pitch which was in perfect condition. Rovers can be proud of their playing surface. The owners of Wembley offered more than £10,000 for the Belle Vue turf in the 1970s but were turned down. Rovers knew the surface was only in such good condition because of the drainage beneath, where the ash lay. It used to be the largest in the league, until manager Billy Bremner, the former Leeds captain, decided his team wasn't fit enough to run around it for 90 minutes. To stop opponents taking advantage of their shortcomings, he had eight yards trimmed off the end!

I was taken beneath the Main Stand into the home dressing room where I met former Spurs and West Ham winger Jimmy Neighbour. He'd just been appointed assistant manager the previous Tuesday. "We can't score enough goals, that's our problem; only five in eight matches so far this season. I want to change that," he said. Neighbour's enthusiasm was infectious.

I told him I'd seen him play for Spurs. "That was a long time ago." His job now was to motivate the Doncaster players. He was writing up the names of the Hereford team on a white blackboard with a marker pen when I interrupted him. The name Wilkins stood out (Graham not Ray). "Have you any special plans for tonight?" I asked. "You know, a man-to-man marker or anything like that." "Not really," said Jimmy.

"I'd prefer to let the other team worry about us, especially when we're playing at home."

I wished him luck on his home debut and went in search of the trophy room. When I asked where the trophies were kept Terry Burdass, the commercial manager, looked at me as if I was winding him up. But I wasn't. I knew from the programme that Doncaster were champions of the Third Division in the '30s and '40s and had won the Fourth Division title a couple of times.

There wasn't a trophy room as such but the boardroom contained a wall cabinet with a few old trophies. Most of them were regional titles, but I was intrigued by a mini replica of the Jules Rimet Trophy presented to the club by the Football Association to mark England's 1966 World Cup triumph. I hadn't seen one before but assumed every League club was given one after our victory over West Germany. They were.

The other interesting item in the panelled boardroom was a caricature of a group of policemen on each others shoulders. They formed a pyramid like you sometimes see in an acrobats' circus act. The policeman on top was shining a torch across the pitch over the caption: "I wish they'd fix those bloody floodlights." "Just goes to show what we have to put up with sometimes," said the commercial manager.

We stopped by the office of the oldest manager in English professional football, 62-year-old Sammy Chung. His makeshift office was in a portacabin in the Belle Vue car park. Hardly inspiring, but it didn't seem to bother the happy-go-lucky Mr Chung. He'd also only recently been appointed and was enjoying life.

Chung joined Reading in 1949 and became an accomplished inside-forward at Norwich and Watford. He then took a job as assistant to Bill McGarry at Watford before moving to Ipswich and Wolves. The partnership at Wolves took them to the UEFA Cup Final in 1972, where they lost to Spurs, and victory in the 1974 League Cup Final.

Chung took over from McGarry when Wolves were relegated in 1976. They were promoted at the first attempt, but Chung was sacked two years later. He has since coached abroad, in Sweden, at Stoke and at Colchester. In 1993 he set up a soccer academy in Wolves and settled back to a peaceful life outside football management.

"I thought someone was pulling my leg when the chairman Ken Richardson rang from Doncaster. I thought it had all gone past me actually. I'd been applying for jobs and was not even getting interviews," said Chung, whose Chinese father came to Britain as an interpreter in 1914.

The Doncaster manager certainly has his own style. "I used to have these big discussions with Brian Clough. He'd say, 'It's all about management.' I would argue: 'No, it's about coaching, about technique, teaching guys the basics, how to head a ball.' Clough said: 'I don't teach them. I buy them because they can head the ball.' This discussion went on until in the end we agreed, 'I make 'em, you buy 'em.'"

I left Chung's office and walked across the car park towards the away supporters who'd just made the four-and-a-half hour trip from Hereford. They were waiting for their team to arrive. Hereford's captain Dean Smith came across the car park towards the players' entrance and was immediately surrounded by fans. The previous day manager Greg Downs, a member of Coventry's 1987 FA Cup winning side, had resigned and assistant manager John Layton was in charge for tonight's match.

The supporters wanted to know what was going on at the club. Smith chatted amiably to the fans. They were a dedicated bunch and they paid his wages so it was in his interests to give them a few minutes of his time. But he seemed genuinely anxious to address their concerns. "The players didn't want the boss to leave. But we're professionals and we just have to concentrate on our football," he explained.

He left to prepare for the match and I asked a young fresh-faced fan what he thought of the latest developments. "Well, the players may not have wanted Downs to leave but I did. We were crap last season and we haven't started well this year either. We need some new faces to turn things around. We just can't score goals right now"

I asked why he followed Hereford all over the country when they had such a crap team. "I also like Arsenal and last season I started watching more of their games. The trouble is I live in Hereford. They're my local team so I have to support them."

And there you have it – fan loyalty. Football is unlike any other product. You can't just replace one team with another like you can when you don't like your wife, your job or your soap powder anymore. The clubs know this and for years they have subjected loyal fans to abject conditions inside Britain's football grounds. It took the law, in the form of Lord Justice Taylor's report, to wake them up to the decline in the facilities. Fans like Oliver Hähnke may never complain, but they shouldn't have to.

SUSSEX IN ESSEX
Southend United v Bolton Wanderers – Roots Hall
24 September 1994

A day at the seaside. Well, not quite. In fact I didn't see the sea - famous as an attraction for East End day trippers. They still come even today. Southend United probably wish a few more made their way to Roots Hall to support the local football team. With gates averaging less than 4,000 they could do with the extra ticket sales.

The south end of the old village of Prittlewell, near the mouth of the River Thames, grew into the resort of Southend-on-Sea from which the club takes its name. Its existence is due to the Prince Regent who, in 1809, decided that Prittlewell, now a suburb of Southend, would provide a healthier climate for his wife, Princess Caroline. She stayed at the south end of the village and that became the town's official name.

Southend's population of 150,000 are spread across most of the nearby towns along a seven-mile stretch of sand and stones facing south onto the Thames Estuary. The football club's nickname, the Shrimpers, therefore requires little explanation. At the old cockle sheds in nearby Leigh-on-Sea you can eat a plate of shrimps as well as cockles, the local delicacy, mussels, whelks or crabs. Visitors either take home the fruits of the sea for their tea or eat them by the water with a pint of beer.

They are also attracted by the Kursaal amusement park, where Southend once played, the crazy golf and the world's longest pier. You can walk or take a train to the end of the one-and-a-half mile pier – not that there's much to see when you get there. Along the seafront Kiss Me Quick hats vie with pink candyfloss. Fortune tellers predict your future. The tacky bright lights of endless amusement arcades line the Eastern Esplanade. The culinary choice is mainly between fish and chips and bangers and mash.

The classier part of the town is along the Georgian Royal Terrace, with its wrought-iron verandas, which runs along the embankment above the seafront. Princess Caroline stayed in two of the houses during her rest there. Nearby is the Royal Hotel – the resort's social centre during the nineteenth century. Nowadays, the socialising goes on in the restaurants and pubs dotted around the town.

Money finds its way to Southend, but not a lot goes to the local football club. Southend United rely on commercial activities to boost their takings. Like the £400,000 earned each year from the use of the main car park outside the stadium as a market. The members' bar, decorated like an Essex pub, also brings in much needed revenue, along with the main restaurant.

Like all clubs, Southend are desperate for funds to develop their Roots Hall ground, named after the house which once stood on the site. The supporters originally bought the ground and the club moved back there in the late 1950s after leaving the greyhound stadium. Parts of the ground had been closed but it's all open again now, including the new £1.5 million South Stand.

Former West Ham star Brian Dear was on hand to serve meals before the match. Nice as it was to see Brian looking so well, it was rather sad that a former professional footballer was waiting on tables. There should be a fund for old players to ensure they don't fade and die like the bubbles in the Hammers' theme song.

One player who hadn't yet faded or died was former Liverpool star Ronnie Whelan, recently arrived on a free transfer. Southend's form had begun to improve since his arrival. A win against Bristol City was a glimmer of hope after thrashings by Wolves and Stoke. Today's visitors were Bolton fresh from a 3-0 Coca-Cola Cup win against Ipswich at Portman Road. They were tough opponents, but Southend showed they had spirit in an entertaining match.

Before the game I was introduced to the then-Southend manager Peter Taylor, a former England international who played for Crystal Palace, Spurs and Orient before moving into management. He joined Southend from Watford where he was assistant to Steve Perryman, who went on to become assistant manager under Ossie Ardiles at Spurs.

Taylor liked his sides to play attractive football and, on their day, Southend had the players to perform. The exciting touchline trickery of Ricky Otto; the strength and aerial power up front of Dave Regis, a new arrival from Birmingham along with Roger Willis in a deal which took Gary Poole and Jon Hunt to St Andrews.

Unfortunately, Nigerian international Dominic Iorfa, known as the Lion of Lagos, was sidelined with a medial ligament injury picked up against Luton. As we sat in one of Southend's executive boxes to watch the match I asked him how long he would be out of action. "I'm hoping to be back for Nigeria's match against England at Wembley on November 16th." His team-mates thought he was being hopelessly optimistic. He was.

Iorfa was well-built, though not as stocky as Nigerian team-mate Daniel Amokachi, Everton's £2 million signing. He'd spoken to Amokachi the previous Thursday to see how he was settling in. Everything was fine except for Everton's form. They couldn't win a match.

Iorfa joined Southend from Peterborough after a spell in Turkey with Galatasaray, conquerors of Manchester United in the 1993 European Cup, and, before that, at Queen's Park Rangers. I asked why he left Galatasaray. "Well, the money was good. I was on a two-year contract worth $200,000 a year. But my wife was unhappy. She wanted to come back to England. I didn't have much choice".

He was doubtless earning less at Southend where the players could expect to pick up about £500 a week, or £25,000 a year. Salaries vary widely between First Division clubs, but the average weekly wage is just under a grand a week. Those backed by rich chairmen, like Derby, can pay a lot more. Southend are not so fortunate. "It's a living but you can't save much for the future," said Andy Sussex, the Shrimper's 30-year-old midfield schemer and penalty taker. "It's only top players that can secure their future outside the game."

Sussex had been at the club for four seasons. He had worked his way up the League ladder after an apprenticeship at Leyton Orient and a spell at Crewe. Sussex planned to learn the 'knowledge' so he had something to fall back on when his football career was over. He was out of the side today with a calf injury but had to report to the ground at 11.30 for treatment.

At Orient he played alongside Southend manager Peter Taylor. Sussex was a young apprentice while Taylor was in the twilight of his career. "I used to go down the betting shop at ten to three to put the bets on the horses for Stan Bowles," he recalled. "Mervyn Day (the former West Ham, Leeds and Carlisle keeper) was there as well. They'd all be watching the racing in the dressing room just before going out onto the pitch."

I'd met up with Sussex in Southend's restaurant where we tucked into a full English breakfast for lunch! He was eating with a young player just signed from Tottenham. No doubt it was difficult for any apprentice to make the grade at a club like Spurs where internationals were ten-a-million. He'd come to Southend because there would be more opportunities.

He seemed like a model professional. Sharply dressed in shirt and tie; well spoken; dedicated. He was ribbed by the other players because he wasn't sure he would be going out on the town that night. A cup of cocoa and Match of The Day seemed more likely. He was also out through injury and would join us in an executive box later.

I asked the players about the changes in football since Lord Justice Taylor's Report. "It has improved the game a lot," said Sussex. "The stadiums all needed modernising and that is happening." The worst

36

ground he'd ever played at was The Shay at Halifax – no longer members of the Football League and fighting to survive.

Sussex's fondest memory was putting Crewe in front against Liverpool at Anfield in the Milk Cup. They lost 5-1! He also scored in the second leg, which they lost 4-1! His best season in the goalscoring stakes was 16, two coming from the penalty spot. Sussex's approach to the game obviously engendered loyalty among supporters. He was amazed to discover that the guy who sponsored his kit at Orient stayed loyal when he was transferred to Crewe. But he didn't followed Sussex to Southend, where the intriguing Lieutenant Colonel J. Boorman had taken over as his sponsor.

After a few beers in the members bar it was time to take up our position in one of the club's executive boxes. It was like being in the treatment room since I was surrounded by Southend players on the injury list along with some of the reserves. Their comments during the game were as colourful as they were revealing.

Footballers do not like to watch football. They are trained to play and that is what they do best. It must be good experience for a job in management to have to watch the team rather than orchestrate the proceedings from the middle of the park. When Southend were awarded a penalty early in the first half Andy Thomson stepped up to take the spot kick. "I don't fancy him taking this," said Andy Sussex. His hunch was right. Thomson missed.

Thomson was later to redeem himself with the winning goal after an opportunist header from mercurial winger Ricky Otto, the subject of much transfer speculation involving Premier League clubs. (He said he was happy to stay at Southend, but would be sold to Birmingham later in the season.) That equaliser came after a stunning 25 yard drive from Bolton's Richard Sneekes had put the away side ahead.

As the match moved into the last few minutes Southend's players became increasingly nervous. Iorfa stood up, teetering unsteadily on his plastered left leg. "Come on, we need this one badly," he said. He knew what it was like to struggle from his time at Peterborough and didn't fancy the experience again.

I looked across at Southend chairman Vic Jobson in the executive box next door. He was pensive, brow furrowed, concentration intense. The club desperately needed three points to move up the table. Otto took the ball over to the far touchline near the corner flag at the Bolton end. Foot on the ball, he hopped and twisted, trying to keep possession while the Bolton defenders tried to get the ball off him.

Finally, the whistle went and everyone breathed a sigh of relief. We watched the results of the other matches coming through on Grandstand in the executive box before heading for the players' bar. That week's results proved again that, as Jimmy Greaves would say: "It's a funny old game". On Wednesday night Bolton had beaten Ipswich 3-0. Today Southend beat Bolton 2-1. And Ipswich? They beat Premier League Champions Manchester United 3-2!

Few of the Southend team came into the players' bar after the game. Many of them preferred to mix with the fans in the members' bar. Others were exhausted and just wanted to go home after their day's work. One player who did emerge was Southend full-back Mark Hone. "You look tired," said his wife as he joined her and their two sons. "I'm completely knackered," said Hone, as he sat back in his chair puffing. The game had taken its toll.

His small boys had been watching the highlights of the game on the TV in the bar. "Look there's dad," said the older one. "There he is again," said the smaller one. They were excited to see him on television, though he had to compete with crisps and cola for their attention.

The players' bar was an extension of the pub-like atmosphere in the members' lounge. The trophies on the wall were a real mixture. One from the early 1980s, presented to the club's top goalscorer, stood beside a bowl given to every club by the Football League in 1963 to celebrate its 75th anniversary. A few of the pieces had been glued back together. It had clearly seen better days.

I was non-plussed by the figure of a man with a gun. It was given to the winner of a clay pigeon shooting championship. A former player perhaps? I was also intrigued by the cup awarded to Southend as runners-up in a match against the Sri Lankan President's X1. "Cricket?" Sussex suggested.

Above the bar hung pennants given to Southend by famous European teams like Borussia Moenchengladbach. The contrast with the old framed fixture list hanging from the wall was striking. It included matches against teams like Rochester just up the road. Southend had certainly seen the highs and the lows since their first match at Roots Hall, in September 1906. The team's only major honour is the Fourth Division Championship they won in 1981 – a season in which they set 17 club records, including 30 wins and 985 minutes without letting in a goal. But they remained in the bottom two divisions from when they joined the League in 1920 until they were promoted to the old Second Division in 1991. Even England's World Cup-winning captain Bobby Moore couldn't help the Shrimpers land a major trophy when he took over as Manager in February 1984.

GUNNED DOWN
West Ham United v Arsenal – Upton Park
25 September 1994

West Ham v Arsenal. East London against North London. Poor against Rich. And it showed. The Hammers just couldn't match the Gunners. Not that they tried very hard. With the exception of the exceptional John Moncur they lacked artistry and determination. Arsenal were efficient rather than spectacular. Two headed goals from captain Tony Adams and Ian Wright, Wright, Wright were enough to secure the win.

I'd parked near East Ham underground station on the district line and taken the tube one stop to Upton Park. Away supporters often get confused about the tube stops because West Ham is not the closest station to the ground. That explains the signs at the Upton Park tube which tells you to get off there for West Ham United Football Club. I walked along Green Street picking up a copy of the fanzine On a Mission from God.

There were lots of handy pocket-sized fixture lists being given away with "Kick Racism Out of Soccer" plastered over the front. The campaign may have been having some effect, but it hadn't registered with all Hammers' fans. One season ticket holder had returned his book of tickets to the club in protest at the anti-racism campaign! The ethnic mix runs thick in the Upton Park area and obviously caused tensions. The local papers often reported racial attacks from both sides of the black and white divide.

I didn't have a ticket for the match, which was all-ticket. I'd called the ground to be told that it was a sell-out despite being Sky's Super Sunday game. I'd decided to take a chance and try to buy a ticket at the match. I wandered around the West Ham Supporters' Club and noticed a group of Arsenal fans in red and white replica shirts standing in the corner by the bar. I couldn't believe they were allowed into the members' club. It wasn't as if you could mistake them for Hammers supporters! Maybe it was a sign of the improved atmosphere at football. I couldn't imagine it happening in the 70's or early 80's without sparking a whole lot of trouble.

I bought my ticket from a bloke called Bob, a tall, gangling chap with thinning hair combed across his head like the Baldie Man on television. He was milling around outside the Supporters' Club looking for a punter without a ticket. His mate couldn't come to the game and he just wanted face value. Bob was a football fanatic. He'd got divorced about a year ago and I sensed this had freed him to do what he loved best:

watching football. Not just the Premier League, but non-league too. Bob explained that he'd used his new-found freedom to see matches at four grounds over one weekend: Walsall, Birmingham, West Brom and Coventry.

Funny isn't it. Women and football just don't seem to mix. Some women like football. But not that many. And those who do probably go to see the dishy looking centre-forward with the sexy legs. How many women would have adored Gary Lineker if he was a bald, bespectacled beanpole with skinny pins? Did they watch him because he was the greatest goalscorer in English football since Bobby Charlton? What do you think?

Sky Sports isn't just another channel. It's man's revenge. Germaine Greer eat your heart out. Men may change their homes, their jobs, even their women. But their football team, never. It's in-bred. Loyalty reigns supreme. If you change your club then you cannot claim to be a serious supporter. You're a casual. A floating fan. If you care about football, you care about your team. And it's your team. No matter that you have to share it with a few hundred, a few thousand, or, in the case of Manchester United, 45,000 at Old Trafford and possibly millions of fans across the globe.

As if to make the point about the relationship between women and football, the West Ham programme contained the results of a survey sponsored by Carling and conducted by Leicester University. It found that females were "under-represented" at Upton Park. Only 9.6 percent of the crowd was female, compared to the national average of 12.7 percent. But that national average is itself a small percentage, though by all accounts a growing one. And there are now even a few female football presenters (no commentators that I know of, mind - there are limits!). But progress is very slow.

And even when a woman does like football it doesn't mean your problems are over. Nick Hornby in Fever Pitch tells how he thought he'd struck lucky when his girlfriend loved watching Arsenal - until they started thinking about kids and she said they'd have to take it in turns to see home matches. And if you don't have to worry about looking after the kids, your woman invariably supports the wrong team.

As Bob and I passed through the main gate to the West Stand I saw Brian Dear, the former West Ham star I'd been introduced to at Southend the previous day. Brian played under Ron Greenwood at Upton Park. But West Ham has been a breeding ground for managers over the years, with Frank O'Farrell, Malcolm Allison, Dave Sexton, Noel Cantwell, Jimmy Bloomfield, John Bond and Ken Brown among the star studded list of successful football brains from the Hammers Academy. The club has only had nine managers in its history. Brian signed my programme and I made my way, with Bob, to the turnstiles.

The West Stand had little character from the outside but from previous visits I knew that inside it was quite an imposing structure. A little further along Green Street is Castle Street which has a sweet little chapel on the corner - a reminder that the ground stands on what was once all church land. On the next corner is the Boleyn pub on Barking Road. Most football fans believe West Ham play at Upton Park rather than The Boleyn Ground, but Upton Park is the name of the district in which the ground stands rather than the name of the stadium itself.

The name Boleyn Ground comes from a house which stood next to the ground on Green Street until the 1950s. Built in 1544, the house had two turrets and was known as the Boleyn Castle taking its name from King Henry VIII's wife Anne Boleyn.

The house was used as a reformatory, a Priory and as the headquarters of a bowling club but when West Ham built a new main entrance to the ground in 1958, following promotion from the second division, the last remaining turret of the Boleyn Castle was demolished. The house was falling apart but it still seems sad that it could not be preserved given its historical significance. The school behind the South Bank on Castle Street now stands on the site of the Boleyn Castle.

I grew up a bus ride away from Upton Park in Dagenham, home of England 'coach' Terry Venables and the England and West Ham captain Bobby Moore. I'd seen West Ham play at Upton Park many times in my younger days. All my school friends were keen Hammers fans but, as a Spurs supporter, my spiritual home was White Hart Lane.

Meanwhile, at this afternoon's match against Arsenal a man dressed as a hammer was wandering around the pitch entertaining the crowd. To my left I could see the half-finished North Bank. Its predecessor had been demolished over the summer and builders Robert McAlpine were putting up a brand new construction similar to the new 7,600 seater Bobby Moore stand rapidly filling up on my right.

The late West Ham and England captain would have been proud of his stand. Moore is the only one of the club's famed World Cup Winners to have a stand named after him at Upton Park. The North Bank would be called The Centenary Stand - at the suggestion of a supporter - since it was completed during the Hammers' 100th year. It would be opened by Labour Party Deputy Leader John Prescott before the match against Everton the following February to cheers from 3,500 local school-children allowed in free to watch hundreds of claret and blue balloons drift into the evening sky.

The Bobby Moore stand - a two-tier construction with 20 executive boxes, modern kiosks, betting booths, toilets, club offices and the prestigious "66 Club" on the upper tier - contained a bust of the great man inside the main entrance. Fans were peering through the glass doors to see the sculpture before the match. On the wall to the right was a replica of the famous number six shirt worn with distinction by England's World Cup Winning captain. Who could forget Moore lifting the Jules Rimet Trophy on that glorious summer's day back in 1966. All Our Yesterdays. I watched the final in my uncle's flat on a small black and white television amazed that grown adults were jumping and dancing around the living room over a football match. I was six-years-old.

There were "innovative concourse areas" in the Bobby Moore Stand, popular with fans who came early to watch the close circuit televisions the club were linking up around the ground. "When I think of the old South Bank facilities - awful toilets, one kiosk and a shed as a bar - I'm delighted with the improvements we've made," said Peter Storrie, West Ham's Managing Director.

Once the North Bank was finished at Christmas the ground was supposed to hold 26,001. "The architects told me the capacity would be 25,999. I asked them to find me one extra seat, and they came up with two!" said Storrie. When I returned to Upton Park in February to see the official opening of the new North Bank the capacity was given as 26,014 - it seemed the architects had managed to find an extra 16 seats in all!

West Ham, their tightly packed ground tucked away in a small corner of East London, had spent £11.5 million modernising Upton Park and had no plans to expand the stadium. Perhaps the club likes the fact that its fans are so close to the pitch that they almost breathe down the necks of their opponents. In fact, the West Ham pitch is 8,064 square yards - the eleventh smallest in the league. However, somewhat surprisingly, it's larger than the pitches of North London rivals Arsenal and Tottenham. In fact, Highbury has the smallest pitch in the league.

"There's no room to extend the East Stand because of the flats behind, said Storrie. We could redevelop the West Stand, but if we closed that for a year the capacity would drop to around 18,000. We could try to join up the corners, but that would cause all sorts of problems because the stands are different heights. It would cost us a lot more money without providing many more seats. If you look at our gates over the last few years, though, we've rarely needed a capacity of much more than 25,000."

The cost of a new West Stand works out at 500 pounds a seat. Fifteen thousand seats equals 7.5 million pounds, or one Dennis Bergkamp, depending on how you look at it. The West Stand was built in 1925 after West Ham's success in 1923 when they were promoted to the First Division and also played in the first Wembley Cup Final, losing 2-0 to Bolton. They joined Bolton, Barnsley, Huddersfield and Wolves as second division clubs which had been beaten in the Cup Final. But the Hammers were to enjoy success as a second division team in the 1980 Cup Final.

West Ham's first major honour was the Second Division Championship of 1958. They were to grace the First Division for the next 20 years. In 1965 West Ham emulated Tottenham's achievement a couple of years earlier by winning the European Cup Winners Cup. And in 1966 the crowning glory was the World Cup as England beat West Germany 4-2 with three goals from Hurst - the only man to score a hat-trick in a World Cup Final - and an enormous contribution from Moore, as captain, and Peters, who scored the other goal. Hurst was such an all-round sportsman that he found the time to play cricket for Essex as well!

In 1969 the club spent £170,000 on a new East Stand. That was towards the end of a decade which saw the name of West Ham United etched on the country's mind for ever. The triumvirate of Bobby Moore, Martin Peters and Geoff Hurst brought a huge amount of success and fame to the homely East End club.

Tottenham pop up again in West Ham's history since in October 1970 they were the opposition when the club's official attendance record of 42,322 was set for a First Division match. In 1975 West Ham won the FA Cup again beating Fulham in the final. It was the club's first trophy for 10 years. Ironically, former idol Bobby Moore was wearing the white shirt of Fulham in that match. How strange he must have felt playing against his old club.

West Ham triumphed 2-0 with both goals coming from Alan Taylor, a £40,000 buy from Rochdale. I remember watching the match with my dad and a noisy bunch of friends at a flat in North London. Amidst the beers and cigarettes it was a disappointing final I recall with the Fulham goalkeeper, Gerry Payton, allowing Taylor to squeeze the ball through his legs for one of the goals.

In 1980, they returned to Wembley as a second division team to beat Arsenal 1-0 in the third all-London cup final with a rare headed goal from Trevor Brooking and an appearance from Paul Allen - the second youngest player ever to appear in a Wembley FA Cup Final. That was the last trophy the Hammers lifted, though in 1983 they registered their record victory with the 10-0 defeat of Bury in the second leg of a second round league cup match .

West Ham have never been a club to splash out large sums for players. Indeed, the club set two transfer records just before and after the First World War when they sold Danny Shea to Blackburn Rovers in the first £2,000 transfer in 1912 and Syd Puddefoot to Falkirk in the first £5,000 deal in 1922. Much later, in 1970, the club sold their World Cup hero Martin Peters to London rivals Tottenham for £200,000 in the first transfer of that size.

After the club received its record transfer fee of £2,000,000 from Everton for Tony Cottee in July 1988 they had enough money in the bank to pay Celtic £1,250,000 to bring Frank McAvennie back to Upton Park in March 1989. Cottee and McAvennie were brilliant when they played together and had helped West Ham challenge for the championship in the 1985/86 season. Apart, they weren't so effective. When McAvennie broke his leg during his second spell at West Ham the writing was on the wall. and he would never be the same player again

Peter Storrie is the man who greets the match and club sponsors for a tour of the ground. (West Ham, to their credit, are one of the few clubs who give ordinary supporters a free tour if you arrange it in advance.) He takes you up a flight of stairs towards the West Stand. At the top, on the wall to the right of the Ron Greenwood Suite, hangs a picture of Bubbles - a pretty little girl with curly blonde hair who used to star in Lux soap adverts. I wondered how many Hammers fans knew the origins of the Bubbles song which reverberates so often around Upton Park.

Once in the West Stand you're invited to sit the directors' box to hear about the club's past, present and future. My tour was conducted against a backdrop of torrential rain which threatened to drown out Storrie's pre-match pep talk. At this point Wally, a Chas 'n Dave sort of character, took over as our guide and led us into the dressing rooms underneath the West Stand. Those dressing room walls must have heard some stories over the years.

The players' shirts were hung on pegs around the walls. MARTIN, DICKS, MONCUR, MIKLOSKO. The stars of today on parade. Bobby Moore's famous number six shirt always hung beneath the clock on the back wall. "He was immaculate," said Wally. "Bobby didn't leave his kit here for the laundry to wash. He took it home and washed it himself. He'd even take his laces out of his boots and wash them. People said he was smarter when he left the ground than when he'd arrived."

Wally showed us the showers and the bath. "We used to put the water on in the second half, but then Julian (Dicks) started playing for us and we had to turn it on at quarter to three," said Wally, referring to the full-back's reputation of being sent for an early bath. "But he's a reformed character now since he came back to us from Liverpool and we don't have to do that anymore."

Wally's next story was apocryphal - I think. He told us about the Arsenal player who'd always struggled to score goals. He said the striker had notched up only 3 goals in 68 matches. The player had always been a Hammers supporter and had therefore asked his relatives to make sure that when he died his ashes were spread over the West Ham pitch. His wish was granted and the ashes were spread on the turf just outside the penalty area. "You'll never guess what happened," said Wally. "A gust of wind came along and blew them over the bar!" I spotted a cabinet in the corner of the lounge which contained a few trophies and mementoes - testimony to West Ham's travels in Europe. On the wall was an old print of a ship built at the Thames Ironworks where the team was founded. West Ham's origins in London's East End docks explains where the nickname 'The Hammers' comes from since hammers symbolise the tools used by shipyard workers.

West Ham were formed in 1895 by Arnold F. Hills, owner of the largest surviving shipyard at the time - the famous East London shipbuilding company called the Thames Ironworks. The players helped to build HMS Warrior, the first ironclad warship.

The Arsenal match was a scrappy affair. The visitors always looked the more composed and were dangerous on the break. Paul Merson linked up well with Alan Smith and Ian Wright, Wright, Wright, the darling of the Arsenal supporters. The first goal saw Smith nod on to Adams who had the simple task of beating Ludek Miklosko in the Hammers' goal from the edge of the six-yard box. In the second half Wright sent an acutely angled header into the top right-hand corner beyond Miklosko's flailing arms.

At 2-0 the Arsenal fans behind me in the top left hand corner of the West Stand gave full voice to their Ian Wright repertoire. The West Ham fans responded in kind with their own version: Ian Wank, Wank, Wank. It was hardly original. Their sense of humour came out, however, when the Hammers' fans in the South Stand began to sing "We're going to win the League." The Arsenal fans responded with "We all agree West Ham are better than Tottenham," which wasn't saying much given Tottenham's form.

MEMORIES OF LEEDS
Colchester United v Bury - Layer Road
1 October 1994

The first I saw of Colchester's stadium after driving through the Essex countryside in the rain was the floodlights looming up ahead like the ones at Stalag 14 in that old black and white film about the German prisoner-of-war camp. They're huge great things which overshadow Layer Road, the ground and just about everything else.

Today I was the guest of Colchester's Match Day Club for kids. Being a big kid myself I felt perfectly at home. I was the guest of Micky Cook, the club's Community Officer and a member of the squad on that illustrious day back in 1971 when Colchester United did the unthinkable by knocking the mighty Leeds United out of the FA Cup in the fifth round. At the time that result was sensational and is still talked about today.

Micky did a sterling job coaching and organising children's football at the club and in local schools. A seasoned pro who spent 16 years at Colchester as a player, and holds the club record for number of league appearances (613 between 1969 and 1984), he commanded the kids' respect. They look up to him and with good reason, He seemed disciplined but fair. Just the sort of defensive midfielder you'd want in your side.

Most of the kids had already arrived at the Soccer Centre for their day out. By the end of it they would have had a tour of the club, a question and answer session with some of the Colchester players who were not in the first team for today's match, a coaching session, a six-a-side match on the Layer Road pitch before the main match and lots of chocolate, coke and crisps. Above all they would have had a whole lot of fun.

The boys sat there with anticipation etched across their faces. They were all Colchester supporters but you wouldn't have known it from the kits they wore. The assortment included both Manchester clubs, Spurs, West Ham, and only one or two Colchester shirts. The talk around the tables was not about the visit of Third Division pacemakers Bury, but about Old Trafford, Stamford Bridge and Selhurst Park. Even the Colchester players who politely answered the kids' questions supported other teams.

I tagged along behind the kids and their dads for a tour of the ground as we were taken around the perimeter of the pitch from the Popular Stand to the Main Stand. "Look at that pitch," said Micky. "It's like a snooker table. The ball will stay nice and true and consistent. So if I'm going to support someone and they roll it back to me I've got every chance of hitting it first time into the box."

"Now on a lot of pitches, I may get that situation, it comes back takes a bobble and I end up putting it up there," said Micky pointing towards the seats at the top of the Main Stand. "Some say that I found the stand a few times when I was playing as a pro. But it's a lovely pitch to play on." The dad's around me laughed at Micky's reference to his playing days. Many had seen him play for Colchester and some remember coming to the Leeds game as small boys to watch their local heroes topple the country's best.

We climbed the terrace steps towards the sponsors lounges and directors room at the top of the Main Stand. We passed the groundsman who had earlier been praised for his pristine pitch. "Stadium manager you mean," one of the dad's corrected Micky with a laugh. "That's right, stadium manager," said the groundsman.

The sponsors' lounge was newly decorated and very smart, though a bit small. "If you look at Premier Division clubs and the facilities that they have, all these lovely boxes and everything else, well this is our equivalent," said Micky surveying the sponsors lounge with its bar and freshly-made sandwiches. There was no sign of an executive box anywhere, but that may come one day. The club has been talking for years about moving to a new purpose-built stadium. It hasn't happened yet, but you never know.

Leaflets headed "U's on the Move" were prominently placed in the Soccer Centre inviting supporters to become members of a scheme which offered a guaranteed top prize of £500 in a weekly draw. The rationale behind the scheme was clear. "When the U's leave the Layer Road ground... to develop a new stadium we need to raise a substantial amount of money. We hope to provide excellent facilities... for our supporters and the local community. We're also hoping the new scheme will help to purchase new players and develop and expand our youth team policy." Oh, is that all!

I thought that the club must have adopted the motto that it's better to live in hope than die in despair. I was surprised they didn't plan to use funds from the scheme to purchase Romario for their forward line as well. Until those vast sums came rolling in they had to make do with buying players like centre-forward Steve Whitton. He was brought to Layer Road just before the previous season's transfer deadline for a five-figure sum (£10,000) from northerly neighbours Ipswich Town.

"It costs a lot of money to run a pro club. We're no exception to that so we have to generate as much income as we can. So we rely on businessmen to come and watch our games and have a bite to eat and they sponsor the games and footballs," Micky explained to the boys. More sponsors would no doubt be welcome at Colchester and most other clubs. Only two companies – Techni-Flo Services Ltd Coggeshall and Roger Dicker, Tokyo UFO – were listed as players' kit sponsors in the programme

I'm not sure that the under 10's took on board the full extent of the cash crisis facing most club's in the 1990s but they listened politely. They would be more interested in our next stop: the directors' room which doubled up as a trophy room. The trophies stood on the sort of sideboard that most people have in their front room. There wasn't a lot of silverware on show, but the club were proud of their modest achievements.

"We're not Manchester United, we're Colchester United, obviously, but what you see here are a few of our success stories over the years and we're very proud of what you're looking at there," said Micky. One of the kids at the front said he wanted a trophy to take home. Which kid wouldn't.

One of Micky's favourites was the FA Trophy won by Colchester in 1992 when they beat Whitton 3-1 at Wembley. "We had about 25,000 people who went down the A12 to see the match. What was nice about that was that it tells you that if we can be successful there is the support in the town. And it also tells you that it's a successful product that people want to come and watch. It was great."

He then pointed to a bronze football boot on top of a ball: a replica of the GM Vauxhall Conference Championship trophy. Micky asked the kids whether they would rather win the FA Trophy or the GM Vauxhall Conference trophy. Their decision was unanimous. They all wanted to play on the hallowed turf in a cup final at Wembley.

Micky had other ideas. "From a footballer's point of view, this is the trophy they will cherish the most," he said, holding up the Conference trophy. "The reason is that this trophy represents 42 games of football. Every game that we played was equivalent to a cup final because we were a Football League club, we dropped down out of the League, and every Football League club was saving their best game for Colchester United. They thought, 'We'll show that old pro's team'. So they had to serve up a good level of performance, game-in, game-out for 42 games over six to seven months. But in their heart somewhere will be a special place for that Wembley appearance. "

Micky then ran through the trophies won by Colchester's impressive youth team both abroad and in domestic competitions against Blackburn, Fulham and Crystal Palace . "Because we're a small club we need to have youngsters come here and want to play for Colchester United. And you young man," said Micky pointing to the kid at the front who wanted a trophy to take home, "may be our first million pound player. And if you were... we'd be in good shape as a pro club." "But I'm rubbish," said the kid to roars of laughter from the dads. "If you practice you might be surprised," said Micky offering encouragement.

One of Colchester's greatest triumphs was their victory over First Division West Bromwich Albion in the 1971 final of the Watney Cup - the League's first sponsored tournament. They won the match 4-3 on penalties after a 4-4 draw in what was the first-ever penalty shoot-out. The Watney Cup was a pre-season competition for the two highest scoring clubs in each division other than those promoted or in Europe. There was a photograph of the trophy next to the Giant Killer's Cup which Colchester also won that year to mark their win over the Baggies.

"We built -up over the years a good reputation for giant killing. And I go around the schools a lot and we talk to the kids and they think giant killing," said Micky. "When the FA Cup comes round there's always a little air of expectancy. You think who have we got now, who are we likely to take on. We've had some great games; of course there's Leeds, but it goes back further than that, to Blackpool in 1948. We got thumped 5-0 but they had a very good side."

Indeed, Colchester first made an impact in that 1948 FA Cup competition through an amazing sequence of giant killing acts. They were still members of the Southern League when they knocked out Huddersfield Town and Bradford, who themselves had beaten Arsenal, before eventually losing to Blackpool in the fifth round. Their manager at the time was Ted Fenton who later took West Ham back to the old First Division.

The publicity surrounding that impressive cup run and a further run of good performances resulted in Colchester being elected to the Football League in 1950. Twenty years later Leeds United came to Layer Road. That Leeds team had won the Championship two seasons before and were runners-up in 1969-70. The side was packed with internationals in all positions bar one. Colchester's side was known as Grandad's Army since seven of their players were over 30. They didn't have a hope.

Leeds were then at their peak with the most feared team in the country. "Everybody thinks of Leeds," said Micky. "I was on the subs bench that day. Ironically, when you talk about how you progress in football, I'd just broken into the first team and I played in all the league games and we went to Rochdale. We were losing 3-1 and the guvnor gave me the call and said come and sit with me (on the bench) and another guy went on and we drew 3-3.

"We brought them back here and he kept the same team. There were a lot of old heads in the side in those days, and we thumped Rochdale 4-0. And then we went into three league matches, and I played in all three. Then Leeds came out of the hat so there was a buzz of expectancy. And he gave me a nudge and said 'Micky' – no actually he didn't say 'Micky' we weren't that close – 'you're on the subs bench son, I'm going for experience'. You didn't argue with him and I said 'Thank you boss'."

"There were 16,000 out there. We doubled up on the revenue, so we had a big pay day at the equivalent of 32,000 people effectively. They were coming out of the rafters," recalled Micky. Colchester burst into an astounding 3-0 lead and eventually won 3-2 to join the ranks of the greatest giant-killers of all time. Unfortunately, they lost 5-0 to Everton in the quarter-finals. Never mind. They had savoured their moment of glory.

Each group of Colchester's Match Day Club boys in twos and threes were given a minder for the afternoon as they made their way to the family enclosure to see today's match. I made a quick detour to pick up a jumbo hot dog (good value at £1.60; Chelsea charged £2.50 for the same delectable cuisine at Stamford Bridge the following day) before joining the youngsters on the terraces.

The crowd were warming up with sophisticated chants like: "Shit On Bury, We're gonna Shit on Bury." Well, it is pretty rural in the wilds of Essex. Behind me were a group of locals who obviously attended all the home matches together. They had broad Essex accents and were all in need of a decent haircut, not that they had much to cut between them. These were the bread-and-butter fans of football teams like Colchester. They would come rain or shine, whether the team was brilliant or rubbish, in good times and in bad. They were real characters and the game would be lost without them.

Colchester had given some meaning to their nickname, the U's, with their performances in the Endsleigh League's lowest division They lost their first six games but were unbeaten in their last six. According to then-manager George Burley (now at Ipswich), a replacement for Roy McDonough after he was sacked by his father-in-law, there was no magical reason for the change. They simply persevered with their short passing game.

It was hard to imagine Colchester playing with any style since Gus Caesar, the Arsenal defender held responsible by many fans for the

North London team's defeat in the 1988 League Cup Final and the man immortalised in Nick Hornby's Fever Pitch, was the bedrock of the U's defence. As it turned out, he played OK. He even picked up the knack of scoring goals later in the season to defy his critics. Fancy running into him at Layer Road. It was a shock I must admit. I thought he'd been consigned to the depths of the Scottish League for ever. Arsenal fans must be shuddering with the memories.

Towards the end of the first half against Bury Colchester's Mark Kinsella left the pitch to get some stitches in a head wound. He returned, heavily bandaged like a modern-day Terry Butcher, to a round of applause. But as soon as he made his way towards the centre circle the referee blew his whistle for halftime. The crowd fell about laughing as Kinsella did an about-turn and made his way back to the dressing rooms.

Each issue of the club programme features a question-and-answer profile on a Colchester player. When Kinsella is featured and asked to "Tell us about a funny moment at Colchester United" I'm sure he will recount his short-lived return against Bury. In the second half, he was joined by one of the Bury players who also had his head bandaged. It was beginning to look like a hospital out there on the pitch.

The deadlock was broken in the second half by the tallest player on the pitch, defender Peter Cawley. Colchester were awarded a free-kick about 25 yards out. The supporters around me were calling for Cawley to step up and take the kick. He duly obliged, thumping the ball into the top right-hand corner of Kelly's goal.

The match report in The Times on the Monday after the match, written by Alyson Rudd, said Colchester would be pushing for promotion if they avoided injuries. No doubt, Bury would also be up there at the end of the season. They could have done with the presence of former Bolton and Everton star Peter Reid, now the manager at Sunderland, but then a summer capture from Notts County. But his pay-as-you-play contract was proving to be as unrewarding as this trip to Layer Road: he had managed only six minutes all season.

THROUGH THE LOOKING GLASS
Coventry City v Ipswich Town - Highfield Road
10 October 1994

This was Football Through The Looking Glass. The Premier Club, Highfield Road. Monday night. The visitors, Ipswich Town. Both teams struggling at the bottom of the Premier League and desperate to pick up points as the spectre of relegation already hung over managers Phil Neal and John Lyall. The Sky cameras were here to bring an early season dogfight to your screens. Pressure, what pressure?

I arrived just before kick-off as the last trickle of supporters made their way through the dimly-lit streets of back-to-back houses which snuggled up to the ground. I had a seat in Coventry's new Premier Club, opened at the start of the season. For £1,000 per double membership you could watch all first team home league and cup matches in the comfort of "luxurious theatre-style seating in warm and comfortable surroundings".

There were plenty of spare seats for tonight's match, both in the Premier Club and in the real world outside. In fact, the Sky Blues were playing in front of only 9,526 - their lowest crowd of the season so far. The locals had either decided that Ipswich weren't an attraction or they were sitting at home by the fire with a cup of hot chocolate watching Sky. They could have joined me in the Premier Club for £40 a seat.

It was like a cross between a hotel and a cinema. I was welcomed at reception like a hotel guest on a weekend break. "Could you give me your name please," said the receptionist. "Thank you. Here's your ticket, Sir." It was so civilised. Hard to imagine I was about to watch 90 minutes of blood and thunder Premier League football. Still, an interesting concept. And not at all surprising that Coventry are at the forefront of new innovations.

The club was formed in 1883 by workers at the Singer's bicycle factory and first played as Singer's FC. The name was changed to Coventry in 1898 and the following year they settled at Highfield Road. They joined the League in 1919 as members of the Second Division and moved between there and the Third Division.

Then, in 1958, when they were relegated to the old Fourth Division for the first and only time, a certain James W. T. Hill, recently retired from playing the game, became manager. What followed was nothing short of a revolution and the period is still called the 'Sky Blue era'. Under Hill's guidance City went from the Third Division to the First in six years. They became the only club to have played in six divisions of the Football League (Third Division North and South plus all four of the mainstream divisions). The team played in a new Sky Blue strip, which is how they got their nickname.

But it wasn't just success on the pitch which attracted attention to the Sky Blues. The off-the-pitch changes were equally remarkable. The Thackhall Street Stand on the north side of the ground was replaced in the early 60s with a revolutionary new pre-fabricated construction known as the Sky Blue Stand. This futuristic concept was put together by a company called Banbury Grandstands. It was like something out of Marks & Spencers: made to fit any size. The cost: £120,000.

The next innovation was an electric scoreboard given to the club by the Coventry Evening Telegraph. The League's first executive club was launched in the Main Stand with a membership at 100 guineas a year. Radio Sky Blue kept fans entertained before matches alongside the dog handling displays, pop concerts and netball matches! And the club began to televise away games on large screens at Highfield Road.

After promotion as Second Division Champions in 1967 a double-decker West Stand was built for £85,000. Coventry had clinched the title in a Championship decider, beating Wolves before a record crowd of over 51,000. The club also launched the Sky Blue Match Day Magazine, just a little ahead of its time. It took most other League clubs some 20 years to realise what a good idea such a broad publication was.

In 1968 the Main Stand was destroyed by fire along with the Second Division Championship trophy. City immediately replaced it with a large version of the Sky Blue Stand – only this one had a restaurant on the first floor.

But the most dramatic innovation, and again an idea ahead of its time, was the decision in 1981 to turn Highfield Road into the country's first all-seater stadium. The conversion required an extra 8,000 seats and cost £400,000. It reduced the capacity from 38,500 to 20,616 (present capacity is 22,600). The main aim of this momentous undertaking was to tackle hooliganism which the club believed had undermined the family atmosphere.

The club's proudest moment came in 1987 when they beat Spurs 3-2 in extra-time to win the FA Cup for the only time under manager John Sillett and his assistant George Curtis, the club's former centre-half. Since then the club has built a new stand at the Kop End and extended the roof to the Sky Blue Stand at a cost of £6 million. In 1994, the new 5,000 all-seater East Stand was built.

But what of today's innovative approach to professional football at Highfield Road. Mark Jones, Director of Sales and Marketing, was planning Coventry's version of Air Miles for supporters buying goods in the club shops or spending money in the Premier Club with a club card. "Football Miles" would be redeemed for merchandise or match tickets. Great idea.

But that was the future. Tonight I'd experience the luxury of the Premier Club. Soft royal blue padded seats. Plate glass window separating well-heeled supporters from the fans outside. Crowd noise piped in through speakers embedded in the ceiling, like skylights. The atmosphere was almost surreal. "It's a totally different game from in here," said a bald-headed man with a greying moustache and glasses sitting next to me. "Sure is," said his bearded friend.

The speakers were turned off before the match and at halftime so as not to disturb the diners in the Premier Club restaurant. When I arrived they were tucking into a selection from the Matchday Menu – basically a carvery. If you didn't want to leave the restaurant, it was possible to see the whole match from your table. All the comforts of home. But is this any way to watch football? Coventry had so far sold more than half of the Premier Club memberships so the demand seemed to be there.

Outside, the game had started. Midway through the first half Coventry's Paul Cook swung in a corner which was headed down by Roy Wegerle bringing a good save from Ipswich keeper Craig Forrest. Outside the "real" fans reacted with an "Ooooohhh". Inside, the patrons of the Premier Club clapped politely as if they were registering their appreciation for a movement at a symphony concert or the finish of a crescendo at the opera. There was about as much passion as afternoon tea at The Ritz.

I could see the lights of the carvery reflected in the plate glass separating me from the majority of the Coventry supporters. Staff in royal blue bow ties and white shirts with royal blue waistcoats scurried around behind me preparing for the halftime refreshments. The supervisor was decked out very smartly in a sky blue two-piece suit. Just before halftime the chef made an appearance in his tall hat. The bulk of his work was over for the evening. He could relax now.

The four men in the front row ahead of me had decided to give Coventry defender David Rennie a bit of stick. "You're so mobile Rennie," said one. "Come on Rennie let's see what you can do now," said the other sarcastically. As Coventry began to get on top the criticism became more muted. Just before halftime, they scored. Julian Darby broke down the right and Ipswich captain John Wark, making a desperate attempt to block the cross, only succeeded in stabbing the ball into his own net.

"Johnny Wark, Johnny Wark, Johnny Wark," rang out from the Coventry fans as the two teams left the field at halftime to be replaced by Sky's dancing girls. So they did still exist. Auntie Beryl at Ipswich had told me they'd been dropped from this year's Sky repertoire, but there they were. Resplendent in their sky blue leotards with matching pom poms. I wished I had binoculars to get a closer look!

The Warwickshire cricket team paraded around the pitch at halftime with the four trophies they'd picked up from their wonderfully successful season: three winners trophies and one runners-up. They received a warm reception from the home crowd.

Inside the Premier Club, the punters were tucking into tea and biscuits as they watched Alan Parry on the television monitors beaming Sky Sports' Monday Night Football to all corners of the suite. I took a cup of coffee and returned to my comfy chair to watch the second half. Expensive cigar smoke wafted over my head from the front row. The atmosphere was like a posh London men's club.

Coventry keeper Steve Ogrizovic saw more action in the second half and came to the rescue four times. He snatched the ball from the head of Chris Kiwomya, dived at the feet of Claus Thomsen and Stuart Slater and then stopped a close range header from Steve Sedgeley. "Oggie, Oggie, Oggie," chanted the crowd. (I knew that's what they were chanting because of the speaker positioned just above my head.)

One of the liveliest players on the pitch was American World Cup star Cobi Jones. His dreadlocks flowed all over the pitch as he jinked and twisted and turned his way into space. His lightning pace was unsettling the Ipswich defence leaving gaps for Coventry's other American, Wegerle, and £2 million summer signing Dion Dublin. The former Manchester United star had scored six goals in six games since his arrival at Highfield Road, but he did not add to that tally tonight.

"Pass it to Cobi," said a young lad in the front row. "Give it to Cobi," he repeated, as if the young American was his best friend. Jones had arrived at Highfield Road for a £500,000 fee but his contract would come up for discussion at the end of the season. One official thought he'd leave to join America's new Major League Soccer circus. "He's pretty homesick here," she said. Jones was still living in a hotel. "But he's also overwhelmed to be playing in the Premiership before thousands of people every week."

The supporters next to me were discussing the cost of advertising on the club scoreboard. "They rang me and asked if I'd like to advertise," said the bearded one, obviously a local businessman. "They wanted £150 to flash an ad on the scoreboard at every home game up to

Christmas." "You wouldn't get an ad in The Evening Telegraph for that," said the bald man. "That sounds cheap to me."

Not cheap enough. "The trouble is the fans aren't watching the scoreboard, they're looking at the football. That's why I didn't have it in the end. Mind you, I've heard people say they've seen my ad at the match. I had it last year. It cost me £150 for the season." He might have had a chance of selling them something from the scoreboard tonight. The football being served up was distinctly less appetising than the carvery.

One of the few flashes of brilliance came from Ipswich keeper Craig Forrest who denied Wegerle after 68 minutes, but it was only a matter of time before Coventry scored again. It came from a Paul Cook penalty after Wegerle was bundled over by Gavin Johnson.

Towards the end of the match a cheer went up for substitute Peter Ndlovu as he began to warm up. Surprisingly, manager Phil Neal took off Cobi Jones. Ndlovu's arrival, after a long lay off with injury, cheered the home fans. "Down with the Leicester, you're going down with the Leicester," rang out across Highfield Road. A couple of weeks before the Ipswich players had been serenaded by supporters from Norwich who sang "Down with the Walker, you're going down with the Walker." Different companions, but the same message. Ipswich were in deep trouble.

The match over, I grabbed a drink from the bar and asked an official to call me a cab. After half-an-hour she'd had no luck. I said I might take the advice of the taxi driver who'd dropped me outside the ground and walk into the city centre to hail a cab there. "I wouldn't walk through the back streets at night on your own," said the official. "It's not too safe around here on your own at night. The stadium is on the border of the Hillfields district of Coventry, an area of town notorious for crime."

Perhaps crime is the result of the depressed and downbeat atmosphere in the city now its car industry, first established in the 1890s, had suffered badly. Or maybe it's because Coventry is plagued by some of the ugliest urban planning in England, including the shopping precinct and inner ring road, which resulted from the rebuilding of the city after bombing raids in 1940. The Germans destroyed the armaments factories and devastated much of the old town, including Highfield Road which took three direct hits and was closed for 18 months.

As I was leaving the ground one of the club's security guards added credence to the warnings I'd been given about the safety of the area. When the Coventry official, smartly dressed in a sky blue two-piece suit, offered me a lift to the station I gratefully accepted.

FAREWELL TO THE COUNTY GROUND - AGAIN
Northampton Town v Mansfield Town - The County Ground
11 October 1994

"The lights will go out at the Country Ground tonight," said the local Northampton Chronicle & Echo under the headline End of an Era. "Tonight signals a landmark for Northampton Town Football Club," said the Cobblers' manager John Barnwell. It was billed as one of the most exciting and eventful weeks in the club's history. After nearly 100 years Northampton were leaving the County Ground and moving across town to the new £5.2 million Sixfields Stadium. Mansfield would be the ground's last visitors.

Of course, the fans had seen it all before. 'Last Game 11 – The Sequel' was being shown at the County Ground tonight by virtue of the fact that the first 'last game', if you see what I mean, was supposed to have been played against Chester the previous season. The Cobblers won that match before more than 6,000 fans on an emotional 'final' day at the ground they'd shared with the cricket and bowls club for 97 years. However, their new 7,646 all-seater stadium wasn't finished on time bringing yet another curtain call.

I'd arrived in Northampton earlier that afternoon to soak up the atmosphere in the town on this historic day. As I checked into the Moat House Hotel near the station, a white concrete 1960's monstrosity with about as much warmth as the Arctic Circle, there were no signs that this was a special day for the people of Northampton. No banners to greet me at the station. No posters advertising 'The End of An Era'. Only the local paper had made any effort to drum up excitement about the move in what's a pretty sleepy town best known for its shoe industry - hence the club's nickname: the Cobblers.

As the night began to draw in I left my hotel and walked through the town square past the market stalls and the paved shopping area towards the Northampton Town Football Club and County Cricket Ground. Young fans were already making their way to the stadium to bid the old ground farewell. Mind you, the Chronicle & Echo's Special Report on the last game didn't sound as if it would miss the club's old home. "Tonight the curtain comes down at the tatty, three-sided County Ground – a joke venue for football fans over several years – and this time there will be no encores."

At least it had the distinction of being the only three-sided ground in the Football League! Ironically, that accolade was bestowed on the Cobblers after Sheffield United built over their cricket pitch in 1974.

United's Bramall Lane had recently returned to its former prominence of having only three sides by virtue of ground redevelopment resulting in the demolition of one of the main stands. But that was a transitionary phase and didn't really count.

The local Northampton paper's back page Sports Chronicle section echoed the feelings expressed in the Special Report. "Sixfields, in all its splendour, is lying in wait in Northampton's West End. And the boys from the soccer slums will be kicking their last ball in the ramshackle hovel that has been home for far too long." It wasn't for nothing that the ground's 'temporary' Main Stand was known as the Meccano Stand. It looked as if a group of young kids had been let loose for an afternoon with their nuts and spanners.

As I turned into Roseholme Road, past the Abington Park Brewery Co. on the corner, I could see the County Ground floodlights. They'd replaced the old-style lights a decade ago after they blew a fuse during their final appearance, causing a match to be abandoned. I wondered if the same thing could happen again tonight. The Sports Chronicle, then as now, had almost prophesied the disaster with their statement that, "The lights will go out at the County Ground tonight". They certainly did that night.

The back of the ground displayed a sign which said, 'Northamptonshire County Cricket Club' in gold relief letters on a maroon background either side of the entrance. Signs inside the cricket ground entrance said: "Dr Martens Air Wair Welcomes You to the County Ground". There were tiny turnstiles to the left and right. All seemed to be decorated in gold and maroon – except for the Mansfield team coach parked over to my left in a corner of the tiny car park.

The eight-and-a-half acre site started out as farmland before being converted into a cricket pitch in the 1880s. The football club used the cricket pavilion on the condition that they could not play before September 1st or after May 1st – a condition that remained in force until the Cobblers left for their new stadium in the autumn of 1994.

I soon realised that the main ticket office was on the other side of the ground on Abington Avenue and not at the entrance to the cricket ground, even though it was used by football fans who wanted to stand on the touchline across from the Meccano Stand. I backtracked and walked around to the front of the stadium. Suddenly, the atmosphere began to fill me with excitement and anticipation. There were thousands of people queuing outside the Hotel End in a long line stretching halfway up the road.

"There'll be 6,000 here tonight," said one fan who passed by me among the rush of supporters heading for the main entrance on Abington Avenue. The maroon-coloured Main Stand was now half its original height after the club had lopped off the top section in November 1985 because some of the steel roof girders were deemed to be unsafe and it was too expensive to replace them.

Maroon balloons decorated the directors' entrance in the middle of the Main Stand. Paper sellers were flogging Special Editions of the Chronicle & Echo. 'Farewell County Ground – Picture Special' was stamped on billboards displayed around the ground. Fans in the club shop were enquiring about tickets for County's opening match at the new Sixfields Stadium against Barnet on the coming Saturday. 'Carpet Supacentre - Official Sponsors of Northampton Town Football Club' welcomes you to the County Ground on this side of the stadium.

Camera crews were milling around outside the ground to film the line of supporters waiting to get in at the Hotel End – so-called because of The County Tavern pub in the corner between that end and the Main Stand. The pub was packed and the fans inside were in good voice. I joined the queue to get into the Main Stand, if you could call it that. An attractive young woman was selling newspapers alongside a billboard which read: 'County Ground Special: End of an Era'.

"What's your most memorable visit to the County Ground?" one television reporter asked an elderly grey-haired man in the queue. "He hasn't got one," interrupted the fan in front of me. The old man thought for a moment. "When we beat the Arsenal," he replied. "That was in 1958 wasn't it?" said the reporter. "Aye. The glory years," said the old man. "I must have missed those," quipped the man in front of him. "Oh yes, I remember, when we kept a clean sheet against Bradford." The supporters around him laughed. It's tough at the bottom.

And that's where Northampton were - almost. An unbeaten run of five matches had pulled the Cobblers from 92nd place into 90th position in the League's basement division. Things could only get better. Manager John Barnwell certainly hoped so. "Of course, we're all looking forward to the move to Sixfields. After such a long wait for a new ground, it's a dream come true for everyone involved with the club, and it will be a big asset. The players trained on the pitch on Tuesday and they loved it. I'm sure that the club can now realise their full potential at such a ground."

The first match at the County Ground was in September 1897 against Earls Barton from the Northants League in a pre-season friendly. The Cobblers secured their first win in their first competitive home game in a 3-1 win over Rushden Reserves. The gate receipts were nine shillings and fourpence, about 47 pence. Tonight's match against Mansfield was expected to net £30,000 from the fans.

Northampton progressed from the Northants League (now the United Counties League) through the Midland League (1899 to 1901) and the Southern League (1901 to 1920). Their first success was as Southern League champions in 1909 under the great Herbert Chapman, who was later to guide Huddersfield and Arsenal to First Division titles. Town became founder members of Football League Division Three in 1920, but the Southern League was their only trophy until they won the Third Division championship in 1963.

And that's where they were now, though today it's effectively the old Fourth Division. In between they had scaled the lofty heights of the old First Division in the 1965/66 season after enjoying a dramatic rise beginning with promotion from the Fourth Division in 1961, from the Third in 1963 and, finally, up from the Second in 1965. They were the first team to rise from the Fourth to the First Division and they did it in a remarkable five years. But they lasted only one season in the top grade before being relegated in front of a record crowd of 24,523 versus Fulham. Their final home match was against Sunderland.

By 1969 they were back in the Fourth Division and even had to apply for re-election in 1972. One of their most famous matches was in the fifth round of the FA Cup in 1970 when Manchester United were the visitors. Georgie Best scored six goals as the Reds slaughtered the Cobblers 8-2 in a game shown on Match of the Day. It was one of Best's virtuoso performances. Who could forget the goal he scored after seemingly beating the entire Town defence before dummying the keeper and nonchalantly knocking the ball into the back of the net before raising his arm in triumph. It was one of football's magical moments.

The game was the only one in the County Ground's history watched by supporters in stands all around the ground, since a temporary stand was put up along the cricket pitch side. That's why it grossed record receipts at the time of £17,000. Those who turned up had seen a genius at work in the shape of Georgie Best. They'd never see anyone like him again. And certainly not tonight against Mansfield.

The crowd were warming up with chants of "Come on you Cobblers". The atmosphere was beginning to build up as the kick-off approached. At the Hotel End I could see a few fans watching from the top windows of the pub, beers in hand, as the teams came onto the pitch.

On the opposite side of the ground a handful of people lined up a few yards back from the touchline behind a rope which separated the pitch from the rest of the cricket ground. I could see the cricket pavilion in the distance, with the scoreboard on the left. The football and cricket pitches overlapped by about 20 yards and, during the summer, the football pitch was used by cricket fans as a car park.

To my left was the temporary Meccano Stand. It was the strangest looking stand I'd see all season and basically looked like a lot of scaffolding. It was almost as if Northampton were in the process of building a new stand, except that they weren't. Barnet manager Ray Clemence and then Luton, now Sheffield Wednesday, boss David Pleat stood in the Meccano Stand near the touchline with their hands in their pockets on what was a chilly night. Northampton would play Barnet in their first match at the new Sixfields Stadium the following Saturday. Clemence had come to check out the opposition.

To my far left was the Spion Kop – a name used at many grounds around the country but never applied to such a strange End as the one at the County Ground. The Kop didn't quite reach the far corner of that end of the ground, but disappeared near the edge of the penalty area. From the Kop you could see the bowling green off to the left behind the cricket pitch. The far touchline cut across the outer edge of the cricket field as it marked out the football pitch – the longest in the League at 120 x 75 yards.

The local fans were now filling the ground. Mums and dads with their kids; a father and son wrapped in claret and blue scarves; three young girls on a night out; a group of lads standing behind me; and behind them the old guard, die-hard supporters who'd seen the best and the worst of times at the County Ground but who still came back out of habit and a sense of loyalty to their local team, even if the football was sometimes dire.

At least it was better than the food. 'Simply the Best' said the sign advertising caterer Tony Ansell's fare. I was sure they could have been done under the Trade Descriptions Act. 'Simply the Worst' was more like it .The cheeseburger I bought from 'The Family Cabin' refreshment hut, served up by a woman who looked just like a farmer's wife, was the worst I'd ever tasted, and by now I'd tasted quite a few. "Where's the Beef?" I wondered. I had some good advice for the young couple queuing behind me. "Try the pasties," I told them, "they can't possibly be worse than the hamburgers." Could they?

The ground was getting full by now, though there was still room on the terraces in the Family Stand and on the Spion Kop where the travelling Mansfield supporters had gathered to cheer on their team. The Hotel End was a different story. It was packed to the rafters now.

The Family Stand terrace was filled with kids along the front, standing on two reverse steps made of chipboard constructed so the little tykes could see the match. The back of the stand was also full since the view was good.

Two young Northampton apprentices wandered through the crowd before the kick-off raffling a signed football. The draw would be made at half-time. I bought a ticket. Number 59. Would I be lucky? What do you think?

Midway through the first half smoke drifted over the Main Stand. The home supporters thought it might be ceremonial. "Maybe they're cremating the stand," said one fan. "Or the directors," said his mate in the gold-rimmed glasses wearing a check lumberjack shirt and quilted tank top jacket.

The game started and the ball soon came over to the near touchline. Mansfield's Kevin Noteman shouted "Fucking hell" after tussling for the ball. The crowd complained at him and he suddenly realised there were lots of kids lined up along the front of the terraces. He held up his hand to apologise.

Town manager John Barnwell hoped his team could bid the ground farewell with a win. "It's sure to be an emotional night in many ways, and it would be nice to sign off with a victory." But, as so often happens on these occasions, Mansfield spoiled the party by taking the lead after 20 minutes when centre-forward Steve Wilkinson scored with a shot which went in off the post. Northampton pressed for an equaliser, but it never came.

The fans were asked to stay off the pitch at the end of the match, but there was little chance of that happening tonight. When the referee blew the final whistle the fans at the Hotel End swarmed onto the pitch joined by the young lads at the front of the Main Stand. The celebrations were finally broken up by police on horseback – a bit extreme since it was very good natured and there was not a hint of trouble.

So that was that. The End of an Era. Town manager John Barnwell was certainly looking forward to the move to a new stadium, but he was also sad to see the club move from their old home. "History is history and I'm sure a lot of fans will have fond memories of the ground. For example, the teams associated with Dave Bowen and Graham Carr certainly served up their fair share of memories. " But Barnwell also had a word of warning. "...I've said before that supporters won't pay to watch a new stand, or a new ground. It's all about what happens on the field..."

After the match I walked back around the ground, passing a group of young lads carrying part of an advertising hoarding and a sign - mementoes of the last game at the County Ground. They could show their grandchildren and tell them they were there the night the curtain came down.

I finally reached the station to catch my train to London. There were only a few fans on the platform, but one middle-aged man appeared smarter than the rest. He wore a blazer with a Mansfield Town club tie. His name was Sandy Whetton and he was a Stags' director. In fact, tonight he was the only Mansfield director at the match. We started talking about the game and football in general. My journey home would be fascinating.

Sandy lives in London and works for a publishing company but he still manages to watch about 35 Mansfield games a year. His wife is very understanding and goes to many matches with him. Sandy is, like myself, a football fanatic. His passion for the game was clear. "I was that archetypal little kid kicking a ball against the wall in my back garden," said Sandy. Lacking the talent of a Georgie Best or Rodney Marsh, Sandy had settled for a career as a Mansfield Town supporter.

After following the Stags all over the country as a fan, he got to know the players, manager and directors, Eventually, his commitment to the cause confirmed, he was invited to join the board. When the club reached the Freight Rover Trophy final in 1987 Sandy was so emotional that he cried when the teams walked out onto the Wembley turf. "I got control of myself, but then the national anthem started and I was bawling my eyes out again," he told me as our train trundled towards London.

One of the highlights of Sandy's football supporting career was Mansfield's 3-0 Fifth Round FA Cup win over West Ham in February 1969. The Third Division side astounded the football world that day by beating a Hammers' team including their three World Cup stars Bobby Moore, Geoff Hurst and Martin Peters and a young Trevor Brooking. Brooking later described the defeat as one of the worst of his career.

Sandy had moved to Putney in West London, within walking distance of Fulham's ground at Craven Cottage. One day, as he left his house early in the morning to go to work, he noticed a fair-haired man walking his dog. It was Bobby Moore. They exchanged good mornings and then, just as Sandy was about to drive off, the England World Cup captain motioned to him to open the car window. "Is that your Mansfield sticker on the window?" enquired Moore. "Yes," said Sandy. Moore looked at him with a glint in his eye. "You mean I've got to walk past that every bloody morning!"

A more recent giant-killing in the cup – this time the Coca-Cola version – resulted in Sandy acquiring one of his prize possessions. Mansfield recorded one of the biggest upsets of the 1994/95 season by knocking out Leeds 1-0. After the match, the sponsors couldn't decide who to nominate as 'Man of the Match'. The players also refused to vote for one player. Nobody was chosen and the award of a Coca-Cola jacket, usually given to the best player, complete with 'Man of the Match' logo embroidered on one side and the Coca-Cola logo on the back was instead awarded to Sandy in recognition of his services as a Stags' director. He cherishes it to this day.

Sandy's one remaining ambition was too see his team play in Europe. "That would top everything off nicely, travelling abroad with Mansfield." He had hopes of a match in the Anglo-Italian Cup someday, but was realistic enough to realise that he might have to settle for a pre-season trip to Majorca! Where would football be without the passion and commitment of people like Sandy Whetton? Now here was a director whose love of the game was total. The Alan Sugars and Barry Hearns may have the money, but the Sandy Whettons have the loyalty and the heart.

THE GODFATHER
Leeds United v Tottenham Hotspur - Elland Road
15 September 1994

On the morning of the match I woke up to hear alarming headlines on the radio: "Twenty-two policemen have been hurt in clashes with youths on the rampage in Leeds," said the announcer. "Cars have been overturned and set alight and 26 police vehicles have been damaged in the Chapeltown area of the city." Great, I thought, just the time to be travelling north to watch United play Spurs.

Leeds fans have not had the best reputation over the years and rioting in the city was hardly the prelude I needed for my first game at Elland Road. Apparently, the trouble started when two policewomen were attacked by a 20 strong mob as the officers tried to arrest a youth. That number grew to nearer 200 by the time the rioters began stoning police and other vehicles.

"The incident in Chapeltown was totally unprovoked and at one time clearly co-ordinated by a hard-core of youths intent on causing as much trouble and injury to police as they could. The vast majority of people in this area are law-abiding and supportive of police. But there is a hard-core of youths who have no respect for authority whatsoever."

Those statements from Inspector Stuart Cuthbert could have been used to describe the football fans who once followed Leeds United on an orgy of violence across Britain and Europe. But not today. The fans at the Tottenham game were impeccably behaved. It wasn't the friendliest ground I'd visited (Doncaster took that accolade) but, nevertheless, the atmosphere was friendly and not at all hostile, unless you were one of the players on the pitch wearing the navy blue change strip of Tottenham Hotspur.

I'd driven to Leeds from London - an easy task since the M62 passes within 100 yards of Elland Road. But anyone arriving at Leeds City station by train will be welcomed by Joshua Tetley. Not personally, of course, but his name is on the station's welcome sign. Tetley's Brewery stands on Hamlet Road and, according to one local guide, the beer is to Yorkshire what Guinness is to Ireland. There's a special visitors centre on Dock Street and twice-daily tours of the brewery itself. Supporters probably know as much about the local beer as they do about the football team.

In 1847 Charles Dickens called Leeds "the beastliest place, one of the nastiest I know". Much has changed since then. The city has been cleaned up and urban renewal is the buzzword. Leeds is today one of the fastest growing cities in Britain. The city, built across a basin of the River Aire, was traditionally a centre of the textile industry. The main industries, including engineering, are concentrated on flat ground south of the river, while the suburbs stand on the heights that ring the city to the north.

The Leeds Markets area, on the east side, is impressive, particularly the Kirgate Market, the largest in the north and a descendent of the medieval woollen markets that made Leeds the focus of the region's textile industry. The outdoor market is where Michael Marks set up his stall in 1884 with the slogan "Don't ask the price, it's a penny." It was the forerunner of Marks and Spencer. Leeds is also the home of Harry Ramsden's famous fish and chips - now being franchised all over England. I was to enjoy Harry's fare, but not at Leeds. It would have to wait for my visit to Blackpool.

But Leeds is probably more famous for its football team than anything else, especially the great Leeds side of the '60's and early '70's which included stars like Billy Bremner, Johnny Giles, Jack Charlton and Allan Clarke. Their all white strip was adopted under the management of the legendary Don Revie, nicknamed the Godfather, who wanted his team to look, and play, like Real Madrid. Revie, an England international and Footballer of the Year in 1955, took over as player-manager in 1961 when Leeds were in the Second Division. They won the title and promotion in 1964.

Revie's team captured their first major trophies in 1968 when they collected the League Cup and the European Fairs Cup. The following season they were First Division Champions with a record 67 points (teams got two points for a win back then), many of which were chalked up during a run of 34 matches without defeat. In 1970 they were on track to record a remarkable treble of European Cup, FA Cup and League Championship, but lost in the European Cup semi-final, against Chelsea in the FA Cup Final and came runners-up to Everton in the League.

But the team's strength of character ensured further successes and in 1971 they won a second Fairs Cup followed by the FA Cup in 1972 (1-0 against Arsenal with an Allan Clarke strike) and a second League Championship in 1974. They became only the third British team to reach the European Cup final the following year, but lost 2-0 to Bayern Munich and were banned for three years from European competition because of a riot by their supporters after the match in Paris.

That was the swansong for the great Leeds team built by Revie, though he'd left by then to take over as England manager. He quit the

England job in 1977 amid controversy following secret negotiations to take over as manager of the Arab Emirates national team. But he'll always be remembered as the manager of one of the greatest club sides ever assembled. It's remarkable that they reached the final stages of 17 competitions but only won six major honours during Revie's reign.

Three times they came close to the double (1965, 1970 and 1972) but defeat in the FA Cup final snatched it away on the first two occasions and, when they eventually won the cup in 1972, they could only manage runners-up spot in the League. The FA Cup was also a competition in which Leeds were often the fall guys to a giant killing. Odd-goal defeats from Fourth Division Colchester in 1971 (see Colchester United v Bury), Second Division Sunderland in the 1973 Final, Bristol City, another Second Division team, in 1974, and Third Division Crystal Palace in 1976 had embarrassed the team that Revie built throughout their glory years.

Success on the pitch led to changes at the ground: Elland Road. The road from which the ground takes its name runs west to the town of Elland, near Huddersfield, while Leeds Road (the name of Huddersfield's ground before they moved into the futuristic McAlpine Stadium – see Huddersfield v Hull) brings you east to Leeds.

A new West Stand had already been opened in 1957 after a fire destroyed the Main Stand. It cost £150,000 – an enormous sum at the time. But it was the rising attendances, and soaring gate receipts, accompanying the Revie revolution that heralded further changes at Elland Road. The open Kop End on Geldard Road was replaced by a £250,000 covered terrace in 1968. (The North Stand, as it was called, was made all-seater at the end of the 1993/94 season for just over £1 million). A new South Stand replaced the small scratching shed at the Elland Road End in 1974 for £400,000 and executive boxes, the first at any club in Yorkshire, were installed at the back of the stand in 1983.

More recent developments include a family stand and executive boxes, costing £500,000, built during the 1989/90 season, a new south-east corner, constructed before the 1991/92 campaign, for £820,000, and a £1.3 million banqueting suite built later that season. The most recent development is the new £6.5 million 17,000 all-seater East Stand, which replaced the Lowfields Road Stand. It has the largest cantilever roof span of any ground in Europe.

So impressive is the new Elland Road that it was chosen as a venue for the 1996 European Championships and Leeds had already been told they'd host one of the four seeded teams. "We obviously don't know who they are at the moment but you could be talking about the likes of

Holland, Italy and Germany if the form guide goes to plan during the qualifiers," said United general manager Alan Roberts. When you consider seven of the last eight in the World Cup came from Europe, we're going to have some tremendous football in this country in 1996."

The capacity at Elland Road is around 40,000 but the number of tickets for the European Championships that would be available to the public would be between 20 and 25,000. The rest would go to the participating countries, VIPs, television people etc. Leeds were therefore urging supporters to buy tickets early to avoid disappointment. United chairman Leslie Silver made a presentation before the Spurs game to the first season-ticket holder to secure his Elland Road seat for Euro '96.

The day after the Tottenham game the club would honour their legendary former manager with the official opening of the North Stand under its new title of the Revie Stand. Don's widow, Elsie, would unveil a plaque in her husband's honour alongside the entire Revie family, United players past and present, the backroom staff associated with the Revie years and 200 supporters lucky enough to have bought a special programme distributed at Leeds' last home match against Manchester City.

"The stand and the plaque will stand as a fitting testament to the work and success that Don Revie brought not only to Leeds United but the city," said general manager Alan Roberts. "The chairman and directors sanctioned that it should be called The Revie Stand and I think most supporters will appreciate that – and certainly the Revie family will. There will also be a memorial wall in the stand with pictures, newspaper cuttings highlighting Don Revie's success and achievements."

One player from the Revie era, who'd regularly struck fear into the heart of strikers, had today returned to the scene of his greatest crunching tackles to provide the colour commentary for radio on the Spurs game. Norman "Bites Yer Legs" Hunter looked the picture of health as he made his way to the main entrance signing autographs as he went. He was still famous here and recognised by most of the crowd around me. Hunter's looks had fared well over the years. He was a little greyer, but that's all.

Hunter had strong views about the new Fifa rules outlawing tackles from behind - an art form he'd perfected. "Obviously, it's right to outlaw the sort of tackle in which the defender just clatters into the back of his opponent - the one that let's him know you're there, as we'd have said in my day. But what about the tackle in which you're genuinely going for the ball? Say it's your first tackle of the game, and you've only got to mistime it slightly and you could be sent off. That can't be right. And you have to remember the pace the game is played at nowadays. Mistakes are bound to happen."

"Tackling is an art form - just as much a part of the game as any of the other skills. And I think that if the physical side of the game gets lost, then you really are in trouble. Football is a physical game. There's nothing better than a good challenge, a good 50-50 ball. You have to have that sort of competitive edge or the game loses something vital."

Norman should know. He was one of the fiercest tacklers the game had seen and won the fist Player of the Year award in 1973. Leeds and England trainer Les Cocker once said: "Norman Hunter phoned me once to say that he'd gone home with a broken leg. I asked him, 'Whose leg is it?'"

Inside the ground Spurs' Chairman Alan Sugar sat behind me up in the directors' box. He had a glowering look about him, as if he thought he was surrounded by enemies waiting for the chance to stab him in the back. I wondered if he'd seen Terry Venables in the crowd. Sugar's serious demeanour remained with him throughout the match, even when Tottenham scored. At halftime he was asked for his autograph by a young girl and duly obliged after straining to hear her over the front of the directors box.

Sugar was flanked by Tony Berry, the longest-serving member of the Spurs board who'd survived from the regime of Irving Scholar. Tottenham's previous chairman. Berry's picture was splashed across the next morning's Sunday Times following the withdrawal of a Department of Trade and Industry investigation into his role in the so-called Blue Arrow affair. The story alongside reported that Amstrad, Sugar's electronics company, was expected to report a loss of £5 million. That would be substantially lower than the previous year and a good few million short of his investment of more than £8 million in Tottenham Hotspur Football Club.

The Leeds supporters next to me in the old West Stand looked round at Sugar after each incident in the match to gauge his reaction. Before his joint bid with Venables for a controlling stake in Spurs he was known to only a handful of football supporters. Now, he was a household name. I assumed he craved the attention, though judging by his face he didn't seem to be enjoying the match.

Spurs dominated the opening exchanges and went a goal up through Teddy Sheringham. The Romanian midfielder Ilie Dumitrescu cut back a precise pass after his shot was parried by Leeds keeper John Lukic and the England striker carefully sidefooted the ball into the top corner from the edge of the 18-yard box. Tottenham then created two super chances to tie up the match, and missed them both. Nick Barmby, now at Middlesbrough, and Gheorge Popescu were the culprits.

The second half was to be a different story. Dumitrescu was the first out onto the pitch after the halftime break; or, more precisely, during the interval. He re-emerged a full 10 minutes before his colleagues. The Romanian international squatted near the centre-circle either to soak up the atmosphere or perhaps to escape the half-time team talk. The then-Spurs manager Ossie Ardiles surely wasn't screaming abuse at his players; after all, they were 1-0 up.

As the match went on the home fans became more impatient. "There's a joke going around about Brian Deane," said the Leeds fan from Derby via Devon sitting next to me. "They say Brian Deane can turn like an articulated lorry." At first, I wasn't sure if the joke had finished. But it had. Unable to drum up enough enthusiasm to laugh I responded with a joke I'd heard about Everton's Nigerian international striker Daniel Amokachi. "Why is Amokachi like a taxi? Because he's big, black and carrying a load of passengers." It went down better than the one about the articulated lorry!

As the second half unfolded Leeds began to pile on the pressure. Spurs' keeper Ian Walker was playing out of his skin, spurred on, no doubt, by the fact that Erik Thorstvedt was sitting on the substitutes bench waiting for his chance to return to first team action after injury. Walker had made three blinding saves in the first half and was equally impressive in the second. He was finally beaten by Deane in the 62nd minute.

The football over I walked past the home fans in their blue and white scarves who were spilling out of the ground and returned to my car. My next stop was the village of Haworth in Bronte country to the west of Leeds and Bradford. The bustling village sits on the very edge of the Pennine moors like a gritstone fortress. The moors had changed little since the time of the Bronte sisters. There were crumbling drystone walls, a few old farms and lots of sheep. The grass and heather are still buffeted by the wind and rain. There was mile after mile of awe-inspiring, yet forbidding, emptiness.

More than a century ago, when the Reverend Patrick Bronte came to be minister at Haworth Parish Church, the village was little more than a collection of stone-built weavers' cottages huddled together for protection from the harsh winter winds. But within a few decades, a series of books, including Wuthering Heights and Jane Eyre, caused this obscure Yorkshire village to become a major centre for literary pilgrims.

All six of the Bronte children died from illness while still young, but during their short and sad lives the three youngest sisters - Charlotte, Emily and Anne - spent long hours writing in secret, leaving a priceless legacy of novels. Thousands of visitors now come to Haworth to see the sites and buildings which provided the inspiration for the sisters' books and to experience the atmosphere of the surrounding moors. Three miles outside Haworth stood a ruined farmhouse in a remote moorland spot called Top Withens which is thought to have been the inspiration for Wuthering Heights.

The steep Main Street, lined with shops, cafes and galleries, led down to one of Britain's best preserved railways, the Keighley & Worth Valley Steam Railway, where films like The Railway Children and Yanks were made. The Main Street, paved with stone setts, looked as if it had come straight out of a Hovis ad. I stayed at a small guest house called Heather Cottage on Main Street. It was formerly two weavers' cottages built about 260 years ago.

The next morning I went for a walk around the village. As I looked up the hill on Main Street, I could imagine a young lad cycling down with a loaf of bread under his arm. At the tope of the hill was the Black Bull Hotel and the Druggist's Store – a deadly combination for the Bronte's brother Branwell who died from a deadly concoction of drink, from the pub, and opium from the druggist's.

THE LION OF VIENNA
Bolton Wanderers v Oldham Athletic - Burnden Park
16 October 1995

My next stop was a famous old club whose President was an England star of the 1950's known as the Lion of Vienna. Bolton Wanderers' centre-forward Nat Lofthouse still worked as a miner down the pits after making his debut for the Trotters in 1939. He'd get up at four o'clock in the morning and work an eight hour shift before playing for Bolton in the afternoon. He was aggressive, yet courageous, and thought nothing of knocking goalkeepers into the back of the net with the ball.

Lofthouse came from the same town as that other legendary centre-forward Tommy Lawton, a star with Everton and Chelsea, and followed him into the England team in 1950. Lofthouse was voted Footballer of the Year in 1953, after scoring in every round of the cup, including the final when Bolton played Blackpool in one of the most famous domestic matches ever staged at Wembley. The game is remembered as the 'Matthews Final' after Sir Stan's achievement in gaining his first winner's medal, but Lofthouse also stamped his name on the record books with his goal a game record.

Mind you, with 20 minutes to go and Bolton leading 3-1 it didn't look as if Stan would emerge clutching that treasured medal of victory. Of course, Blackpool fought back to win 4-3 (see Blackpool v Birmingham). And their manager? Joe Smith, Bolton's record holder for most league goals scored in a season – 38 in 1920/21! Lofthouse emulated Smith by becoming the club's top scorer in the First Division in 1956 and captained Bolton to victory over a depleted Manchester United team in the 1958 Cup Final following the tragic Munich air crash (see Manchester United v Tottenham Hotspur).

His role in that '58 final was particularly controversial because he forced the keeper over the line with the ball for his second goal which won the match. Lofthouse also scored the last of his 30 international goals in 33 appearances – a club record – in 1958. He retired in 1960, because of injury, with a career total of 285 goals in 485 matches.

I'd driven across the Yorkshire moors from the village of Haworth to reach Bolton a couple of hours before the game against rivals Oldham to the south-east. Bolton is a city of almost 150,000 people surrounded by other football towns like Blackburn to the north, Wigan to the south-west, Bury and Rochdale to the east and the two Manchester clubs, United and City, plus Stockport to the south. There must be more

League clubs concentrated in Greater Manchester than any other part of Britain.

Bolton itself was a textile manufacturing centre specialising in wool and, later, cotton. Nowadays engineering and chemicals have taken over as the main industries. The football club was formed in 1874 by boys from Christ Church Sunday School in Blackburn Street, led by their master Thomas Ogden, and was called the Wanderers because in the early years the team had no particular home ground. Their peripatetic state also accounts for the club nickname, the Trotters.

In 1877 they broke away from the Church after a dispute with the vicar and changed their name to Bolton Wanderers and became founder members of the Football League. They lost their first FA Cup Final at Goodison Park in 1894. They reached their second Cup Final in 1904 where they became the first Second Division team to lose in the final in a match played at Crystal Palace. Some of the money earned from that Cup run was used to start building the first section of the Main Stand, on Manchester Road, at a cost of £3,500.

Starting with the White Horse final at Wembley in 1923, Bolton won the cup three times between that first Wembley final and 1929 without conceding a goal at Wembley. They beat West Ham in 1923 (2-0), Manchester City in 1926 (1-0) and Portsmouth in 1929 (2-0). Bolton were to get their hands on the cup again in that 1958 final remembered for Lofthouse's second goal.

Bolton have never won the League Championship but as long ago as 1905 they came runners-up to Liverpool. They have won the Second Division title, in 1909, but finished bottom of the First and were relegated once more in 1910. After gaining promotion again in 1911 Bolton stayed in the top flight for 22 years. In 1987 they escaped from the Third Division – into the Fourth for the first time in their history!

That relegation promoted them to equal third in the list of Most Relegated Football League Clubs in history – a distinction they share with Birmingham and Grimsby (only Notts County and Preston have been relegated more often). They bounced back straight away and in 1992 secured promotion to the Second Division which is how they ended up back in the First Division. Did you all follow that?

Bolton's most recent success was in 1989 when the club won the prestigious Sherpa Van Trophy (which has absolutely nothing to do with sherpas or vans, though there is a trophy for the winners!) Among the club's famous players are strikers Frank Worthington and Francis Lee. When Lee made his debut at 15 on the right wing he scored a goal, was booked and comforted in tears by Lofthouse.

The Lion of Vienna was Bolton's manager between 1968 and 1970 and again in 1971 when he resigned. He took over again briefly in 1985 and the following year accepted the post of club president. The memory of Lofthouse permeates Bolton's Burnden Park ground on the Manchester Road. Pride of place in the club trophy room goes to the shirt he wore in the 1958 FA Cup Final. Lofthouse says he's done everything at the Wanderers from making the tea to scoring cup final goals.

Other features of the trophy room were a huge photograph of the 1923 'White Horse' Final and a mini FA Cup in the trophy cabinet to mark Bolton's 2-1 win over West Ham in the first final at Wembley. One of the Wanderer's goals was scored after the Hammers' full-back ran into the crowd lined up along the side of the pitch after chasing a ball. He couldn't get back on the field because of all the people and in the meantime Bolton had taken the throw-in and scored.

Bolton's oldest fan, James Bradley, 105 years old, whose father played for the club remembered that 1923 final. He would be at Wembley in early April to see the Wanderers in the Coca-Cola Cup Final against Liverpool 72 years after that first FA Cup Final at the Theatre of Legends. Sadly, Bolton would lose the match 2-1.

Bolton's ground was less impressive than I'd imagined. The main entrance was in the Manchester Road Stand. It was almost hidden behind the club's offices, social clubs and executive facilities along the front. The car park and the back of the stand were painted by Lowry in his work Going to the Match, complete with matchstick men and matchstick cats and dogs. The original painting is in private hands, but would fetch about £100,000 at auction. Limited edition prints signed in pencil by Lowry cost about £1,000, but again, they are rarely for sale. Football supporters are also art collectors it seems! The wooden stand was typical of those built in the early 1900s.

A group of teenage girls were waiting in the car park for the Bolton stars to arrive. They were on the lookout for their idols Alan Stubbs and Jason McAteer. McAteer, now at Liverpool, was then being chased by all the big Premier League clubs, after his stirring performances for the Republic of Ireland in the World Cup Finals in America, as well as his teenage fans. One problem for the girls clamouring for his autograph was that he had a steady girlfriend. They arrived together, but McAteer, looking very smart in a trendy black trenchcoat, was happy to sign autographs outside the ground.

Bolton originally moved to Burnden Park in 1895 when the site was a complete mess. One end backed onto a railway and the land itself was a stagnant mixture of chemicals from the nearby works and dumped refuse. The pitch was apparently built up on old barrels and cotton bales and had the most cambered surface in the League.

Bolton played their first game at the ground in September 1895 with a benefit match against Preston. In 1901 the ground staged the FA Cup Final replay between Tottenham and Sheffield United. The first game at Crystal Palace attracted 114,815, England's first six figure attendance. But the replay was watched by an official gate of only 20,740. And even though the actual attendance was higher, perhaps as many as 30,000, this is still the lowest crowd at an FA Cup Final this century.

In 1915 the Main Stand had an extra wing added at the Southern End. In 1928 Bolton began to build The Burnden Stand which cost £20,000 and should not have been beyond the means of a successful club which had just played in two packed Wembley finals. However, there was uproar when cup-winning hero David Jack was sold to Arsenal in October 1928 for a then-record fee of £10,340.

The ground was taken over by the government during the Second World War with the pitch used by the Education Authorities and the stands by the Ministry of Supply. The Burnden Stand was still full of food when an event which was to stand out in the history of football ground tragedies took place on 9 March 1946. It was the precursor to Ibrox, Valley Parade and Hillsborough – The Bolton Disaster.

The match itself was unusual because in the season immediately after the War all cup ties up to the semi-finals were over two legs. The extra games helped to compensate clubs since League matches did not begin on a proper basis until September 1946. Bolton won the first leg of this quarter-final tie at Stoke 2-0. An estimated 85,000 squeezed into Burnden Park for the second leg, most of whom knew nothing about the tragic events unfolding at the Railway End.

The disaster was the first inflicted by a crowd upon itself. Thirty three people died, including seven from Bolton. The accident occurred in the Railway Enclosure, so-called because it was formed on the embankment supporting the main LMS Yorkshire to Bolton line.

Pressure began to build up outside the turnstiles at twenty past two and by 2.30 some people in the crush were already trying to move away from the turnstiles. Five minutes later it was impossible for people coming through the turnstiles to pass along the terraces. Shortly after-wards police began to help spectators out of the north west corner onto the perimeter track. People then began to force their way into the ground over the railway line fence and at the eastern end of the enclosure. The crowd continued to clamber over walls and force open doors. A father who wanted to get his small son out of the ground picked the padlock of the exit gate next to the boys' entrance and people rushed in there.

So many people were packed into the ground, some with tickets and some who had forced entry, that when the teams came onto the pitch at five to three the crowd swayed and the spectators in the north-west corner of the terrace were thrown down into the bottom corner. The crush barriers either bent or collapsed as the crowd seemed to sink. People began to pile up and were trodden underfoot. Many were asphyxiated. As the match kicked off hundreds of fans spilled out onto the pitch. Just after ten past three bodies were brought out and the referee was told there had been fatalities. The players left the pitch and the 33 bodies were laid out on it before being taken away to mortuaries. First aid was given to about 500 people.

Hardly anybody who wasn't in the north-west corner of the Railway Enclosure realised how serious the disaster was. The Manchester Evening News commented on the fact that so many people broke into the ground, many of them servicemen. "Possibly the war has left some people with less respect for law than they used to have."

Afterwards, questions were raised which were to result in lower capacities at every ground in the country. After the government report, which did not blame Bolton specifically, the club spent £5,500 modernizing the Railway End, improving the turnstiles and gates and fencing off the railway line.

From my seat in the Main Stand on the Manchester Road I could see the Railway End to my left. In 1986 the 16,000 capacity terrace was cut in half when a superstore was built on the land flattened behind. The famous embankment with its haunting memories and railway at the back was gone forever. The Normid End, as it's now called after the supermarket, is a source of great amusement to away fans and an embarrassment for Bolton supporters. But the change did mean that access to the Burnden Stand and the back of the terrace was improved by the building of a road, car park and new turnstiles along the route of the former railway.

The north-west gangway where the disaster began was in the corner between the Manchester Road Stand and the end terracing just behind the corner flag. It was from here that Burnden Park featured in Arthur Askey's 1954 film Love Match in which a train-driver stops to watch a match played before a packed crowd wearing cloth caps and smoking Woodbines. Today you can't see the pitch at all from there. A few years after that film Bolton's new floodlights were switched on for a friendly against Hearts in October 1957. It was said at the time that they had enough power to light the streets from Burnden to Blackpool!

To my right was the Great Lever Stand, named after the district nearby which I assumed was itself named after Lord Leverhulme, the soap magnate who lived in Bolton between 1851 and 1925. And behind the Burnden Stand opposite the Manchester Road was a modern sports hall and a floodlit artificial playing surface, which cost £150,000 in October 1986 when it first opened.

The crowd were in full voice for the match against Oldham and were ecstatic when Bolton took a two goal lead. When their Finnish star Mixu Paatelainen scored they sang: "Mixu, Mixu Mixu, Mixu Mixu, Mixu Paatelainen" to the tune of No Limit. McAteer was pulling the strings in midfield, David Lee was making surging runs down the wing and John McGinlay looked dangerous up front. Unfortunately, the defence let Oldham back in and they scored twice in the second half to square the match at 2-2. The atmosphere changed from joy to despair, optimism to pessimism. The new mood reflected the view of the fans about how the club was being run off the pitch.

After years of fending off complaints from the Burnden Park faithful about the lack of money spent on the ground's facilities, the powers that be had finally decided to move. However, there weren't any plans to relocate within the town, but to a place called Red Moss, a large expanse of muddy industrial wasteland in Horwich, to the north of Bolton. Simon Jones of the 'Keep Wanderers in Bolton' campaign vented his feelings about the planned relocation in When Saturday Comes. "For many fans the club might as well be thinking of moving to the other side of the moon."

"The news that's filtered out... from the Bolton Evening News has already mentioned 'secret negotiations' with the council and various consortia. The only merits that we can see in the club's backing for this Lancashire San Siro is that it shows that they're ambitious and have a desire to regain the lofty heights we have not seen since Frank Worthington last graced the Burnden Park turf with a full head of hair."

"In the opinion of many Bolton fans, however, the move is ill conceived, ill advised and, sadly, a prime example of the gulf of communication that exists between the boardroom and the terraces. Financial gain and commercial interests look like triumphing over tradition and loyalty once again at Bolton." Could he have been referring to the Railway End and its Normid supermarket? I wonder.

A CLASSIC
Manchester City v Tottenham Hotspur – Maine Road
22 October 1994

"The finest display of attacking football from both sides that I've seen in many years," was how the BBC's Match of the Day commentator John Motson described the events at Maine Road, Manchester on a sunny autumn Saturday in October. The game between Manchester City and Tottenham Hotspur had everything: world class internationals from Germany, Romania, England and The Republic of Ireland; seven goals; an almighty downpour; and some of the most exciting football I'd ever seen.

Then-City manager Brian Horton's programme notes were prophetic. Under the headline "This could well be a classic" he wrote: "A visit by Tottenham Hotspur to Maine Road always promises to be one of the highlights of the season. Ossie (Ardiles) plays the game the way spectators love football to be played, and with his recent overseas signings he has been able to produce some marvellous attacking soccer this season."

I'd arranged to travel with the Manchester City London Supporters club – MCLSC to the initiated – thanks to a former colleague. He'd followed City as a boy and usually took his mother, now in her 80's, to most home games. She'd been afraid to go alone since the late '70's after a mugging by City fans who ran off with her handbag. Such things were, hopefully, less likely to happen today, but she'd still only go with her son. Some scars take a long time to heal. After the match, he'd usually catch the bus to Manchester-Piccadilly and a train to London, while his mother went home in a taxi.

I arrived at London's Euston station just after nine o'clock to catch the 9.50 to Manchester. Small groups of football fans in their team colours were dotted around the main concourse. The red and white of Liverpool alongside the blue and gold of Wimbledon. They were playing at Anfield. The sky blue and white of Manchester City could be seen at intervals in the long queue for the train to Manchester. It wound its way like a snake from the platform entrance towards the centre of the station. The match at Maine Road was a sell-out, although because of the rebuilding of the Kippax Stand the ground only held just over 25,000 compared to an eventual total of 40,000.

The MCLSC had close links with the other supporters clubs in London and we'd be joined today by Plymouth, Stoke and Bolton fans for the journey north. Plymouth were playing Stockport, Stoke were at

Oldham and Bolton had a match at Port Vale – all stops along the way. It was cheaper to travel in large numbers, but each supporters club needed at least 10 fans to get a discount. City were the only team to reach that magical figure today, hence the link up with the other clubs.

The presence of fans from around the League made for a colourful spectacle. There were scarves and hats of all colours: the green and black of Plymouth, the red and white of Stoke and the white and black of Bolton. There were also badges, bags and shirts in team colours. Harmony at last among football supporters. The recurring theme throughout my journey was that the bad old days of football violence were past. Even if occasionally there might be an incident or two, we'd not return to the full-scale war mentality that reigned when I watched football as a boy.

There was one shirt – blue and white – which I couldn't recognise. It wasn't until the journey home after the match that I discovered from the Plymouth supporters that it belonged to a Gillingham fan. I grabbed my copy of the famous Manchester Evening News sports supplement The Pink to find out who they were playing and why this fan had travelled north for the day. Table-topping Bury was the answer. I wondered whether Gills fan Brian Moore, the ITV commentator, was also at the match.

We walked towards the centre of Manchester to catch a bus to Maine Road in Rusholme, on Moss Side – a community that has repeatedly been near breaking point partly because of a high crime rate and the presence of drug dealers. However, The Rough Guide to England noted that "an outsider's view of Manchester is all too often negative, conditioned by stories of inner-city mayhem in Moss Side, where crack-related crime brought a dozen shootings during two months in 1993."

When City moved to Moss Side from their old ground at Hyde Road in 1923 they were closer to Old Trafford which lies only three miles to the west. But there were advantages in settling on Moss Side. The main one was that there was a large population in the suburb and people were moving to the huge new council development. This gave City a large catchment area since it was easy to reach Maine Road from the city centre and South Manchester.

"Traditional images of shabby back-to-back houses, their slate roofs and cobbled streets glistening in the ever-present rain, tend to be reinforced by the suburbs flanking most routes into the city...," according to The Rough Guide. "But this place is very much alive, especially when the country's largest student population is in town, and although the so-called "Madchester" youth culture scene may have peaked, the city still boasts the north's most vibrant nightlife."

The docks and the cotton mills, once the main source of employment in the area, have now gone and the city is a mixture of bleak Sixties architecture, built to fill the gaps caused by German carpet bombing during World War Two, and Victorian buildings. Manchester's campaigns to host the Olympic Games have helped to clean up the city, but much still needs to be done to finish the job.

The image presented by Coronation Street still prevails in many parts of the city, even though much of the programme is now shot elsewhere. Still, you can see the original set if you take the Granada Studios Tour, along with the other three-quarters-of-a-million people who troop through the studios' doors each year to see the sets for Britain's longest-running soap opera. That's almost as many people as file through the turnstiles at Maine Road each year to see the Blues.

As we waited for a number 99 bus from the city centre I noticed lots of posters of Manchester United's star players on sale in a nearby shop – but there was not a City player in sight. A Norwegian football fan asked if he was queuing at the right stop for Maine Road. He was. He'd come over for a week's holiday with his two friends to hit the football grounds and the night clubs. And his wife let him!

The Norwegians were at Old Trafford for United's European Champions League game against Barcelona on the Wednesday night, a thrilling 2-2 draw, and would travel to Ewood Park the next day, Sunday, for the Reds' Premier League match against Blackburn. This little jaunt was an annual event. They just loved watching English football.

At Maine Road I picked up my ticket from the main reception where I saw the BBC's Mottie talking to former Blues' stars Mike Summerbee and Francis Lee. He looked very smart in a dark pink (yes, really) jacket. City had turned things around since Lee became chairman and, with the other member of the famous City triumvirate, Colin Bell, now head of the Social Club, it was surely only a matter of time before they started filling the trophy room. Then again, I could have been wrong.

The famous Bell, Lee, Summerbee trio had spearheaded City's quest for honours in the '60s and early '70s. The golden era began in 1965 when Joe Mercer became manager and Malcolm Allison was coach. Over the next five years the club won the Second Division Championship (1966), the First Division (1968), the FA Cup (1969), a Neil Young goal beating relegated Leicester City, the League Cup and the European Cup Winners' Cup (both 1970).

FA Cup success had been City's before in 1904, 1934 and 1956. The future managers of two of City's rivals played for the Blues in the last two of those games. Matt Busby actually lifted the cup as City captain in 1934 and Don Revie was centre-forward in 1956. Revie was featured in the match programme as part of the 'City Post-War A-Z...' "The early years with City were a struggle until the inception of what became known as 'The Revie Plan'... a version of the Hungarian national team's soccer."

Malcolm Allison returned to Maine Road in January 1979 and, over the next 15 months, £7.5 million changed hands in the transfer market as Big Mal bought 10 players for £4.5 million and sold 13 for £3 million. The £1.5 million paid to Wolves for Steve Daley is widely regarded as one of the worst deals ever struck. The other million pound man, Kevin Reeves, was a better purchase at £1.25 million. Under Allison's successor, John Bond, City reached the 100th FA Cup Final, ironically against Tottenham, in 1981 but lost 3-2 in a replay to a stunning Ricky Villa goal. Since then, City had failed to deliver and divided their time between the top two divisions.

The fans were hoping that Frannie Lee's arrival was the start of a new golden era. The link with the past was there on the pitch as well as in the boardroom. Mike Summerbee's son, Nicky, was on the right wing against Tottenham today. He bore an uncanny resemblance to his dad, with his shirt outside his shorts and his stooped running style. Summerbee junior tore Spurs apart down the right wing, while on the other side of the park an inspired Peter Beagrie tore Spurs apart down the left wing.

The centre of the Tottenham defence was softer than those famous chocolates. You can imagine the half-time team talk in the Spurs dressing room. Ossie: "We have to defend in the second half." The players: "What does defend mean?" They desperately needed O.J. Simpson's lawyer. I was later to learn that Ardiles, desperately looking for help, had asked Spurs' Norwegian international Erik Thorsvedt how Norway defended. Certainly better than Tottenham I can tell you!

Having said all that, Tottenham played some delightful football and should have scored at least five goals themselves. In the event, they could manage only two and that soft-centred defence let in five. City's Paul Walsh, the former Portsmouth, Spurs, Liverpool and Luton striker, now back at Pompey, was outstanding. He scored two goals, helped create the other three and generally caused chaos in the Tottenham defence. Ossie's diamond formation was flawed. His famous five under-mined by his flat-footed back four.

The City fans were happy. Their anthem Blue Moon, the Rodgers and

Hart song borrowed from Crewe, rang out across Maine Road. The City and Spurs fans in the Kippax Stand opposite were getting soaked, despite the white plastic macs City had generously handed out before the game to help keep some of the water off them. It was like a gathering of the Ku Klux Klan. And Spurs were being burned at the stake.

The new Kippax Stand followed the opening of the club's new Umbro Stand in 1993 which replaced the old Platt Lane Stand. (Confusingly, Kippax Street is actually behind the North Stand while Platt Lane is a few streets away). Unfortunately, City fans invaded the pitch the day the stand was opened for an FA Cup quarter-final against Spurs, resulting in 60 supporters being banned. The disturbances haven't helped City's hopes of being a big-match venue and the ground wasn't chosen for Euro '96.

Maine Road was originally a claypit for brick-making and had to be levelled when City first took it over. But when it was ready, at the huge cost of £200,000, it could hold more than 80,000. In those days there was just one Main Stand. Today there is the new Umbro Stand, the rebuilt Kippax Stand, the Main Stand and the North Stand.

The North Stand, which used to be called the Scoreboard End, was rebuilt and covered with a smart cantilever stand during City's halcyon days in the '60s. The Main Stand was also covered by a huge white roof supported by a large steel cross beam. The roof's plastic panels can apparently withstand up to 7.5 feet of snow. Is the weather ever that bad up north during the winter?

Maine Road's use for big matches hasn't been helped by its closeness to Old Trafford, Anfield and Hillsborough. But, ironically, Manchester United's record attendance was not for a game at Old Trafford, but a match at Maine Road against Arsenal in January 1948 when the Reds shared the ground because of bomb damage to Old Trafford in the war. The crowd of 82,950 was the largest ever to watch a League match.

City's record attendance, the highest for any English club match except a cup final, was 84,569 for a Sixth Round FA Cup tie against Stoke in 1934 when the Blues were on their way to a second cup success. The 80,407 fans who packed Maine Road for an FA Cup semi-final replay in 1946 was the highest ever for a midweek game. The following season 2.25 million people saw City and United, plus a cup semi-final and the Northern Rugby League Cup Final, at Maine Road, a record for a League ground.

The crowd today was only 25,473, but that was mainly because of the ground redevelopment. It was City's biggest crowd of the season so far and they could have attracted thousands more for a pulsating encounter. "We played well, we entertained. But the object of the exercise is to win matches," said Ardiles after the match. "We are not defending properly. It's as simple as that. We should have done something to cut out their crosses into the area but we didn't compete hard enough to do that."

Match of the Day and the tabloids were full of praise for the philosophy of attacking football. But the little Argentinian's days were numbered. Bob Cass in The Mail on Sunday summed up the way most people viewed his approach to the game. "Ardiles seems prepared to go to his managerial doom presenting the smiling face of football. If unemployment is to be the Spurs manager's ultimate fate, it will be a tragedy for entertainment and a triumph for those who insist that results are everything." It was.

THE BRADY BUNCH
Brighton & Hove Albion v Bournemouth - The Goldstone Ground
2 November 1994

You may not believe this but the Goldstone Ground, originally called Goldstone Bottom, takes its name from a stone supposed to have been placed by Druids on the site which is now occupied by the pitch. A local farmer got fed up with archaeologists coming to see the stone and in 1834 had it buried. In 1900, the stone was dug up and put in Hove Park across the road from the ground. It was a pity the legend far outshone the football served up on a cold Wednesday night

It was one of the worst games I'd endured so far: a 0-0 draw. Even the introduction of one veteran, 38-year-old Frank Stapleton, for another, Steve Foster, failed to light the sparks that were barely flickering on the pitch in the run up to Guy Fawkes night. Former Arsenal and Manchester United star Stapleton was, however, by far the best player on view and his contribution grew during the match. He'd already done his homework on opponents Bournemouth by watching them play their previous match as a spy for Brighton manager and former Arsenal and Eire maestro Liam Brady.

The Hove, in Brighton & Hove Albion, is an independent borough of 90,000 people west of Brighton where the seafront begins along a seven mile stretch beyond Rottingdean in the east. Brighton, mentioned in the Domesday Book as Brighthelmston or Brithelmeston after a mythical Bishop of Selsey, is the largest town and most famous resort in southern England and is nicknamed 'London by the Sea'. At the centre of town is the Old Steine, believed to be named after the stone where fishermen used to dry their nets. It's an open area with gardens dominated by the Royal Pavilion – the palace built by George IV for himself.

Brighton first became a prosperous town in the mid 1700's when its air and sea-bathing was recommended by doctors. But it grew rapidly after the decadent Prince Regent began visiting the town in the 1770s with his mistress giving it notoriety as a destination for the typical "dirty weekend". The Rough Guide calls it "Brighton's major contribution to the English collective consciousness."

His Pavilion, a mixture of Indian, Chinese and Gothic architecture, is the most famous building in Brighton. The minarets and balconies are Oriental in the loosest sense, but it looks like it came straight out of Bombay or New Delhi. "That's some Indian restaurant," said a pal of mine once on passing the building in a mini-bus full of footballers on a stag weekend in Brighton.

Today Brighton tries to play down its reputation as the town to come to for a bit of 'nookie' and prefers to focus on its Georgian charm, shopping, and thriving conferences. It's a fascinating town partly because of the mix of people from tourists through to the students who fill its many language schools, the art college and its two universities.

I'd arrived in Brighton on a train from London after work. The weather was cold so I was glad the station was only a short walk to the ground. I went into the main entrance to find a copy of a painting of the 1961 FA Cup Final between Tottenham and Burnley on the wall. It was not the first time I would cast eyes on the scene. Many clubs have a copy. On the floor was a blue and white mat decorated with Brighton's club crest - a seagull. I rang the bell on the front desk and was taken to the Seagull Lounge for a cup of tea.

The match officials had already arrived. They were chatting over a cup of coffee and, strangely, the conversation had turned to football. Referee Mike Pierce was making his first appearance of the season at The Goldstone Ground. It was his fifth season as a League referee after moving up through the Hampshire League, the Football Combination and the Football League. Outside football he enjoyed cricket and most other sports. He also worked as an electrician during the day.

Pierce and his linesmen, plus back-up referee, were pondering the new FIFA regulations requiring players to be cautioned immediately for a serious infringement. The balance of opinion seemed to favour the new interpretation of the law, though there was concern that some of the other changes, such as players not being given offside when running back from an attacking position, had made their job more difficult.

Pierce usually refereed two games a week. He mostly handled games in the South. The farthest he'd travelled was to Wolverhampton from Portsmouth to take charge of a game at Molineux. "A wonderful stadium and a fine venue for football." The financial rewards were improving. Pierce could claim £102 mileage for tonight's game and was paid £82.50 for refereeing the match. A Premier League referee gets £300 a match. Not bad for doing something you enjoy.

I asked if a referee had to put in much training. "If you've got two games a week you don't really need to train. But in the summer I go running every other morning. You have to pass a fitness test at the beginning of the season. If you fail they give you two weeks to get into better shape and allow you to take the test again. If you don't pass that they kick you out. So 20-odd years of refereeing could be out of the window just like that."

The physical demands of the job are quite high, hence the fitness test.

"The League give you a stamina test involving sets of sprints between two cones 20 metres apart. The sprints increase in speed as the test progresses. You have to get to level 10,5, which is five shuttles at level 10, to pass. We do one other physical test. You have three cones, 10 metres apart and do 60 metre shuttle sprints with 30 seconds in between. We do six of them within a set time."

The League also check the officials to make sure they're fit and healthy enough to do the job by testing their haemoglobin, heart, cholesterol, weight, blood sugar and blood pressure. "It's a good thing for referees to be seen to be in shape. At least you know you're in reasonable condition," said Pierce.

He welcomed the FIFA rule changes, but said it would be hard to improve on the dedication and professionalism of English referees. The back-up referee agreed. "You take Italy where they have professional referees. I don't think the standard is any higher than it is here. They make mistakes too."

Did Pierce resent any abuse shouted at him when he'd made a decision the crowd didn't like? "They pay their money and they can say what they like, within reason," he said. Was he always aware of the fans barracking him during a match? "You tend to hear it if there aren't many in the ground. If there's quite a few then it's just a mass of noise. But you know when you've made a mistake or something's wrong. You'll soon be told. But you try not to take any notice of it. If you took notice of everybody you just wouldn't get on with the job."

The only downside to the FIFA changes seemed to be the lowering of the retirement age. They're now looking at an upper limit of 40 to 45 and the aim is to bring it down to 40 which would exclude a number of top class referees. "You take George Courtney," said the back-up ref. "He's probably one of the best referees the country has ever had, but he can't do the job any more under the new regulations and that's a loss to the game." The silver lining is that younger referees are finding their way onto the League list much sooner than they would have done. "This will speed everybody up. At 32 or 33 a referee from the amateur game could be on the League line."

Talk then turned to the sacking of Spurs boss Ossie Ardiles, announced the previous day. There was sympathy all round for a nice guy who, like a bad lawyer, just couldn't sort out his defence. "I suppose he had to go," said one of the linesmen. "Inevitable really." At which point he had to go himself to prepare for his night's work.

The Seagull Lounge was starting to fill up as the kick-off approached. Former Crystal Palace goalkeeper John Jackson, now Brighton's goalkeeping trainer, appeared at the tea and coffee bar. It was run by two of the sweetest old girls you could wish to meet. They told me they didn't get to see much of the match when Brighton played at home (and I doubted they travelled to away games at their age) but they ran outside the lounge whenever Brighton scored to find out the goalscorer and soak up the atmosphere. They could save their breath tonight.

The tea ladies went to Wembley in May 1983 for Brighton's only FA Cup Final appearance against Manchester United. "We had a lovely day then," said the one who'd been at the club since 1977. "And Smith must score..." I reminded them of the BBC commentary when Gordon Smith had the chance to win the cup for Brighton in the dying minutes. He missed and, after battling to a 2-2 draw in the first game – a feat which had manager Jimmy Melia dancing a soft-shoe shuffle in celebration – the Seagulls were outclassed 4-0 in the replay. Even Ray Wilkins scored when he deceived the entire Brighton team by curling the ball into the top corner instead of playing his customary square pass to Bryan Robson. You couldn't blame the defence. Who'd have expected "the crab" to shoot?

In the boardroom, once graced by the presence of comedian Norman Wisdom when he was a director, stood the trophy cabinet. There was a faded programme from that great day at Wembley in '83, but no trophy. "The players got medals, of course, but I don't think the club received anything to mark the occasion," said the official who gave me a lightning tour before the sponsors arrived for tea and sandwiches. He must have been wrong. On a later visit to Tottenham I saw a Football Association pennant marking the occasion of Spurs' 3-2 defeat against Coventry in the '87 Cup Final. Brighton must have had one somewhere.

There was also no sign of any silverware to mark Brighton's Third Division (South) title in 1958, the Fourth Division Championship of 1965 or the Charity Shield win over Aston Villa in 1910. There was, however, a plate on the wall presented to Brighton by Arsenal to mark the Seagulls' first League match in the old Division One in 1979. The Gunners won 4-0. There was also a clock engraved with the Arsenal crest to mark their meeting in the FA Cup Fourth Round in the '80s. The Gunners won 2-1.

I left the boardroom with its trophies, long wooden table and bar to look around the rest of the ground. The changing rooms were empty but the players' kit was neatly folded ready for the team to get ready for the task ahead. On top of each kit was a match programme and a packet of Wrigley's chewing gum. "Liam doesn't let anybody near the dressing rooms on a match day," said the club official. I was privileged.

Brady, the mercurial genius loved by Arsenal fans in the '70s, guided the Gunners to FA Cup success in a thrilling final against Manchester United. They won 3-2 after a stirring United comeback from 2-0 down. The Reds were beaten in the dying moments by an Alan Sunderland goal fashioned by 'chippy', as he was known to Gunners' fans. The Irishman had joined the South Coast club after a dismal spell as manager of Celtic had ended in the sack. Happier years had come as a player in Italy at Juventus, Sampdoria, Inter Milan and Ascoli before he returned home to join West Ham.

The tradition of colourful managers at the Goldstone Ground had been upheld by the likes of George Curtis, Alan Mullery, Brian Clough, Mike Bailey and Jimmy Melia. So what did Brady bring to the job? "The first task was to get a bit of confidence back," said Brady. "We worked on getting the players to play in an entertaining way. That got everybody's enthusiasm going again." Trying to instil a flair for entertaining football was just one part of Brady's job. The other was to operate on a tight budget. "We have got money for wages, but not for transfer fees," he said. His main close season signings were two free transfers from Tottenham, Jeff Minton and Junior McDougald.

The official then took me out onto the pitch. Along with Doncaster Rovers' Belle Vue it was probably one of the most run-down stadiums I'd see all season. It was no surprise to hear at the end of the season that the club planned to leave and temporarily share Portsmouth's Fratton Park ground, 50 miles along the south coast, from the start of the 1996/97 season. The club hoped to build a new 30,000 all-seater multipurpose stadium.

The problem with ground-sharing was the distance Seagulls' fans would have to travel to watch 'home' games. "It will be the end of Brighton as we know it. Who is going to travel to Portsmouth on a wet Tuesday to watch them play someone like Crewe," said one fan. The supporters were also sceptical that the club could ever afford a new stadium. Brighton planned to sell the Goldstone Ground to pay off debts "which they cannot contain".

I took my seat in the Main Stand next to then-Preston manager John Beck. He was under pressure at Deepdale after a bad start to the season. I wondered which player he was checking on tonight. Opposite was the open East Side of the ground. I was surprised to see rows of houses overlooking the pitch behind the terraces. They should have sold season-tickets to the residents! The terracing began to drop away towards the South Stand on my right so that there were only a few steps by the corner flag.

Brady's Brighton team had a blend of youth and experience. Players with potential like Junior McDougald and Kurt Nogan, nurtured along by elder statesmen such as 40-year-old player-coach Jimmy Case, the former Liverpool, Southampton and Bournemouth midfielder. Case, the oldest outfield player in England, had just had a testimonial against Liverpool. His Albion X1 included Matt Le Tissier.

Case started out at his home town club, Liverpool, 21 seasons and almost 800 matches ago. His experience had helped Brady since he was a "real presence on the field". He was sceptical about players who retired early, saying they wanted to get out at the top. "That's a load of nonsense. They say they would not enjoy playing at a lower level. But, for me, that's where your enthusiasm for the game comes in. I played at Sittingbourne. Not for money – there's not much around at the lower levels – but because I just love the game."

"When I started at Liverpool, the older pro was Tommy Smith. I would learn off him. If all the older pros packed in at 30, at the top, who's going to learn anything? If you have a team full of 22-year-olds there are certain parts of the game that they have no knowledge about, like concentrating at the end. The older pro is there to protect the younger ones." So how long could Case continue to defy Father Time?

"There is nothing in my head saying this week, or this season, I will stop. I know I can't go on forever. (Brady) will be looking to replace me, if he gets a person who's better than me. That's always been the case. At Southampton Chris Nicholl used to buy a midfield player every year, but I was still there at the end of the season, still playing up to 37."

"If I was playing for Wimbledon, I wouldn't be playing now. Not because I wouldn't enjoy it, but because there would be too much running. I can't keep up but I have other attributes."

So does Case do anything special to keep in shape. "Not really. I didn't look after myself that much in my younger days. But when you are younger and fitter you can cope better with the knocks, whether from football or life. But when you get a little bit older, and get a bit more responsibility, you think 'If I don't settle down here I'll end up on the moon.'

"I used to drink a fair bit. But then a few years ago at Southampton I just said I'd pack all that in. Not necessarily to extend my career, it was just getting in the way with certain things, whether it be home life or whatever. No real big incident, I'd just had enough. Everyone should take stock at some point. I didn't have any alcohol for two-and-a-half years. Now I just have a shandy. In the past, (the drinking) would start straight after games. At no other times, just then." We believe you Jim!

WALKER'S MILLIONS
Blackburn Rovers v Tottenham Hotspur – Ewood Park
5 November 1995

"He wasn't anything special at school," said Jack Aspin referring to his school chum and namesake Jack Walker. But he was certainly something special now. "Nobody would have dreamed he'd take over Blackburn. But football is about money and Jack Walker has it," said Aspin after another Rovers victory on their way to the Premier League title – their first major trophy since their FA Cup win back in 1928. "Every team would like a fairy godmother. We've got one," beamed Aspin.

Jack Walker, owner of Blackburn Rovers Football Club, was the richest man in British sport. A survey by Business Age magazine estimated his personal wealth at £345 million. Some estimates put the figure nearer £400 million – and said even that might be conservative. However, unlike most of his fellows among the very rich, Walker's wealth is diminishing – and Blackburn is the main reason why.

Walker had spent more than £50 million to ensure Rovers would win the Premier League title. Jack Aspin, who attended the same school as Walker between 1941 and 1944, told me he'd put £50 million into a trust for the club so they'd never have to worry about money again. "He looks upon it as his participation in Blackburn Rovers and in the town," said Blackburn Chairman Dick Coar.

Combined with his other hobby, Jersey European Airways, the fairy godmother had invested £100 million in two of the biggest financial black holes known to man – a football club and an airline. Blackburn alone made trading losses of £14.5 million over the previous two years. But Walker clearly wasn't in it for the money. As Martin Luther King might have put it: He had a dream.

His dream was built on the millions he'd acquired from selling the family steel business. His father started out with a sheet metal business, while Jack began with a couple of textile mills acquired with government grants. In 1989 British Steel bought the business for £330 million but, according to Aspin, Walker still owned the largest steel stock warehouse in Europe which he rented out to British Steel for £100,000 a week.

That brought in £5 million a year, or one Chris Sutton. But Aspin reckoned Walker's interest earnings had paid for his investment in Blackburn Rovers. Walker lived in Jersey, but he flew in for every match. His exile meant he could only come into England for 90 days a year, but the days he flew in and out to watch Rovers didn't count. It was a good job he owned the airline – he was saving a fortune in plane fares!

When Howard Kendall was manager of a cash-strapped Rovers from 1979-81 he was asked to economise by not using too much milk in the players' halftime tea and to send his mail second class. Ewood Park's old brickwork and turnstiles were the backdrop for a Hovis ad depicting the timeless traditions of northern England. But all that had changed now. The club even had a fanzine called Loadsamoney now that Jack was picking up the tab for multi-million pound players and a refurbished stadium.

"Jack Walker's commitment is total," said Dick Coar. "Without his backing, (Blackburn's) recent rise to prominence would not have been possible." Paul Warhurst, Tim Flowers, David Batty, Graeme Le Saux and Chris Sutton had cost Walker £12.3 million. Then-manager Kenny Dalglish had been given a total of £27 million to play with. The wage bill in 1993 was £5.3 million and growing. The SAS (Shearer and Sutton) were each rumoured to be earning £15,000 a week.

When Liverpool won the title in the first season after World War Two their team cost just £21,000, worth £420,000 today. Arsenal's League and Cup double-winning team in 1971 cost £165,000. And Manchester United's 1994 double winners cost £15 million. Blackburn were the most expensive team ever to challenge for the title.

"My aim now is for Rovers to be not only the most successful club in the country but also in Europe as well," said Walker. "And there is no reason why we cannot achieve that. It may not happen overnight, but I would like to think it will happen sooner rather than later." Baroness Margaret Thatcher of Kesteven, the club's honorary vice-president, no doubt firmly supported the ambitions of the entrepreneurial Walker.

Rovers had waited a long time for success. That 1928 FA Cup victory was a dim and distant memory, remembered by few. The match programme had a feature on the 'Tireless Kingpin' of that cup winning team, Harry Healless. He was the only Blackburn captain ever to lift the FA Cup at Wembley and for that alone was worthy of a place in Ewood Park's Hall of Fame. He was the only Blackburnian in the side.

When Rovers reached the cup final again in 1960 Healless was one of the eight survivors of the 1928 team to go back to Wembley as official guests. Sadly, he didn't see the blue and whites lift the cup that day and died, aged 78, some 12 years later. Being a proud Blackburnian, Harry Healless would have been delighted to share his achievement with another Ewood captain.

The FA Cup had been the almost exclusive property of Blackburn Rovers in the late 1800s. They won the cup in three successive years, 1884-86, and again in 1890 and 1891. Rovers were awarded a special shield to commemorate their hat trick of FA Cup victories. It was displayed in the Ewood Park boardroom for those lucky enough to get a glimpse behind the scenes.

Thirty seven years after that 1891 triumph Healless lifted the cup at Wembley. And that was the last major trophy to find its way to the Ewood Park boardroom, if you exclude the Full Members' Cup in 1987. Jack Walker had waited a long time for success at the club he'd supported since he was a boy.

Rovers were original members of the Football League in 1888 and won the Championship in 1912 and 1914. In between, around the turn of the century, the club's namesake Fred Blackburn, who was born near the town, made 204 League and Cup appearances as a winger. His brother Arthur also had a spell with Rovers.

The club stayed in the First Division until 1936 and then spent most of their time in the Second Division. Their fortunes slumped to a new low in 1971 when they were relegated to the Third Division for the first time. The return to the big time started in 1980 when they regained their Second Division place.

Two of Rovers most capped players since the Second World War – England winger Bryan Douglas and half-back Ronnie Clayton – were guests of the club today and were treated to a tour of the transformed Ewood Park. Douglas had appeared in 36 internationals and Clayton was just one cap behind. However, his 580 League appearances between 1950 and 1969 were still a club record.

The ground they saw had changed beyond recognition from the one they played in during the '50s and '60s. There were two new all-seater stands at the Blackburn and Darwen Ends, each holding 8,000 and the new Jack Walker Stand on Bolton Road which had replaced the old Nuttal Street Stand. The only side not renewed was the Riverside Stand, now called the Walker Steel Stand after the company that Jack built. Its original name came from the narrow River Darwen which runs behind the stand.

Until Walker arrived Ewood Park, which, like much of industrial Lancashire, was built in the late Victorian period, had been desperately in need of modernisation. The main Nuttal Street Stand was built in 1906 for £24,000, a huge sum at the time, and opened on New Year's Day the following year against Preston. The double decker Riverside Stand was built between the two League Championship years of 1912 and 1914.

The archetypal northern setting of Ewood Park, complete with cobbled streets, terraced houses, tramlines, mill and old-fashioned turnstiles, made it the ideal setting for Hovis ads in the '80s. Today the glass fronted Main Stand would be more at home in an ad for Microsoft computers. Blackburn, with a population of just over 100,000 people, still looks like a mill town. But its football club is no longer in a backwater, struggling to keep up with its rivals to the south in Liverpool and Manchester.

Blackburn was once the greatest cotton-weaving centre in the world but, despite the mill buildings and chimneys, particularly by the Leeds and Liverpool canal, it now depends more on engineering than textiles. One of the fanzines, 4,000 Holes, takes its title from the Beatles' song, "A Day in the Life" which includes the line "4,000 holes in Blackburn, Lancashire" in reference to the coal mines in the area. But it was Rovers, rather than the town's historic industrial might, that now put the place on the map.

"People forget how far we've come in the three years since Kenny Dalglish took over," said the club's chairman Dick Coar. "In that time we have virtually trebled our average gate from 8,000 to the low twenty thousands." The match programme confirmed the transformation. Ten years ago Rovers beat Brighton at Ewood in a Second Division encounter before a crowd of just 7,341. Twenty years ago nearly 14,000 turned up to see Rovers against Crystal Palace in a Third Division game. That's progress!

Incidentally, 40 years ago to within one day of the match against Spurs was a game for all Blackburn fans to remember and one which went down in history. It brought a record-breaking 9-0 victory over Middlesbrough. Eddie Quigley and Frank Mooney got hat-tricks and there were two goals for Eddie Crossan and one for Bobby Langton.

There was no chance of a repeat score against Spurs today but the London side, with former captain Steve Perryman in temporary charge after the sacking of Ossie Ardiles earlier in the week, were clearly vulnerable. I feared the worst as I took my seat in the Darwen End, next to the away supporters. The stand was named after a small town four miles from Blackburn which once had its own League club in the 1890's.

The noise from the travelling Spurs fans to my left was incredible. The chanting was sustained throughout the match, even when they'd gone 2-0 behind after goals from Jason Wilcox and an Alan Shearer penalty. They were either stupid or hopeless optimists. Still, I suppose when you've driven from London to Blackburn, as I'd done earlier that morning, you've got to make it worthwhile even if your team is losing.

Basically, Spurs' new five-man defence performed as ineptly as the four-man defence which superseded their three-man defence! Before the end of the season they'd probably have an 11-man defence and still concede goals!

The Blackburn fan next to me worked at the local Mercedes dealership. He told me that Kenny Dalglish and Alan Shearer had stopped by recently: Dalglish to pick up his dark blue 200 series Mercedes, registration number K7 KMD (the M is for his unusual middle name – though I still don't know what it is) and Shearer to purchase a dark purple 190 series Merc, registration number A9 ALS, for his missus. England's centre-forward drove a Rover himself – it was gratis which explained the choice.

The Tottenham players had left their expensive cars back in London and had travelled up by coach. But Sol Campbell, the young Spurs and England under-21 international defender, said he wished he'd driven to Blackburn. He told me he wasn't looking forward to the long journey home as I accompanied him through the main gates at Ewood Park towards the car park. Hands in pockets, head bowed, he was clearly bitterly disappointed at the way Tottenham were playing. "I don't know what's going on," he said dejectedly. "We've just got to keep plugging away I suppose."

After the match I browsed through my Loadsamoney fanzine as I waited for the Blackburn players to emerge from the main entrance. Under a feature called Back to Basics the fanzine insisted it did not want to be accused of being ageist, sexist, racist or any other thing ending in ist that's deemed to be derogatory to minority groups. It had therefore decided to rename various football teams.

"Sexism is the first issue to be addressed and the following changes will be effected as soon as possible: Motherwell becomes Parentwell, Queen of the South becomes Monarch of the South and Queen's Park Rangers becomes Monarch Park Rangers. Mansfield Town becomes Personfield Town, and obviously Manchester City and United become Personchester City and United. Cowdenbeath become Bovine-quadruped-enbeath, whilst Peterborough will alternate with Petraborough on a strict rotation basis.

"Club nicknames will be alternatively sexed with: Leicester City being known as the Vixens, Derby become the Ewes, both changing week and week about, whilst Everton will be renamed the Toffeepeople. In order not to widen the north-south divide, Southampton and

Northampton Town will in future be known as Hampton and Hampton Town, with Preston North End becoming Preston End. Middlesbrough will be called whatever you feel like at the time.

"As we do not wish to offend vegetarians or people with special dietary needs, West Ham United become West Kosher United and Rotherham United will be known as Rotherlentil United. Religious bigotry will become a thing of the past as Falkirk rotate through a list featuring Falchapel, Falsynogogue, Faltemple and Falmission. Bishop's Stortford will similarly be Priest's Stortford or Gurus Stortford, dependant on where during the rota a particular game falls.

"So as not to take sides in the anti-abortion debate, Bournemouth will be henceforth referred to as Conceivemouth. Finally, slang words for parts of the body will not be allowed to feature in club names. Arsenal will become Rectumnal, Bristol City and Rovers become Mammary City and Rovers, as it would be impolite to refer to the clubs as a nice pair of Bristols. And Scunthorpe United will be asked to resign from the League altogether!"

Meanwhile, a large group of Rovers fans stood in the light rain, autograph books to hand, hoping some of Blackburn's stars would sign for them or stop for photographs. The SAS appeared along with Flowers, the most expensive goalkeeper in the world. They were immediately surrounded by youngsters attracted like bees to honey.

The players signed and posed while their wives and girlfriends stood patiently by the smart four-wheel drives and executive cars their men drove around town. Trappings of the rich and famous. One young fan approached Flowers. "Could you sign this Chris?" A bemused Flowers duly obliged. When the fan had left he turned to the rest of us and said, "He just said 'thanks Chris'. He thinks I'm Chris Sutton. Am I that ugly?" I approached Sutton and told him what had happened. "Tim said he wasn't too pleased about it," I told him. "I'm not too pleased about it either,' said Sutton.

As the supporters gradually drifted away and the rain continued to fall the women grew impatient. When the last photo had been snapped and the final autograph signed Shearer, Sutton and Flowers were able to go home. Their women gave a look as if to say at last and they sped away into the night.

Most of the players had left by now but a group of five young girls lingered around the exit from the ground. "Who are you waiting for?" I enquired. 'Graeme," they replied in reference to Rovers' England inter-national full-back Graeme Le Saux. One of them had Le Saux's name on her blue and white halved Rovers shirt. Another had Shearer above the red number nine feared at Premier League grounds around the country.

After what seemed like an age the fresh-faced pin-up finally emerged from the splendour of Ewood Park. His fan club gathered around him as if he was a pop star. "Graeme, Graeme could we take your picture," they cried. Le Saux posed with his fans while I took a picture. "Thanks Graeme," said one. "You were great today Graeme," said another. "You're a lucky man to have all these fans," I said. "Great," said Le Saux, as if a mob of squeaky-voiced teenage girls was the last thing he needed.

Walker's school chum Jack Aspin had stood outside the main entrance to the new Ewood Park along with all the other fans hoping to get a glimpse of the most famous chairman in the Premier League. "My daughter presented Walker with a picture of me and Jack playing snooker when we were young boys before a match last year (1993)," said Aspin. "And you know what Jack said? 'Where have the years gone?'" It seems the King of Ewood Park has always enjoyed life. Blackburn Rovers have seen to that.

SAMBA COMES TO BOUNDARY PARK
Oldham Athletic v Tranmere Rovers – Boundary Park
6 November 1994

On Sunday morning I slept in as late as possible. I was tired from the long journey to Blackburn and the beers I'd drunk the night before with the Leeds and Burnley fans at my hotel. I wandered down to breakfast just before 10 o'clock to enjoy a fry up complete with black pudding. There was just me, a woman and her son. They'd been to a wedding nearby and were also suffering from the night's festivities.

The hotel was near Accrington and the woman told me she'd seen their last ever match in the old Fourth Division in the 1950's. Her only other link to football was that her other son's girlfriend's sister had nursed Gary Lineker's son George who was thankfully recovering from leukaemia. "She (the nurse) was very discreet about it. She would never discuss the boy or talk about his problems." I should think everyone in the country was concerned about the little lad's health when they heard of his illness. He has since recovered and the Lineker's have now added a second child to their family.

It was a beautiful sunny morning. Just perfect for a drive through the countryside and an afternoon's football. I was headed for Boundary Park, the home of Oldham Athletic. Their success in the early 1980s, which culminated in the 1991 League Cup Final (lost to Nottingham Forest) and the 1994 FA Cup Semi-Final (lost to Manchester United after a last minute Mark Hughes goal secured United a replay and eventual victory), had given way to relegation and the current struggle for promotion.

I didn't know it at the time, but Oldham manager Joe Royle, the longest serving boss in the League after 12 years in charge at Boundary Park, would shortly be leaving to replace Mike Walker and turn things around at Everton where he starred as a centre-forward in the 1970s.

Royle had taken Oldham as far as he could on limited resources. He needed a fresh challenge. Sorting out the mess at Goodison would require all his managerial skills, but big Joe had already performed miracles at Boundary Park. Nothing was beyond him. Oldham, meanwhile, would have to battle on without their mentor. Royle was a hard act to follow.

I drove past an old mill, a reminder of the area's historic links to the cotton industry. The importance of King Cotton to the town is shown clearly by the fact that Oldham once boasted the largest number of spindles of any cotton town in the world. Nowadays there are only a few cotton mills still working, though there are lots of other textile mills. This was definitely the archetypal mill town. I half expected a young lad to cycle up the hill carrying a loaf of Hovis under his arm.

I parked in the club's huge car park behind the home supporters end. Oldham have plans to develop the car park into a rugby ground with the Main Stand backing onto the football stadium. The rugby and football clubs would share the same end stand which would cater for about 12,000 football fans on one side and 8,000 rugby supporters on the other side.

I'd arranged to meet the club's public relations manager, Gordon Lawton, for a tour before the match. After wandering to various parts of the ground I eventually found him and he treated me to an extensive look behind the scenes. I was taken first into the directors' room where one wall was covered with caricature drawings of the board of directors. This lot must have had a sense of humour. A glass case on one wall contained the silver spade used to cut the first piece of sod for the pitch in 1896.

I was taken through the dressing rooms, noticing that the away facilities didn't include a bath. "We try to make it as uncomfortable as possible," joked Gordon. The Tranmere players' shirts were all in a line, hanging on pegs but, unlike most Premier League teams, they didn't carry the name of a sponsor or the players' squad numbers. John Aldridge's boots were laid out, but he played no part in the afternoon's proceedings because of injury – much to Oldham's relief.

There were a couple of signed footballs in the Oldham dressing room to be given away to two lucky television viewers in a competition on Granada. Some of the Oldham players were being treated in the physio's room. Sean McCarthy jumped off the physio's treatment table to replace Andy Ritchie in the starting line up. Although McCarthy was receiving treatment he felt fit enough to play and he lasted the whole match. Joe Royle later explained why he played instead of a bitterly disappointed Ritchie who was not even brought off the bench in the second half.

Next stop was the kit, or laundry, room, "probably the busiest place in the club". Gordon ran through the training kits and explained the significance of the different colours used by each team. "Everybody has three kits, three training kits. Purple is for youth team players, black is for the pros, blue is for the senior staff. " Each kit was embossed with the player's club number, though Oldham had gone back to 1-11 on the pitch instead of the very confusing squad numbers used by most teams.

The executive boxes at Oldham may not be as big as those at Old

Trafford, but Oldham pride themselves on their friendly service. "We've had a lot of people in here who obviously, with being close, have gone to the Manchester Uniteds and the Liverpools. They've always said that our facilities may not be up to the size of those like, say, Leeds have got, but the actual service and the meal we give is better. We try to give that little bit more attention," said the club official responsible for looking after the sponsors.

Among today's executive guests were a local bread manufacturers, and Invincible Double Glazing, one of the main match sponsors. They could look forward to a four-course meal with wine, a free bar before the match, at half-time and after the game, plus the chance to win a signed football or a bottle of champagne by guessing the attendance. The main sponsors were also allowed to pick their man of the match and could rub shoulders with the chosen one and a couple of his teammates who'd come up to see them after the game.

The boxes were a portacabin-style construction, complete with speakers which pipe in the crowd noise so executive guests can soak up the big match atmosphere in comfort. Unfortunately, Oldham were now in the First Division after relegation at the end of the 1993/94 season so there were few big matches for the crowd to get excited about. That had affected the atmosphere, along with the development of Boundary Park into an all-seater stadium.

The club was so concerned about the subdued atmosphere that a Brazilian samba band had been invited along for today's match to stir up the supporters with a Latin beat accompanied by whistles and drums. They certainly added an exotic touch to a brisk winter afternoon. The Oldham chairman was so enthusiastic he wanted to sign them up for every game.

"They did a trial run on Friday and the BBC filmed it and everything. The idea is to get the crowd going because it's gone so quiet," explained Gordon. "We thought there'd be five or six, maybe eight of them. But there's 52 of them. The manager's not very happy. The commercial manager had arranged it but when Joe Royle found out he wanted to cancel the whole thing."

I ran into the band before the game as they were taking up their positions. "They don't sound very Brazilian," I said after hearing their north-east accents. "How much do they get paid?" "They don't. They're doing it for nothing," said Gordon. "They're all Oldham fans."

Granada were using 11 cameras to cover a match for the first time. Normally, they only used eight ."There's one in each goal. One at the side of each goal. That's four. One at the side of the gantry, which is five.

Two on the bottom gantry, seven. Two on the top, nine. One on the side, 10. And where's the eleventh? Oh, yes, the tunnel," said Gordon. "The referee's really going to get it today." "They've got no chance have they?" I replied.

We retraced our steps out through the main entrance and into the club shop. It was a busy little enterprise selling every article of merchandise you could imagine being associated with a football club, including a range of cosmetics called LATIQUE, after the club's nickname, the Latics from Athletic. There was also a lucrative travel business organising everything from trips to away games to fully-fledged holidays for supporters to places like Australia – a far cry from Oldham.

There was just time to meet Joe Royle in his office and grab a quick photograph with the big man before heading to the players' lounge for lunch. Royle is not quite as tall as me and he guessed correctly that I played centre-half. He was clearly ticked off by the presence of the Brazilian band because he was still complaining about them under his breath as he left to get his players ready for the match.

I thanked Gordon for the tour and sat down in the players' lounge for lunch served in the best northern tradition: meat and potato pie, mushy peas and red cabbage washed down with strong tea. Former Manchester United star Lou Macari, now manager at Stoke, was Granada's match summariser. He sat talking to former Liverpool full-back Jim Beglin

Norway's assistant manager and his wife were also having a drink in the players' lounge. They'd come to watch Gunnar Halle, Oldham's Norwegian full-back. He'd play an important role in the European Championships' qualifying tournament which would lead to the 1996 finals in England. He told me that Tottenham manager. Ossie Ardiles, had asked Spurs' Norwegian keeper Eric Thorsvedt how the national team organised their defence.

Thorsvedt explained that Norway played twice as many attackers against their four defenders to put them under pressure. At his next training session Ardiles organised a practice match in the same way. The problem was he didn't ask how the Norwegians actually coached the defenders. At Tottenham, they seemed to train without the key ingredient: coaching. That explained a lot about Spurs' defensive problems. A few weeks later Ardiles was sacked.

The game itself was a bore draw. One Latics fan offered £50 of his £800 half-time jackpot to the Oldham match-winner. The problem was, there wasn't one. "He wouldn't have been in any danger if he had tendered the entire winnings of the National Lottery," said The Sun.

Except for a brief spell at the beginning of the second-half, when the home side laid siege to Tranmere keeper Eric Nixon's goal, the punter's money couldn't have been safer inside the Bank of England.

Royle was aware of the need for his team to get on the goal trail. "We need a goal," he said to reporters huddled together in a small ad-hoc press room underneath the Main Stand. "We have had four clean sheets in our last five games but have only scored once. We've got to start scoring again." I wished they'd started against Tranmere!

HOW SWEET IS MY VALLEY
Charlton v West Bromwich Albion – The Valley
13 November 1994

Charlton had not won a live televised match since the 1947 FA Cup Final so the arrival of the London Weekend Television cameras for this Sunday afternoon game was greeted with apprehension by the home supporters. As they could have told you before the match, their team was again unable to break the sequence in a game they completely dominated. The die-hard fans know only-too-well the sense of self-delusion that takes over when they think Charlton have a game sewn up.

The teams ran out onto the pitch to the sound of that old Al Jolson classic 'When the red, red, robin goes bob, bob, bobbing along'. Charlton have a number of nicknames, one of them being the Robins because of their red kit. Among the others are the Valiants, after their home ground, The Valley, and Haddicks or, more commonly, Addicks. The fishy tale is that the players once used a room above a 'chippie' in East Street as their base and the owner, a keen Addicks fan, used to come to matches armed with a haddock nailed onto a piece of wood which he waved about during games. Inspiration for the inflatable haddocks used at Grimsby?

The Charlton team certainly needed all the inspiration they could get. Cult hero Carl Leaburn had returned after recovering from knee and calf injuries, but had little impact on the match, while leading scorer David Whyte was still out of action and sorely missed. At least Kim Grant put the home side ahead after a long kick downfield by keeper Mike Ammann resulted in an attempted clearance by West Brom centre-half Paul Mardon which hit Grant's shin and rebounded into the net.

The West Brom fans had turned up in large numbers and occupied at least half of the South End. Their team had given them little to cheer about after a disastrous start to the season which had seen manager Keith Burkinshaw sacked and Alan Buckley recruited from Grimsby. They were second from bottom of the Second Division at the start of the match, but gave their team lots of encouragement even when, at one point, it seemed they'd gone 2-0 down before Mark Robson's goal was disallowed for offside.

Just after half-time The Baggies brought on substitute Carl Heggs and within two minutes he'd set up an equaliser for the prolific Bob Taylor who volleyed past Ammann. Charlton's biggest crowd of the season –

10,876 – groaned all around me. They knew it was coming even in the first half when their team managed to miss eight good chances. The inevitability of an equaliser was there from the moment Charlton scored. The home fans had seen it all before.

It was a far cry from the Charlton team of the 1930s which became one of the top sides in the country under manager Jimmy Seed. They won the Third Division (South) in 1935, for the second time, and the following season went up to the First Division as runners-up. They went one better in 1937 when they were the second best team in the country and, after coming second in the 1946 FA Cup Final, they won the trophy in that televised 1947 final, beating Burnley, though Seed dropped the cup and broke the lid.

Charlton's most famous player of all time is probably their goalkeeper of that era, Sam Bartram, who many people believe is the greatest goalkeeper never to be picked for England. Sam was honoured at The Valley with the Sam Bartram Gate at the Main Entrance and the Sam Bartram Close. Jimmy Seed's contribution was recognised in 1981 when the club named the new South Stand after their former manager.

But a Hall of Fame poll in the club's match programme Valley Review put striker Derek Hales, the club's top goalscorer with 168 strikes, just ahead of Bartram, whose 623 games for Charlton are a record. The race for third place was won by Robert Lee, now captain of Newcastle and an England international, but who made more than 350 appearances for the Addicks over an eight-year spell scoring 60 odd goals.

Eddie Firmani, a former Charlton player and manager, and an Italian international, was fourth, just ahead of fellow South African Stuart Leary, whose 158 League goals are a club record. In sixth place was the man who had made more appearances for the club than anyone except Bartram, present reserve team boss Keith Peacock, who played 591 senior games for Charlton over 17 years, much as captain. Keith was also one of only five players to score more than 100 goals for the club.

The Robins' most capped player and the third in terms of appearances (530), John Hewie, came seventh in the poll. He also won 19 caps for Scotland. And last, but by no means least, was Allan Simonsen, who finished just ahead of Peter Shirtliff, Mike Flanagan and Colin Powell. Simonsen's Valley career was short, but the former European Footballer of the Year made quite an impact with nine goals in 17 games.

But while the present-day team may have faltered, the dedication of the supporters has never been in doubt. The club are now firmly re-established at the ground they called home for almost 66 years before being forced to leave and shack up with Crystal Palace at Selhurst Park on the other side of South London, and then West Ham at Upton Park in East London.

Memories of those dark days could be brought back on your VCR by purchasing the video of the "last ever" match at The Valley on 21st September 1985 when almost 9,000 saw them bid farewell against Stoke City. At £11.99 it was a snip from the Supporters' Club representatives in the VIP lounge.

Their club came back to The Valley in 1991 with promises to restore their old home ground after the damage caused by vandals and nature. The stadium re-opened on 5th December 1992 when Charlton beat Portsmouth 1-0.

But the bitterness about the way the club was forced out of The Valley lingers on. The irony of their departure was that Charlton won that "last ever" home match 2-0 and went on to gain promotion to the top flight. They stayed there for four years and it seems sad that their most recent spell among the elite occurred at a time when they couldn't play at their spiritual home. Thankfully, the exile has ended, restoring to North Kent, one of the most densely populated areas in the South East, its only League club.

The Valley sits in the middle of a chalk pit which was once in the centre of what was then known as Charlton Village. The pitch was levelled by an army of volunteers who built the terraces from rubble excavated from a nearby hospital. Apparently, there were a number of bones unearthed at the time, some of which made their way to the ground. It's obvious why it was named The Valley. From the Main Stand you have the sense of being in a large bowl with buildings above and around you. It was surprisingly windy given the natural shelter afforded by the steep banking.

It was hard to imagine the stadium was once the largest club ground in Britain with a capacity of probably close to 80,000 and that more than 75,000 fans packed the ground when Charlton played Aston Villa in the Fifth Round of the Cup in 1938. It was even considered as a venue for the FA Cup Final.

The redevelopment which has transformed the ground into a smart modern venue, including the new 6,000 all-seater East Stand, has also cut the capacity to 15,000. The atmosphere has suffered but then it has been some time since Charlton pulled in large crowds.

The development hasn't finished yet. Or, at least, I hoped not since the players changed in portacabins behind the Main Stand and ran onto the pitch from the corner by the North, or Covered, End which houses the more fervent home fans. "We 'ate Millwall and We 'ate Millwall," they sang in recognition of their "Souf" London rivals.

The fanzine Voice of The Valley gave its Optimist of the Month award to defender Alan McLeary for thinking Charlton would do the double over the Lions. "Most Charlton fans would settle for getting out of The New Den with all their body parts intact, but you can always hope." Charlton seemed such a friendly club that I feared for the safety of their supporters if there was any trouble during their derby matches with their assailants from the Old Kent Road.

After the match one Baggies fan in a deep embrace with his girlfriend outside the ground attracted a crowd. It wasn't his Romeo act that was pulling in the punters, but his T-shirt which reflected the Midlands rivalry with the slogan: "If you're a Wolves fan you must be very sad". Maybe, but challenging for promotion beats the battle against relegation any day. Who would be laughing at the end of the season I wondered?

GREEN CARD
Sheffield United v Southend United - Bramall Lane
26 November 1995

This match was all about a green card, and I don't mean the piece of paper which gives you the right to work in the States and was the title of the movie starring Gerard Depardieu and the gorgeous Andie Macdowell. This green card was the one held up by about 90 percent of United's fans to protest against Chairman Reg Brealey. The A5 slips of paper urged him to "Go and go now". Their main complaint was the lack of resources made available to strengthen the team.

Quite what the Southend supporters were doing joining in the protest is anyone's guess. I suppose supporters generally don't get on too well with football club chairmen who they believe are not in it for the love of their team, though there are one or two exceptions like Jack Walker and Sir John Hall. Reg Brealey clearly felt he had more feeling for the club than the supporters. He'd arranged to meet the Independent Supporters' Association on the morning of the match but pulled out more than a week before saying they didn't have the club's best interests at heart. Someone was wrong!

The Blades' manager, Dave Bassett, had tried to sit on the fence throughout the dispute but was clearly angry that the team wasn't getting the support he felt they deserved after three straight home wins. "If they roared their support for United while the game was on and kept their arguments with the board for before and after the game it would be different, but people are beginning to take out their frustrations on the team when their frustrations lie elsewhere."

Brealey had been involved in a long-standing run-in with the fans. But at least he said he knew what running a football club was all about. He certainly knew that there was no alternative to rebuilding the John Street Stand which had been demolished over the summer leaving Bramall Lane with three sides, reminiscent of the days when United shared the ground with the Yorkshire county cricket club and only had three stands.

"Those who have responsibility for control must never forget that the club belongs to the supporters," said Brealey. Funny that, since the fans were convinced it belonged to the chairman, the board, and the other shareholders. "The shares might belong to individuals. But the ground is the home of the supporters and if I protect their 'home', I protect their club," insisted Brealey. He must have known his days were numbered though since he was determined to restore Bramall Lane to its rightful place in football before he departed. "If that is the last thing I do for this club then I shall be satisfied, whatever the supporters may think." Does that sound like someone on their way out?

I'd arrived in Sheffield by train from London having passed through some of the most depressed industrial areas I'd ever seen. Sheffield is the fourth largest city in England, with a population of just over half-a-million, and the biggest city in Yorkshire as well. But some people refer to it as the county's second city after Leeds. No wonder there's such a great rivalry between the two United's not to mention Wednesday.

Sheffield stands at the foot of the Derbyshire hills, where the River Sheaf meets the River Don. It once prospered on steel, particularly cutlery, which explains United's nickname of the Blades. The city was renowned for its knives and fine blades from as early as the fourteenth century, and by the 16th century had about 60 hallmarks. It was famous for high-quality steel from the 1700s when the crucible process was invented.

In 1742 Thomas Boulsover discovered that silver could be bonded to copper and then rolled into sheets, producing Old Sheffield Plate, the forerunner of electroplate. By the nineteenth century the great steel works stretched all along the Don valley to the north-east through the suburbs of Attercliffe, Brightside and Tinsley to Rotherham. The city's first football team doesn't quite go back that far but Sheffield FC, formed in 1857, is still the oldest club in the world.

Advances in steel production techniques soon turned the city into one of Britain's main centres of heavy and specialist engineering. It became a mixture of Victorian splendour and abject poverty. Falling demand for steel has, sadly, eroded Sheffield's industrial might. According to The Rough Guide "to approach the city by road or rail is to make a journey through some of the most dispiriting landscapes imaginable". Nevertheless, it now claims the cleanest air of any manufacturing city in Europe and the city centre has been transformed by new developments in recent years, much like Bramall Lane.

The ground was originally used by the Sheffield Cricket Club, which was formed in 1854 and secured a 99-year lease from the Duke of Norfolk. Yorkshire County Cricket Club first played there in 1855 and Sheffield Football Club first set foot on the pitch in 1862. However, Bramall Lane's place in history was secured when the first game under floodlights was played there in October 1878. Two local teams played under four lights powered by two generators and equivalent to 30,000 candles. Although only 12,000 actually paid to see the match, there were about 20,000 people at the game.

The lucrative gate receipts from an FA Cup semi-final between Preston and West Brom persuaded the cricket club that football was a profitable business and Sheffield United was formed in 1889. In 1892 they joined the Second Division in the same year that Wednesday were elected to the First Division. United were promoted within a year and won their only League title in 1898. The following year they formed a limited liability company and bought Bramall Lane from the Duke of Norfolk for just over £10,000.

I'd arrived at the ground by taxi from Sheffield station and was dropped off at the entrance to the car park on Cherry Street in front of the South Stand. It was packed with posh vehicles of all kinds from Range Rovers to Mercedes, BMWs and the odd Roller. The South Stand, which cost £750,000 and opened in August 1975, is a full-length cantilever seating 8,000 with no posts to obstruct the view. It's certainly impressive from the outside with its announcement of Sheffield United FC in big white letters over the main entrance.

The car park covers what used to be the cricket pitch used by Yorkshire until August 1973 when, after 150 years of cricket, the men in white flannels were forced to leave Bramall Lane. Northampton Town thus became the only League club in the country with a three sided ground. They have since moved to their new Sixfields Stadium. The only clubs with three-sided grounds now are those awaiting further development such as Huddersfield's McAlpine Stadium and, ironically, Bramall Lane.

The demolition of the John Street Stand, built by Archibald Leitch in 1890, had left a clear view of much of the city including St Mary's church, built 50 years earlier, which is distinguished by its four Gothic pinnacles. The bulldozers had achieved what the Luftwaffe could not for, despite being hit by German bombers in World War Two, resulting in the destruction of half the stand and its marvellous tall mock-Tudor gable, it was completely restored – even though it took eight years to complete the job.

United had already decided on the design of the new cantilevered John Street Stand which would cost around £4.2 million and seat just over 6,500 fans. The club newspaper Blades News outlined the shape of things to come: "The first tier is general seating; the second tier is a dining and lounge area with front rows of seats in the central area which will be behind a glass screen; the third tier consists of private boxes with external balcony seating. A feature... will be the return of the central clock, reminiscent of the past cricket era at the Lane."

But that was the future. Today United's aim was to win three successive home games for the first time this season. A 2-0 win over Southend left them in the ironic position of doing so just as the protests against their chairman reached new heights. "The players could have been forgiven for wondering just how important this victory had been in the context of what was going on around them," said The Yorkshire Post. "The reality is that they are doing their bit to keep United's season alive, but to expect them to do so indefinitely is unrealistic." Or is it?

WELCOME TO THE KOHLERDOME
Luton Town v Derby County - Kenilworth Road
11 December 1995

"Luton Chairman Ready for a Stretch Inside" was the headline in The Sunday Times. Yet another misdemeanour in the Season of Sleaze? One more bung in a brown paper bag at a motorway service station off the M25 uncovered at the 12th hour by the football authorities? Nothing of the sort. This was an article about what Luton Town's Chairman calls the Kohlerdome.

The Chairman in question is David Kohler and his "dome" is the code name for a project to build a new multi-purpose indoor stadium near Junction 10 of the M1 that will seat 20,000 at a cost of about £30 million. The key to his plans is a moveable grass pitch which would follow in the footsteps of the Pontiac Silverdome, the indoor stadium in Michigan touted as the wonder of USA '94 and an example of American ingenuity. It was the first, and so far only, World Cup venue to feature indoor soccer on real grass.

Laying a grass pitch inside the Silverdome was a major exercise. Two thousand hexagonal sections of grass were brought in by forklift trucks. It took three days to bring in and three days to take out. That's obviously far too long for a stadium to switch regularly between grass and other surfaces for different events. Under Kohler's plans the Luton pitch would be installed in five hours and removed in three, using hovercraft technology.

Basically, the playing surface is divided into nine large sections, each held on a steel tray weighing about 375 tonnes. These are moved by four small hovercraft, manoeuvred by four people, instead of the dozens needed at the Silverdome. The hovercraft are placed under the corners of each section, raising it up and floating it out of the stadium on a cushion of air. The grass therefore grows outside the stadium and must be stored in natural conditions until it's floated in. Luton thus need an extra area the size of a football pitch to store the grass.

It will take about five hours to set up for a football match, or any other activity requiring natural grass. The pitch will be seven feet above ground so workmen can move it and make the necessary drainage connections. "The technology is regularly used by Boeing and British Aerospace," according to Dr Stephen Baker, research officer at the Sports Turf Research Institute (STRI) which has given the Kohlerdome its seal of approval.

The STRI says the concept of trays being moved in and out so the grass can be grown in suitable open conditions is very exciting. "Currently, pitches in new stadiums are suffering from the large surrounding structures and in particular the effect of shade." Moveable grass overcomes this problem. The greatest challenge is therefore not growing the grass in trays, but moving the trays and placing them in such a way that you end up with an absolutely perfect surface. The key is knitting the grass together

"This is where the design has been clever," says Kohlerdome architect David Kierle. "The grass comes together at the edge, and each tray is separated by a plastic mesh which stops the grass matting together. After you put the trays in all you do is roll it, cut it and mark it."

Blackpool are considering a similar system for their International Colosseum complex which they hope will replace their decaying Bloomfield Road ground which stands in the shadow of the Blackpool Tower a few hundred yards from the sea on the north-west coast.

Any plan to play football in an indoor stadium requires the approval of the Football Association, the FA Premier League and the Football League. Kohler has presented his plans to all three and has received, in principle, a favourable response. Jimmy Hill, a League director, says his colleagues have an open-mind. "It could solve a lot of problems and there was certainly no resentment on the League's board."

The supporters also seem to favour the proposed Kohlerdome after rejecting plans for a move to Milton Keynes. The editorial in the fanzine Mad As A Hatter clearly gave the scheme it's backing. "Some of those opposed to the new stadium are suggesting that the existing... ground should be redeveloped. It is clear that these are people who have not stepped inside a football ground for may years, and have no appreciation of how poor our ground now looks in comparison with many others in the (First) division. To improve the ground significantly would require the purchase of many houses around the ground and that process alone could take many years. The only way ahead is a new stadium, at a new location, and it will be up to us, the supporters, to give the proposals the backing they need to come to fruition."

The club's lease from Luton Borough Council on its present home at Kenilworth Road runs out in May 1996 and Luton have made no secret of their desire to move. A planning application for the new stadium has already been lodged with the council. The Kohlerdome would take about three years to build and Kohler says it could open the door for ground-sharing.

The Kohlerdome Corporation, formed by Kohler to "realise his vision", joined forces with Whitbread and in April 1995 formally announced the launch of the £30 million scheme. The PR machine called the complex "an out-of-town multi-purpose leisure facility for the 21st century". That means a stadium outside Luton which can be used for all sorts of things in the years ahead. It will include hotel, restaurant and leisure facilities, which explains the association with Whitbread, described by the club as "one of the country's leading food and drink leisure operators".

"Its creation will provide Luton with a first-class community, cultural and leisure facility which can be used throughout the year in all conditions, and will endorse the club's reputation as one of the most innovative in British football," says Luton.

The club's reputation for innovation comes from the installation of an artificial pitch in 1985 and the controversial members-only scheme introduced the same year partly in response to the chaos caused by rioting Millwall fans. The club was banned from the fizzy drinks cup, then the Littlewoods Cup, in 1986 as a punishment for breaking the tournament's rules. Luton got their revenge when they won the trophy by beating Arsenal 3-2 in 1988. They were also runners-up the following year.

News of the plans for a super stadium was first unveiled in October 1994, since when discussions have been taking place on a possible site. Kohler clearly has a vision. "...we at Luton Town have a dream that one day we can move from Kenilworth Road, our home for the past 90 years, into a new stadium. The reasons for the move, apart from our lease running out in 1996, are obvious to all who have visited us."

In fact, Luton have been trying to find a new home since the end of the Second World War. In the 1970s there was talk of moving to Milton Keynes, 23 miles up the M1. During the 1983/84 season the club announced that, because of road-building plans affecting the ground, they would be forced to move. Milton Keynes was again the planned location, but the supporters organised protest marches and it never happened.

The need for a move is obvious to anyone who visits the ground. Michael Heatley and Daniel Ford in British Football Grounds Then and Now point out that Kenilworth Road was not an ideal location even by the standards of 1905 when it first opened.

Simon Inglis in The Football Grounds of Great Britain says that until you have been to Kenilworth Road "you cannot appreciate how cramped is 'cramped'. One side is hemmed in by a railway with houses on two of the other three sides." But things have got worse. Heatley an Ford point out that: "In the 1990s the situation is considerably worse:

add the traffic generated by a football crowd and you have an area of the town that comes to a complete standstill every other Saturday."

I went to see the Hatters (Luton was once a straw hat-making centre) play Derby in a televised match screened live on a Sunday afternoon and the traffic was appalling. Queues of cars blocked the approach roads around the ground and the journey was one big headache. Clearly, improved access was impossible at Kenilworth Road.

I eventually arrived at the ground and was ushered into the Eric Morecambe suite. A portrait of the genial star of the Morecambe and Wise show hangs on the wall. Morecambe was a Luton Town director from 1976 to 1983 and brought a lot of sunshine to the club and its supporters. He was sadly missed. The club still play 'Bring Me Sunshine', the theme tune which used to bring the curtain down on the hit television show, when the Luton players run out. Sadly, they failed to deliver any rays at all.

The Morecambe & Wise theme was more in tune than the local church band. They were out on the pitch to get everyone in the Christmas spirit with off-key versions of several festive favourites. On-loan midfielder Paul Allen from Southampton must have wished he'd stayed on the south coast, or at least brought his ear plugs along.

I was in the Main Stand on Maple Road, built in the 1920s after a fire destroyed its predecessor. The centre-section was bought from Kempton racecourse. A railway line runs parallel to the stand and its assortment of offices, social clubs and guest lounges. It only covers three-quarters of the length of the pitch because of the lack of space due to the railway line and the relief road which cuts across the south-east corner of the ground by the Kenilworth Road End.

Opposite was the North Stand on Beech Hill Path which replaced the Bobbers Stand in 1986. It once cost a 'bob' (a shilling, or five new pence) to stand on the terraces, but today they've gone, replaced first by seats and now by executive boxes. Kenilworth Road is the only ground with boxes along the whole of one side of the pitch. Like those at Watford, box holders and their guests can sit outside on a private balcony if they prefer to watch the match in the elements. Luton got the idea from Lord's Cricket Ground where sliding glass doors provide access to the seats outside.

To my left was the all-seater Oak Road End with its unusual three-tiered roof rising up to meet the roof of the Main Stand. Away fans are allowed into Kenilworth Road now after the lifting of the club's ban imposed in 1986. I walked around the back of the stand before the match for a first hand look at how cramped the ground is. The entrances actually run through terraced houses, along a pathway and up a flight of stairs looking over a row of back gardens.

The Middlesbrough fanzine Fly Me To The Moon summed up the attitude of away fans to this end of the ground. "One thing I don't like is the fact that if the away end ever totally sells out then the front row is under pitch level and so far below the hoardings that you can't actually see the pitch. One thing I do like is climbing down the steps to the rear of the stand and being able to get a good insight into the kitchen and bathroom hygiene of the citizens of Beds." Whatever turns you on!

The home fans were underwhelmed by Luton's display against Derby. The match ended goalless, though it was more exciting than the previous day's game at Gillingham. (After watching the Gills even snooker player Steve Davis would have had me jumping out of my seat.) At least I got to see Marvin Johnson, the Luton number 3 who, according to the fanzine, "looks like a clown, defends like a Tottenham full-back and attacks like a Brazilian". Nice combo.

The contrast between this performance and Luton's record win back in the 1930's couldn't have been sharper. One of the guest suites is dedicated to the hero of that game, Joe Payne. "Ten Goal" was the nickname given to Luton's reserve wing half who in 1936 scored a League record 10 goals against Bristol Rovers in a 12-0 win. Payne had never previously played centre-forward. He described his afternoon's work as "just one of those days". Offers flooded in from other clubs, but he remained at Luton to score a record 55 goals the following season. He eventually left to join Chelsea, West Ham, and Millwall, earning an England cap along the way, before retiring in 1948.

Payne was a reminder of better days for Luton. The following year they were promoted from the Third Division as champions, though they had to wait until 1968 for their next taste of glory when they won the Fourth Division title. The Second Division Championship followed in 1982 and then a series of close encounters of the First Division relegation kind, including a last-gasp win over Manchester City at Maine Road in 1983 thanks to a goal from Raddy Antic in the closing minutes. Luton eventually ran out of luck and dropped down into the First Division (the new one) in 1992.

Perhaps a new super stadium will bring the good times back to the Bedfordshire team. Kohler hopes so. "On my office wall I have a picture of the proposed 'Kohlerdome' with the words: "If you will it, it is no dream". He sounds like a cross between Martin Luther King and one of those flash foreign car ads and has yet to deliver his dream to the people of Luton. But David Kohler is working on it.

POSH THEY'RE NOT
Peterborough v Cambridge United – London Road
31 December 1994

Derby matches usually call to mind places like Merseyside, North London and Manchester but in the Fenlands of South-East England there's another battle which is just as fiercely fought, if less well known: Peterborough versus Cambridge.

Peterborough owed its nineteenth century development to railway workshops and Fletton bricks, but 'planned expansion' had dramatically changed the place and raised the population to more than 150,000. Almost five percent of them would be at London Road for today's derby match against the old enemy from the south.

I had no idea how passionate the supporters were in this part of the country. Peterborough fans call the U's ground The Shabbey Stadium (instead of the Abbey Stadium), but to be honest London Road was little better. Still, FA Cup defeat at the hands of Cambridge had given the POSH fans extra reason for hoping their team would win. It would be a great way to welcome in the New Year.

The clubs had decided to reschedule the match to a midday kick-off so that New Year revellers would have plenty of time to prepare for the night's festivities. They'd no doubt spend much of their evening going over the incident-packed football match they were about to see. There were more twists and turns than an Agatha Christie mystery.

The visiting Cambridge supporters were camped at the Moys Road End of the ground with the POSH faithful at the London Road End. Both covered terraces are identical but their inhabitants couldn't have been more different. The persistent colourful banter between the rival fans was a highlight of the afternoon along with a smashing match.

The atmosphere was not always this passionate judging from the programme notes penned by The Evening Telegraph's football reporter Alan Swann. His In The Press Box column played down the suggestion of the club's chief executive that Lord Lucan had made an offer to take over the POSH.

"At the time of his disappearance 20 years ago, Lucan was in a worse financial state than Peter Shilton," noted Swann "... but I have discovered the origins of this sorry story. Lucan was advised to lay low in a quiet part of the world until his troubles blew over. He has been a Glebe Road (POSH) season ticket holder since 1974."

He followed that with the story of a POSH fan who sold his season ticket after the cup defeat by Cambridge. "That's a pretty rash move, but not as rash as the bloke who bought it," wrote Swann. With that kind of support from the local football writer things must be bad.

Peterborough were in better shape than Cambridge since they were in mid-table, while the U's were only just above the Division Two relegation zone. I got the feeling this local derby was one of the few highlights of the season at London Road.

Peterborough had made an immediate impression when they joined the League in 1960 after gaining a reputation as cup giant-killers and dominating the Midland League in the 1950s. Before their election to the old Fourth Division they'd put together a run of 103 matches with only one defeat between 1955 and 1960!

Their first season was spectacular. They stormed to the Fourth Division title scoring 134 goals in 46 games – still a record for any division – to become the first side to win the championship in the year of their election. Terry Bly got 52 of those goals, the most ever scored in the division; no other player has topped 50 League goals in post-war football.

In 1965 the POSH reached the FA Cup Sixth Round, after beating QPR and Arsenal, and the League Cup semi-final the following year. Their bubble finally burst in 1968 when they were relegated for alleged financial irregularities. Sound familiar? Since when their only real success has been two seasons in the First Division between 1992 and 1994.

Among their former stars were Arsenal's David Seaman and Coventry's Mickey Gynn. How they could have done with either of those two against the U's. "Seaman was an obvious England player from the moment he came here," according to former POSH forward Robbie Cooke. "I phoned my dad the day he had first trained and told him exactly that. He didn't believe me but later had to admit to my being right."

Seaman was at the other end of the spectrum from the current POSH keeper Scott Cooksey. Under the headline 'The Nightmare Continues' the fanzine The Peterborough Effect discussed the merits of the man they called Scott Dropsey. "Even in his better games he dropped balls for no reason whatsoever and mishandled and miskicked with monotonous regularity," said the fanzine.

It seemed that the only real excitement on offer at London Road these days was a derby match against Cambridge. The Evening Telegraph's Alan Swann offered some idea of how much Cambridge mean to POSH fans. In an off-beat preview of what might happen over the next 12 months he tried to warm the hearts of all POSH supporters. "January:

Cambridge are thrown out of FA Cup after refusing to switch their tie with Burnley to London Road on police advice." Instead, they lost the tie 4-2!

The pre-match build up on the local radio station Q103 had already whetted my appetite as I sped along the M11 towards Peterborough New Town. The drive was hardly inspiring as I passed acre after acre of flat farmers' fields as I crossed the Fens. The radio reporter interviewed both managers, John Still of Peterborough and Gary Johnson of Cambridge, but seemed more interested in the boots his mother-in-law had bought him for Christmas than in the outcome of the match.

The man they call "The POSH", Peterborough's answer to the bloke in the red, white and blue top hat and tails who follows England around the world, was also wheeled on for his moment in the sun. (I later learned from a POSH fan called Julian, who I met on a flight from Chicago to London, that the man called "The POSH" was a local celebrity and always ran out on the pitch before home matches.) "The POSH" had been preceded by an interview with "Barry Moore – The Number One Cambridge Fan". Well, someone has to be!

Peterborough's ground was, well, functional would be a kind description. Simon Inglis in The Football Grounds of Great Britain described it as "Born in the 1950s and barely touched since. London Road is the spirit incarnate of British ground design during that unrewarding decade... The basic tenet then was to copy everything that had been done in the 1930s, but replace curves with straight lines, wood with brick. Goodbye character, farewell warmth; welcome efficiency, insurability and long life."

But at least the POSH had the first computer installed in any League ground. The large electronic counter was positioned underneath the Main Stand. The executive suite behind the stand, which overlooked the car park, was opened in 1985.

At the ground the POSH supporters tucked into the London Road End gave a few clues on how they regarded their esteemed neighbours from the university town to the south: "You're just a bunch of wankers" rang out more than once on a bright, sunny New Year's Eve. The "wankers" chant was particularly noticeable after Cambridge striker Jason Lillis cancelled out Ken Charlery's opening strike after about 25 minutes. The abuse began after Lillis was joined in a Klinsmannesque diving celebration by Canadian-born striker Carlo Corazzin. Well, what did they expect?.

The Cambridge fans at the Moys Road End responded with "You're not singing anymore". But Lillis was to infuriate the home fans even

117

more after 81 minutes when he put the U's ahead during a pulsating second half. It was end to end stuff in a typically frenetic derby and no surprise when Charlery, now at Barry Fry's Birmingham, equalised with six minutes left. The POSH fans went absolutely barmy.

Both sets of supporters could at least enjoy their New Year celebrations without having to drown their sorrows over defeat at the hands of the enemy. I had little time to think about celebrating anything since I had to race across to west London for the afternoon game between Brentford and Oxford at Griffin Park. It was a hard life!

THE RETURN OF STAN THE MAN
Brentford v Oxford United – Griffin Park
31 December 1994

Talk about ball skills. This guy was brilliant. Hoops and Hoopla. More tricks than a magician. A true maverick. Hello Stan Bowles. The former Manchester City, Queen's Park Rangers, Forest, Orient and Brentford star was propping up the bar in the executive club after the match. Fag in hand, pint on the bar and doubtless a bet on the 2.30 at Haydock Park.

Stan was larger-than-life. He still had the long locks which all true mavericks sported in the 1970s. They were grey now, but very distinguished. "Do you miss playing?" I asked. "No," replied Stan. "Not really. I loved being out there in front of the crowd and all that. But I hated the training." And he meant it.

Stan was a conjuror on the pitch. A shimmy one way, then the other, and two opponents would be on the floor. I'd grown up watching him on The Big Match with Brian Moore on Sunday afternoons. I'd be straight over the park afterwards imagining I could dribble just like him. I couldn't. But football just wouldn't have been the same without players like Stan Bowles.

He had come back to Griffin Park for the first time since he stopped playing for the Bees in the early 1980's to see his old team-mate David Webb, now Brentford's manager. He wasn't that impressed by the football served up from the current side. "The ball seemed to be up in the air all the time in the first half-an-hour," moaned Stan. "Why don't they keep it on the floor?" Why indeed?

Webb thought Stan and his old team-mate, winger Dave Thomas, could help his young Brentford team to polish some of their rough edges and, just maybe, keep the ball on the deck. "I wanted someone who could impress upon my players the value of their first touch," said Webb referring to Bowles. "I wanted to get him on the training pitch to show my players what can be achieved with one touch of the ball. Stan was a great one touch player. He was so economic with his use of the ball. Simplicity was his game." Thomas was brought in to show the wide players how to cross the ball consistently well. "At his peak, Dave was one of the best," said Webb. "He takes his own little group and works on crossing and wrapping your foot around the ball."

Webb has often used the 'greats' from the 1970s in training sessions. Players like Charlie George and Tony Currie. "We can't live in the past, I know, but my own feeling is that the game has fewer skilful players than 20 years ago. Football has changed so much since I was playing. It's no longer the skill factor that unlocks the door. These days it's more likely to be the pace factor."

Stan finished his career at Brentford and nowadays lives in a council flat across the road from Griffin Park. He won five caps for England and, according to Michael Hart of the London Evening Standard, could "charm the birds from the trees".

"Only two people could have got me back on the training pitch," said Stan. "One is Webbie and the other Gerry Francis. My touch is alright, but I'm having trouble with my breathing. But I love it. What you miss most is the banter and the atmosphere in the dressing room. Ask any old pro. They'd all say the same."

Stan played the day Brentford notched up their record Cup Victory, a 7-0 thrashing of Windsor & Eton away in the FA Cup First Round in 1982. He really turned on the style that day, though he didn't manage to score. It was great to see him looking so well, but his addiction to gambling has hovered over his career like a rain cloud and he still dreams of getting one over the bookies with his dole money.

"Stan is a terrific bloke," said Webb. "A lot of people say he's had his chance but I'd like to get him interested in football again. He'll live his life however he wants to but it's nice to see a smile on his face again when he's playing with my lads. He's got a bit of grey hair now and when he first turned up one of my lads asked: 'Whose side is Dave Allen on?' It was the sort of crack Stan would have come up with as a player. He took it all in his stride."

"Most of my lads had never seen him play, but by the end of the session they knew he was no mug. At his peak I'd have put him up behind George Best. He wasn't as good as George but he was better than Rodney Marsh. And when the going got tough he could get stuck in a bit."

Brentford had recently matched their record score against Peter Shilton's Plymouth – their biggest win since a 9-0 thrashing of Wrexham in 1963. The last time they'd scored seven goals was against Exeter in 1983 during Stan's time at the club. They're the only League club to win all their home games (21 in 1929/30) and were once in the old First Division (1935-47) after a spectacular rise from the Third Division in only three seasons. They were relegated in 1947 and have achieved little since.

Stan's old team-mate Webbie, scorer of that memorable winning goal in the replayed 1970 Cup Final against Leeds, was building a promising team at Brentford after his earlier return to Chelsea alongside Chairman

Ken Bates had been predictably brief. When the phone rang and Brentford Chairman Martin Lange was on the other end asking "How would you like to come and work for a decent chairman?" Webb couldn't refuse. He was impressed by Lange's upbeat outlook and infectious enthusiasm for football.

The chairman's commitment stems from his genuine affection for Brentford Football Club. He first watched them from the terraces at the age of five. Lange's success as a property tycoon enabled him to take control of the club he's "nuts" about. But that doesn't mean he lavishes millions on players à la Jack Walker. Webb had little money to spend and in recent years Brentford had sold their best players to make ends meet.

The most notable transfer was the sale of Dean Holdsworth to Wimbledon for a club record £750,000 in August 1992, but Andy Sinton, Marcus Gayle, Gary Blissett and Joe Allon, leading scorer in 1993/94, have all been sacrificed to raise funds. Surprisingly, Holdsworth was the all-time favourite player in a poll conducted by the fanzine Beesotted with the 'legendary' Stan Bowles in second place.

"Stan, who can still be found in the pubs of Brentford most days (and evenings for that matter!), must surely be the all-time crowd pleaser for his antics on the playing field, and even at the end of his career his class was still there for all to see." Mind you, the most valuable player ever to leave Brentford must be pop star Rod Stewart, an apprentice with the Bees in the early 1960s before he switched careers.

On a very wet Saturday afternoon I was able to cast my eyes over the latest strike force of Nick Forster and Robert Taylor, plundered from Gillingham and Orient. According to Dave Lane, the editor of Beesotted, they are "the first truly potent strike force since the Blissett-Holdsworth era". Webb calls them his 'FT Index'. "My chairman's in stocks and shares and if either of them score I tell him, 'The FT Index has gone up again chairman.'"

But can the club keep hold of their promising young players? They disposed of table-topping Oxford thanks to an impressive display by goalkeeper Kevin Dearden, who made a series of crucial saves in the second half when Oxford applied the pressure. A hamstring injury to Oxford's former Sunderland FA Cup star John Byrne had already removed the visitors' most dangerous striker. When a horrendous defensive error allowed Brentford to score a second goal late in the game Oxford's fate was sealed.

The visitors were kept out despite a hatful of chances in the second half and part of the ad on the roof of the New Road Stand seemed to sum up their afternoon: "Next Time..." it said, adding "Fly KLM". The reason for this, and the "Forward Air Cargo" ad on the Main Stand roof, is that Griffin Park is under the flightpath to Heathrow Airport. The Air Cargo ad is thought to be the largest in the world in terms of area. There must be a bigger one in America surely!

Unfortunately for Brentford, KLM would not be renewing their sponsorship when the deal expired later in 1995. That means the ad will either be replaced or painted over. Beesotted had held a competition to see who could come up with the best slogan. The suggestions were more appropriate to supporting Brentford such as, 'Next Time... Go Shopping with the Mrs' or 'Next Time... drop Westley'.

I left the ground and walked along a very wet Braemar Road past the tiny terraced houses and cottages which surround the stadium in what is a fashionable part of West London between the River Thames and the M4. Legend has it that the game of football began near Griffin Park when Julius Caesar crossed the Brent and kicked the skull of a dead Briton! I passed one of the pubs which makes the ground unique – it's the only one in the league with a watering hole on each corner. The legend probably began with Brentford fans' celebrating a home win in one of them on a Saturday night.

Ron Atkinson, once employed at Griffin Park painting names on the dressing room doors, offices and boardroom, has probably tried them all. So has Stan Bowles whose nights of propping up the bar will no doubt be among the stories in a book he is writing about his life. "It's all in there," he said. "The good and the bad"... and the bubbly – as Georgie Best might say.

GRAHAM'S GLOOM
Tottenham Hotspur v Arsenal - White Hart Lane
2 January 1995

New Year's Day and one of the most fiercely-contested derby's in football, Spurs against Arsenal. Undersoil heating ensured this Monday night fixture went ahead as planned, unlike the match at Orient earlier in the day and the West London derby between QPR and Chelsea at Loftus Road which was to be postponed the following night forcing Sky commentators Andy Gray and Martin Tyler to speed up to the north-east for Manchester United's match against Coventry at Old Trafford instead.

The passions aroused by a North London derby are among the fiercest in the country. I could feel the excitement building as I drove along Tottenham High Road past the Whitehall Tavern and the Hotspur restaurant with its blue and white cockerel sign hanging outside. There was no mistaking who was at home tonight as fans in navy blue and white hats, scarves and jackets made their way to the ground.

The police were out in force to try to prevent trouble. You couldn't miss them in their bright yellow jackets with white fluorescent trim around the middle as they struggled to restrain Alsatian dogs who were trying desperately hard to break free. Police on horseback paraded along the High Street using their higher vantage point to direct operations. They would all be needed to keep the rival fans apart tonight.

I parked behind some flats in a side street off the High Road and walked back towards the ground past a stall selling souvenirs of both teams. Unusually, it was the only one I could see on what was a bitterly cold night. Most of the games in the lower divisions scheduled for the afternoon had been postponed because of frozen pitches.

Tonight's match had been sold out for weeks and television coverage was no deterrent for the faithful who were now arriving in their thousands. I approached the main entrance which had always been a meeting place for fans before the game. They'd congregate inside and outside the White Hart Inn. The pub was famous because Charringtons, the owners, had encouraged Tottenham to settle there in 1900 because of the profits they knew would flow from increased beer sales to fans. To my surprise the White Hart Inn had been transformed into a trendy wine bar called Rudolph's.

Rudolph's neon sign would once have seemed out of place at the entrance to the West Stand but now it seemed to belong there. The tinted glass exterior of the £4.2 million stand, the most costly at any British ground when it was constructed in the early '80s, reflected the dawning of a new age in stadium design. Younger supporters may welcome such changes as progress but to me something irreplaceable had been lost.

As a boy I remember one of my father's best friends, Ronnie Massey, once president of the Spurs Supporters Club, having a drink with Dave Mackay and some of the other players in the White Hart after a league match in the late '60s. The arrival of Rudolph's had dimmed the memory. It was probably the last place you'd find any of today's Spurs team after a match. Then again, times have changed since Mackay pulled on the famous white shirt and the distance between players and supporters has grown wider outside the confines of the players' bar and the sponsors' lounge.

I turned away from Rudolph's and walked towards Paxton Road when I suddenly heard a roar. Rival fans came running across the High Road throwing punches. The police moved in to separate them and dragged at least one supporter away with his arm up behind his back and forced him into a police van. It was the first trouble I'd witnessed on the streets outside a ground in 45 matches!

As the Arsenal followers moved towards the Park Lane End, where they'd be seated for tonight's game, there was more shouting and jockeying with the Spurs' fans. The police had their work cut out to prevent uglier scenes developing. They succeeded, just. The Alsatian dogs and officers on horseback had been enough to prevent more widespread fighting breaking out. It was like a throwback to the '70s and showed that, despite innovations such as video cameras, there was an undercurrent of violence waiting to get out. After all, the pride of North London was at stake tonight!

Having seen enough of the trouble in the High Road I popped into the Spurs kit store to see if I could get a number nine steamed onto the back of the Blackburn shirt I'd bought for my son on my earlier visit to Ewood Park. I couldn't get it done there because they only put numbers and lettering on shirts when there isn't a match on. To their credit, Spurs had the staff on hand to provide the service when you wanted it and that, not surprisingly, was when you were at the ground on match days. It doesn't take a genius to work these things out but then not everyone involved in football is a genius.

Of course, profit is a great motivator and I know the Spurs shop isn't there out of the goodness of Chairman Alan Sugar's heart. But they steamed Alan Shearer's messianic number nine onto my Blackburn shirt for nothing, which was more than I expected. The young lad who did the job, with a steam press resembling a smaller version of those used in a dry cleaners, had a concerned look on his face as he tried to assess whether his equipment would work on an alien shirt. Or perhaps he couldn't bear to work with anything other than the navy blue and white of his beloved Tottenham.

Shirts hung around the shop adorned with the names of the Spurs stars: KLINSMANN, SHERINGHAM, WALKER, BARMBY. The longer the name, the higher the cost. SHERINGHAM would set you back about £10.50 – and that's just the name. Add a number, the Carling Premier League motif and the cost of the shirt and you wouldn't get much change from £50. No wonder there was a sigh of relief from dads everywhere when DUMITRESCU went on loan to Seville in Spain!

I just had time to pick up my ticket from the collection point at the main entrance and skip around the ground to the East Stand before the match began. I passed one supporter drinking a pint of beer as he walked along the High Road! I entered the ground and made my way past a door above which was a sign announcing "The Arthur Rowe Suite" – named after the manager of the great Spurs 'push and run' side which won the Championship in 1951. I climbed the stairs up to a corridor which had executive boxes leading off it on the right. My ticket took me to a box used as an overspill for guests who couldn't be accommodated anywhere else in the ground.

I found myself among a group of Jewish people who'd come to cheer on Ronnie Rosenthal – a replacement for the injured Nick Barmby. Two other guests supporting Jürgen Klinsmann were also in the box along with Millwall boss Mick McCarthy. He was there to check out the Arsenal side which his team would play in the FA Cup Third Round at the New Den on the coming Saturday. I took my seat in the second row of three and sat back in a comfy chair to enjoy one of the year's football highlights.

Watching behind glass really does affect the excitement of the game. I hadn't warmed to the Premier Club at Coventry's Highfield Road because of the sterile atmosphere. It was just as bad, and perhaps worse, sitting in a box. The crowd noise could have been piped in from a speaker at the back but it wasn't turned on. Nor was the TV mounted on the wall just above the speaker. The match therefore kicked off in virtual silence. You could have heard a pin drop.

I was desperate to join the 'real' crowd outside the glass who were in full voice all around the ground. According to Simon Inglis in The

Football Grounds of Great Britain, "White Hart Lane is not just a football ground, it is part of a small kingdom". Tonight the people of the kingdom were paying homage to the family who they believed ruled North London. "I don't think I've been at a match this season where there has been so much noise," John Motson told Match of the Day viewers that night.

As usual the game itself was a close encounter of the passionate kind with little space for flair players like Anderton, Sheringham and Klinsmann of Tottenham and.... now if only Limpar had still been at Arsenal. The only goal of the first half was created by Howells and Anderton and clinically finished by Romanian international Gica Popescu. The Spurs fans went crazy, the Arsenal supporters sat there in silence.

Popescu was called Georghe when he first arrived in England but is now known as Gica. Is that a short form of Georghe or did everyone just get it wrong? Answers on a postcard please. The confusion over Popescu's name continues a tradition at Tottenham. Former coach and then manager Peter Shreeve, now assistant to Ray Wilkins at QPR, was called Shreeves for months after his appointment before he bravely announced at a press conference that there was no 'S' at the end.

It seemed even Gerry Francis had been having a little trouble with names at the club. The fanzine Cock-a-Doodle Doo, whilst welcoming the arrival of the former QPR supremo as the new Spurs manager, noted that "it would have been nice if football's most famous pigeon fancier had got our name right". Francis called the club Tottenham Hotspurs. At least he didn't pronounce the first word as Tottingham like a certain Argentinian star I could mention!

The club's name comes from Shakespeare's Harry Hotspur, a character developed from the fourteenth century ancestor of an aristo-cratic family of landowners called the Northumberlands who were based in the Tottenham area in the 1880s. Hence the name given to nearby Northumberland Avenue. Harry got his name because of the spurs he wore when riding and the club's ball and cockerel emblem is probably also linked to him since fighting cocks used to wear tiny spurs.

At half-time I accompanied one of the neutral guests to the executive club bar for a swift pint. He told me he didn't support any particular team, but seemed to have a soft spot for West Ham and QPR. "Some of my mates are over there," he said pointing to a group of tall blokes on the other side of the bar. "One of them has just got out of jail for murder and the others have been inside as well."

The murderer had been in a pub one night when another man pulled a knife on him. He jumped over the bar, found a knife and that was that. With friends like that, who needs enemies. They'd all grown up in Bethnal Green, a notorious part of East London famous for the boxers it produces. "I don't live there anymore though. I've got two young children, see, and that's no place for them to grow up." Unless they want to be boxers!

The second half was also tight and the Spurs fans began to chant "We Hate Arsenal". "A lot of people would agree with that," said Millwall's McCarthy. Sour grapes over the cup defeat the year before? Ian Wright was closest to scoring when he clipped the bar with a chip over Ian Walker. The Spurs goalkeeper had made a great save by turning away a Wright effort earlier in the half, but was clearly beaten by Wright's chip and looked on helplessly as the ball bounced off the bar.

Walker, barracked by Norwich fans at Carrow Road the previous Monday for being the son of former Canaries' boss Mike Walker, out of a job after being sacked by Everton, had gained some notoriety for showing off his assets in the magazine For Women. "The other lads were just disappointed that they were not asked to pose naked. I suppose we're just not BIG enough stars!" said Spurs midfielder Micky Hazard.

As the electronic clock on the Umbro-sponsored Tottenham scoreboard at the Park Lane End showed the minutes ticking away, the game opened up and both sides could have scored. Klinsmann fired just wide and Sheringham squandered two clear chances - one veered away past the far post and the other was driven straight into the arms of Seaman. Arsenal also applied pressure, but failed to find the net.

Late in the game Stefan Schwarz was sent off for a late tackle on Klinsmann who almost waited for the Swedish international to throw himself at the ball before falling to the ground. It was almost the famous dying swan act, but not quite. The Arsenal fans jeered, the referee held up the red card and Schwarz left the game.

As the Spurs fans whistled for the match to end I glanced at the supporters in the executive box to my left. They were obviously Gooners fans since they had greeted every Arsenal miss with a pained expression and had wrung their hands nervously every time Spurs attacked. The tension had got to them all with the exception of the pretty blonde and even more gorgeous brunette who both looked calm throughout.

Their torment was soon over as the referee blew the final whistle and the Tottenham fans went delirious. The Spurs players hugged each other as if it was a cup final and then applauded the fans. The Arsenal players shook hands with their assailants and left the field dejected. The pressure on George Graham was growing as his side's poor form added to the controversy surrounding his role in the transfer of Danish midfield star John Jensen from Brondby and revelations that Paul Merson was a cocaine addict.

For Spurs fans Arsenal's troubles were like manna from heaven. After all the problems surrounding the Irving Scholar years, Gazza, the bust-up between Sugar and Venables and financial irregularities which led to an FA Cup ban and six point penalty, eventually overturned, the inquisitor's spotlight had at last moved to the arch-enemy.

Under a headline The Arsenal World of Sleaze the Tottenham fanzine detailed an Early History of Arsenal Misdemeanours and a Rogues Gallery of the Seventies and Early Eighties before moving on to The Recent Past.

It's not hard to understand why Spurs fans hate Arsenal when you look at the historical background. A scandalous series of events in 1919 saw the Gooners unjustly take Tottenham's place in the First Division. That year the Football League decided to expand the First Division to 22 teams. However, instead of retaining Chelsea and Spurs, the two clubs who were at the bottom of the First Division before the war in 1915, only Chelsea kept their place as the top two teams in the Second Division were promoted and Arsenal were voted into the First Division instead of Spurs despite finishing fifth in the Second Division. Perhaps that partly explain the animosity.

Tottenham's fate was also sealed by a fixed match in which Manchester United beat Liverpool in 1915 – a result which kept them above Tottenham at the bottom of the table. Some players were suspended but United were not penalised! And everyone complains about corruption in the game today. As always it just seems like things used to be better. Older people tell you how much better things were. Usually, they weren't.

I returned to the bar after the game with my acquaintance from the executive box. We just caught a glimpse of World Cup winner Martin Peters, now on the Spurs payroll as a PR man, leaving the ground. In the bar supporters were listening to interviews with a satisfied Gerry Francis and an under-fire George Graham.

I didn't catch the interviews on Sky but later that night the views of the two managers were aired on Match of the Day. There are times when football is like a war and the comparison wasn't lost on Francis as he told John Motson: "Obviously, John, it was a hell of a battle. We had to dig in there at times. Arsenal came at us with a lot of pride and didn't want to lose the local derby and neither did we. It was obviously going to be very tight. Even before the game started we thought it was going to be like that – maybe one goal was going to win it and, fortunately, we got the goal."

Surprisingly, George Graham was upbeat. The master of disguise. "I was very pleased with our attitude and our overall performance. Really pleased. And we had some chances in the second half. I thought the commitment and effort was there. I think if we'd have got the equaliser things would have been different. They were full of it tonight. As long as we can repeat that a bit more often we won't have any problems."

Motson then asked the question on everyone's lips. "That's only two wins in 12 games in the League now George. Do you think that any of the off-the-field publicity which has been directed towards Arsenal has affected your form or the confidence of the team?" Graham's answer was short and to the point. "No."

I wandered over to the trophy cabinet past a couple of old Spurs favourites. Martin Chivers had retained the stature he had as a player while Cliff Jones, a member of the 1961 double-winning team, looked very smart in a jacket and tie. It was nice to see old stars returning to the scene of their greatest triumphs. It drove home to me how short a footballer's career really is. And I bet they expect it to last forever when they're at the top and making the headlines. It doesn't.

The first trophy I laid eyes on was a silver presentation plate. The inscription said: "Presented by the directors of Watford Football Club to Tottenham Hotspur Football Club on the occasion of the Semi-Final of the Football Association Challenge Cup Competition. Saturday 11th April, 1987. Villa Park, Birmingham."

There was a display of colourful pennants from AS Monaco, FC Metz, Aberdeen, Sparta Rotterdam, Atletico de Madrid and Ajax of Amsterdam – all old-time foes from European competitions over the years. There was also a pennant from a team called Wydad Athletic Club, Casablanca. I wondered if Humphrey Bogart had played centre-forward.

The cabinet also contained the answer to a question I'd pondered since visiting Brighton's Goldstone Ground. At Brighton the only sign of their Wembley appearance in the 1984 final was a dog-eared programme on the bottom shelf of the trophy cabinet in the directors lounge. What does a club receive when it loses an FA Cup Final?

A gold-trimmed white pennant with the Football Association's crest gave me the answer and somewhere at the Goldstone Ground there must be a similar memento. It said: "Runners-up, Challenge Cup.

Tottenham Hotspur FC. Season 1986-87." Not much for all that effort! Spurs had only ever lost one FA Cup Final and held the joint record for the number of wins with eight – the same as Manchester United. The one blemish was in 1987 when they lost 3-2 to Coventry after extra-time when Gary Mabbutt deflected the ball past Ray Clemence.

As I was leaving White Hart Lane I noticed a tall copper ball with a cockerel perched proudly on the top displayed outside the Arthur Rowe Suite. "Was that the cockerel which used to sit on top of the East Stand?" I asked the girl on the front desk. "That's right," she said. "How old is it?" "There's an inscription on the wall. That'll tell you."

I wandered over to the tall weather-beaten sculpture to take a look. "The Tottenham cockerel, manufactured in 1909 by Mr W. J. Scott of F. Brady and Company, London at a cost of £35. Mr Scott had also been an amateur player with the club in 1896. The cockerel was originally positioned in the gable end of the old West Stand and was moved to the East Stand in 1958." Some fans believe the ball contains Tottenham's league registration papers from 1908 as well as coins and old newspapers.

As I walked back along the High Road I could have been in Milan or Madrid instead of North London. Car horns were tooting and flags were waving as the Tottenham fans savoured the victory. Icicles hanging from the roof of an underground parking garage near my car reminded me of the coldness of winter. But for Spurs fans the night was a warm one. They'd witnessed a famous victory – all victories over Arsenal are famous – and were in the mood to celebrate... long into the night.

ECHOES OF FINNEY
Preston North End v Mansfield Town - Deepdale
21 January 1995

I arrived at Preston's ground exactly 120 years to the day after the club, then called Preston Nelson, moved to the Deepdale Farm in 1875. It would be four years before the first football match at the new ground because cricket, rugby and athletics were the games usually played by the members. But Deepdale would soon be famous as the club expanded and the football team took the domestic game by storm.

In their first game at Deepdale Preston were thrashed 16-0 by Blackburn Rovers, the start of a rivalry which is just as fierce today. The current Premier League Champions are not known as Bastard Rovers for nothing in this part of the north-west. The Lilywhites, for their part, are usually called Preston Nob End by rival fans, including those at Blackburn and Blackpool.

The feud with Blackpool is the most intense. Preston had been drawn out of the hat to play the tangerines in an FA Cup First Round match shown live on Sky – the first time the Lilywhites had been on television since the 1964 Cup Final. Preston won 1-0 and their fans went barmy. "This was MEGA. Like birthday, Christmas, first shag, a gallon of Diamond White and winning the lottery rolled into one," wrote one fanatic in the Preston Pie Muncher fanzine. Can anything be that good?

In the early years Preston played some of the great old teams like Old Carthusians and Queens Park and the crowds began to grow. Sheep were still allowed to graze on the pitch but fences were put up around the ground and Preston's policy of allowing ladies to watch for free was abandoned because so many came along to see the new craze of the day.

Preston made their mark in the record books when they beat Hyde 26-0 in the First Round of the FA Cup in 1887 – the heaviest defeat suffered by any club in the competition's history. They were helped by the referee though. He apparently lost his watch and didn't blow the final whistle until 120 minutes had been played!

Preston never looked back and in 1889 became the first double winners in the Football League's first season. Nicknamed the "Invincibles", they won the Championship without losing a match and the FA Cup without conceding a goal. Their double achievement would not be emulated until Tottenham's success in 1961.

Preston were described as "the most perfect, most consistent team in the history of the game" by one newspaper – and we think tabloids are sensationalist today! Since the Football League had only just begun the praise was a little over the top. But they still hold the record for the fewest goals (15) conceded in a season – albeit over fewer games.

Preston pioneered the use of paid players and continued to dominate English football through the early 1890's. The club retained the title in 1890 and were runners-up in the following three seasons. They have not been champions since (though they were second in 1953, by the narrowest of margins, and again in 1958). Preston last won the FA Cup in 1938. George Mutch hit the winner from the penalty spot against Huddersfield with the last kick of Wembley's first extra-time final – the first to be shown in full on television.

There's no doubt that Tom Finney was the greatest player ever to pull on a Preston shirt. One of his descendants ran out onto the pitch at Deepdale before the Third Division game against Mansfield. His Preston shirt carried the name of sponsors Coloroll, the Preston badge with the famous PP, which stands for Proud Preston, and another badge with the word footy. But this young Finney was not in today's line-up. Tom's great, great nephew, four-year-old Matthew, was the mascot.

Tom Finney is the President of Preston. His company, Tom Finney Limited, were today's match sponsors and had taken out a half-page ad in the match programme. It said: "Tom Finney Ltd. A long standing local firm just a phone call away for all your electrical, plumbing and heating problems, however large or small." The firm was certainly long standing. Finney wasn't known as the Preston Plumber for nothing. The man who ranks alongside Sir Stanley Matthews as the greatest English footballer of all time began his business during his playing career.

Finney joined Preston from school and really began to shine after the Second World War when English football entered something of a golden era. He was famous for his dribbling and burst of speed. Finney played for England 76 times between 1946 and 1958, scoring 30 goals and appearing in every position in the forward line.

He was the first player to be named Footballer of the Year twice, in 1954 and 1957, and a host of clubs were after his signature. But Finney remained loyal to Preston despite lucrative offers from clubs like Palermo in Italy which offered him £10,000 plus a car, a villa and a huge salary.

He retired after 569 first-class matches at the end of the 1959-60 season. Despite his legendary status, he never won a Championship or Cup winners' medal ending his career with two League runners-up medals and a Cup runners-up medal. His last game at Deepdale attracted a huge crowd which sang 'Auld Lang Syne' as Finney bade farewell.

Tom Finney is widely regarded as the best footballer Preston have ever had and one of the best players to wear an England shirt. The Pie Muncher said he was "a fine ambassador for the club, country and town. A gentleman, a sportsman and thoroughly nice bloke".

After Finney retired in 1960 Preston's form slumped. The following year they were relegated. The club suffered a slow decline throughout the '60s, though they reached the '64 Cup Final when, as a second division team, they lost to West Ham. Preston then moved between the top two divisions until they dropped into the Third for the first time in 1970.

They have since mostly divided their time between the Second and Third divisions, apart from a brief spell in the Fourth between 1985 and 1987 and relegation to the new Third Division in 1993.

John Beck, former Cambridge manager and arch-exponent of the long ball game, orchestrated the drop to the Third Division. But he took them to Wembley in the play-offs the following season. A dramatic 4-1 semi-final second leg victory over Torquay at Deepdale overturned a 2-0 deficit from the first game at Plainmoor. The fans dubbed that Wednesday night, 18th May 1994, one of the all-time great nights at Deepdale.

Promotion fever gripped the town and 20,000 tickets for the play-off final were sold in one day. Wembley was a sea of blue, white and yellow. Preston lost 4-2 to Wycombe and remained in the bottom division, but the fans were philosophical. "We lost like, but it's the taking part that counts innit?" said the fanzine.

Beck followed some great players into the managers seat. Unfortunately, most of them failed to bring success. Bobby Charlton took over in 1973, but was gone by 1975. Harry Catterick, fresh from a largely successful 13 year spell at Everton lasted three years. Nobby Stiles was in charge until 1981, when Tommy Docherty took over. The 'Doc's' reign was brief. After losing the Preston job he said, "They offered me a handshake of £10,000 to settle amicably. I told them they would have to be a lot more amicable than that." Gordon Lee, former Manchester City centre-half Tommy Booth and Manchester United's current assistant manager Brian Kidd, have also had spells in charge.

The job was clearly a tough one given the club's history of failure since the '60s. The question was could Beck cut the mustard? His reign was highly controversial. The Preston Pie Muncher summed up the feelings towards him in its BiteBack editorial. "The Evening Post's post-match discussion page illustrated more than anything the gulf between the factions that had developed on the Deepdale terraces. Each Tuesday we'd turn to the back page and find two polarised and aggressively articulated views about our maverick manager. 'He's ruined our club'; 'He'll take us to the top'."

Beck was appointed in December 1992. He put the players on a weightlifting programme. They wore tights on Deepdale's plastic pitch. They were faster, fitter. "We played a system whereby the goalie booted the ball out to the winger, he crosses and the big striker shoots. This is repeated until PNE score enough goals to win the match," said the fanzine. By May they were relegated.

Beck's system wasn't working. After all, there was no Dion Dublin to play the big striker's role at Deepdale. The writing was on the wall. The fanzine's match report on the 1-0 defeat by Scunthrope in October 1994 summed up the mood. "The noose is tightening Johnny boy. Four defeats on the trot, new owners, lotsa lolly: it might be bye, bye Becky if things don't buck up soon. Little wrong with the overall performance that a multi-million pound strikeforce couldn't put right." The new owners were local heating giants Baxi, who'd taken control with a proposed £10 million cash injection for team strengthening and ground improvements.

The next game against Hartlepool was worse. The fanzine described the team as "disorganised, disinterested, dispirited, disgraceful. They (Hartlepool) at least tried to play footy, whereas most of our stuff burned up on re-entry." Preston lost 3-1 to register six defeats in a row. In desperation, Beck brought in a gypsy called Paula Paradaema from Blackpool to rid the pitch of negative energy in one last bizarre attempt to save North End's season. But the gypsy didn't turn things around. A month later, on the eve of the FA Cup Second Round, Beck resigned.

So what did the players think of him? New signing Graham Lancashire was asked whether Beck's departure had made any difference to his decision to join the club. "No. The other players haven't really told me about John Beck, but they do say there's a much better team spirit now, and they all enjoy their football more." Precisely.

And what about the fans? "Until December 1992 Preston North End was stagnant. Now there is passion and commitment behind the scenes and on the terraces... he made every player proud to pull on a white shirt. He also divided the supporters, something no other manager has ever done, but at least the feeling was there. John Beck did PNE more good than any manager since the war, and fair play to him. The foundations for success are now in place, and for that we should all be eternally grateful to one person... John Beck." At least some supporters liked him.

Then again, some of the Preston fans are a bit sad. A trawl through the letters page in the fanzine revealed one supporter who disagreed with the old cliche that scoring a goal is like an orgasm. "I play centre-forward for a Sunday league team and believe me there's no comparison." As proof he recalled that "nobody got pregnant when I headed a late equaliser against Acregate Lane Labour Club!" Another letter was from an even sadder case. "I had a dream last night that I was in bed with Sharon Stone. Problem was, we'd left the telly on and I heard the theme to Endsleigh League Goals. What does a guy do in that situation? She had to go."

Beck's assistant Gary Peters took over and had an immediate impact. The fanzine described the 4-2 win over Hereford as "another step along the road from Stone Age football to New Age football".

This New Age football was being played in a stadium which looked as if it had come out of the Victorian era. It almost had. The only English League club to have been at their present ground longer are Stoke. Football was first seen at the Victoria Ground in 1878, three years before it was played at Deepdale. But Preston had been based at their ground since 1875, even though it wasn't used for football at first.

It was dark and wet when I arrived at Deepdale but I didn't care. I was just relieved to get to another match after a washout at Wigan (see Wigan v Hereford). I stood on the terraces in the Pavilion Stand. The ground was somehow magical in the fading light of the winter afternoon. It's hard to explain why it felt that way but it was certainly different to any other ground I'd been to. Perhaps it was echoes of the "Old Invincibles" reaching me from down the years. The fans of both teams were brilliant, probably the best I was amongst all season.

The die-hard Preston supporters were packed into the Town End to my left. A drummer and a trumpeter serenaded them through old classics like "Falling in Love" and new tunes including the obligatory "Go West" by the Pet Shop Boys. These guys were great. Not to be outdone completely, the travelling Mansfield supporters responded with chants of "We are Mansfield, We are Mansfield, Super Mansfield from Field Mill".

Opposite was the elegant West Stand built in 1906 – a unique feature. The old wooden stand was probably the best preserved of its age in the country. It looked majestic in the winter gloom. More a pavilion than a stand, it would have been at home on a cricket ground. Thin white posts, roughly 10 feet apart, supported the roof, giving it an almost delicate look.

Sadly, its days were numbered. By the summer it would be gone. The club was replacing it as part of a £10 million scheme to redevelop the ground along the lines of the Luigi Ferraris stadium in Italy, home to Sampdoria and Genoa. Plans for a public share offer to raise £4 million to strengthen the first team and speed up the development of Deepdale would also be announced before the start of the 1995/96 season.

The stadium redevelopment was made possible by the local council which had given Preston security by offering the club a new 125 year lease, costing over £300,000. The rebuilding plans included a new 6,000 all-seater West Stand, due to be finished by March 1996. The only chance of preserving the famous old stand was to take up a suggestion from one Dutch football enthusiast who believed it should be carefully dismantled, reassembled and preserved as a reminder of football's glorious past.

There was little chance of that happening. But there were plans for a National Football Museum inside the new West Stand. Preston hoped the museum would be open by the time the European Championships began in May 1996. The club would also begin negotiations during the summer with Fifa to persuade football's governing body to place its museum collection at Deepdale. I couldn't think of a better place for a shrine to the world's football legends given proud Preston's place in the history of the beautiful game.

Opposite the West Stand was the Pavilion Stand where I stood to watch the match. Built in 1934, it was originally 50 yards long and straddled the halfway line. There were new offices, guest rooms on three floors, dressing rooms and a lift. The South Pavilion, effectively an extension of the original Pavilion, was built in 1936 - the same year that local firm Abbotts of Lancaster made specially-designed stained glass windows for the boardroom. The name of the South Pavilion often confuses away supporters who aren't familiar with the ground. It's actually on the East side but lies to the south of the original Pavilion. Behind me, between the two, was the club crest proudly displayed on the front of the stand roof.

The pitch was treacherous after all the rain but Preston played neat, attacking football in a lively match and beat Mansfield 2-1. I was just glad the game was played and owed a debt of gratitude to the referee, ironically a Mr Flood, for passing it fit on a day when half the League programme was wiped out by rain. The home fans were certainly happy. The win kept Preston on the heels of the Division's leading pack. What better time for the musicians amongst them to finish with a flourish as they treated everyone to some of the Glenn Miller big band sound and a medley of Brazilian Samba songs. Great stuff.

GRAHAM ON THE RACK
Arsenal v Southampton – Highbury
24 January 1995

Highbury in crisis? The Queen will be filing for divorce next! George Graham could handle it – he'd been there before as a player. Not as a manager though. And certainly not with allegations of taking a £285,000 'bung' hanging over his head. The players? Paul Merson certainly couldn't handle it. He was just back in training after rehabilitation for cocaine addiction. Merson had a strong incentive to return to work though – the need to pay off thousands of pounds in gambling debts. But what about the rest of the team? Arsenal hadn't won at fortress Highbury in 13 weeks and were slipping down the table.

I made my way along Avenell Road towards the East Stand. Above the main doors was Arsenal's AFC insignia and over that the club's red cannon emblem picked out in relief between the tall windows. I entered the ground through the main entrance to the East Stand, famous for its marble halls. A black marble bust of the legendary Herbert Chapman stands in the hall with its sweeping staircase leading to the boardroom and guest rooms on the first floor. (The club's late secretary, Bob Wall, claimed Chapman's ghost walked the corridors of Highbury).

New striker John Hartson passed me in the main hall where former Arsenal keeper and ITV presenter Bob Wilson was talking to BBC commentator John Motson. Lee Dixon emerged from the dressing rooms to the right and shuffled past in his Arsenal kit with stockinged feet. He expertly span a letter under the teller's window in the main office. At the top of the stairs I was greeted by the famous Arsenal commissioners, smartly dressed in their black military-style uniforms with peaked caps. They were there to usher guests to the various rooms and to keep an eye on the trophies displayed on a table to the right. The European Cup Winners' Cup, decorated with red and white silk ribbons, was flanked by the FA Youth Cup and another trophy.

Then it was up another flight of stairs to the trophy cabinets housing the silverware collected by some of the great Arsenal teams of the past, including the one shaped by Chapman which won the League Championship five times and the FA Cup twice in the 1930s. There was a striking figure of a Russian bear presented to Arsenal by a club from the former Soviet Union, a pennant from the Racing Club of Argentina dated 1950 and a silver presentation plate from arch-rivals Tottenham commemorating the first FA Cup Semi-Final between the two teams and the first played at Wembley in 1991 when Spurs won 3-1.

I wandered out into the directors box in the middle of the East Stand where each red seat is personally labelled with the name of an Arsenal director. The Southampton players were already outside inspecting the pitch. Ironically, shortly after they emerged from the tunnel in their smart suits, Highbury's state-of-the-art Jumbotron screens, one in each corner of the ground, began showing highlights of previous Arsenal matches against the Saints. The Southampton players smiled as they pointed towards the big screen where Ian Wright, Paul Merson and Alan Smith were finding the back of the net with the Saints defence in disarray.

I left the East Stand's marble halls and walked around the perimeter of the pitch marvelling at the modern Highbury. The famous West Stand, complete with electric lift, stood opposite. It was opened in 1932 by the Prince of Wales (later Edward VIII). At one end the new North Bank rose steeply into the sky, while at the other the distinguished Clock End with its shimmering executive boxes also towered over the pitch. The Arsenal Stadium wasn't always like this.

A feature in the match programme marvelled at the changes. "They'd be amazed now, those Church Commissioners –the men who sold a 21-year lease on the playing fields of St John's College, Highbury to a struggling south-east London football club in 1913. So would those 20,000 fans who filled the stadium on opening day – September 6, 1913: Arsenal 2 Leicester Fosse 1."

By the time of Chapman's arrival in 1925, Arsenal had bought the stadium outright for £64,000. Chapman transformed the team – and manager and board developed the ground to keep pace with the Gunners' success. In the summer of '31 work began on the most ambitious project yet – the £50,000 West Stand, which opened in December 1932. The Stand remains, with only minor alterations, as it was built 60 years ago. In 1935, the year after Chapman died, his famous clock was moved to the South End, known ever since as the 'Clock End'.

The 1988/89 season saw the start of the first major redevelopment at the ground since 1937. Gleaming executive boxes were built above the Clock End along with offices, banqueting facilities and a new Arsenal Sports Centre. Following the Hillsborough disaster of 1989 and the Taylor Report, Arsenal laid down plans for the North Bank to be turned into a state-of-the-art superstand. On 2nd May 1992 Arsenal played in front of the old North Bank for the last time, firing five goals past tonight's visitors Southampton.

The new £16.5 million North Bank stand opened in August 1993. It includes facilities rarely seen before in this country. If you get tickets for the North Bank today you'll be entertained by a live pop group in the main concourse, you can visit the club shop under the stand, or perhaps walk around the museum containing memorabilia (including Don Howe's tracksuit, replicas of major trophies, England caps won by Arsenal stars of the past, pennants, medals and even a waxwork dummy of George Graham if it's still there!), watch a 20-minute film, The Story So Far, recounting great moments in the club's history (it was narrated by Graham when I was there), or see the man whose goal against Liverpool in the 1971 FA Cup Final won the 'double'.

Charlie George, famous for his flowing locks, flamboyant lifestyle and spectacular goals, works for Arsenal in the museum and is on hand to talk to supporters, autograph photos of himself at his peak in action against Manchester City's Francis Lee and Mike Doyle and pose for pictures. The long hair has thinned and he wears glassed now but there's no mistaking him. "Hello, Charlie. How are you doing?" said two fair haired young lads entering the museum. "I'm fine boys, how are you?" Charlie replied politely. They were far too young to have seen him play but they had seen his goal, and his celebratory slide to the ground, arms outstretched behind him as he waited to be mobbed by his elated Arsenal teammates. North London (well one side of it anyway) was in raptures for weeks. Champagne Charlie had brought home the 'double'.

I would have loved to have talked to him about the old days, how it felt scoring the winner against Liverpool and whether he missed playing but the game was about to start so I was moved on by my guide. He later told me that Charlie didn't miss playing football anymore. I suppose there's a time and a place for everything. In 1971 Charlie George was in the right place at the right time and his goal will live on in the memories of Arsenal fans forever.

I took up my place in the press box – front row, over the halfway line. On my left was a journalist from a Dutch football magazine called Football International. "There is a lot of interest in English football again," he told me. "When English teams were banned from Europe there wasn't so much interest in the game here. But now people back home want to know about the stars they see on television. The Premier League is very fast, very direct and exciting. In Holland there are only a couple of big teams but here there are at least half a dozen Championship contenders. Also the crowds are much bigger and more passionate. It all makes the game more exciting."

Behind me sat the radio commentator for Radio Solent who would be keeping the people of Hampshire up-to-date with all the action from tonight's match. In fact, the first ever radio commentary on a football match took place at Highbury on 22 January 1927 when some bloke called H. B. T. Wakeham covered Arsenal v Sheffield United. The first televised match was also at Highbury when Arsenal played Arsenal reserves on 16 September 1937. Was it a defensive encounter I wonder? The location of the BBC's broadcasting unit at nearby Alexandra Palace, from where the first-ever television pictures were broadcast, was the main reason for Highbury being chosen.

According to an article I'd read in The Independent the week before the first radio broadcast also involved a blind man and another commentator. The blind man's job was to nudge the main match commentator if he wasn't getting enough information about what was going on in the game. Meanwhile, the other commentator kept track of where the play was on the pitch according to a grid of squares over the pitch published in that week's Radio Times to help listener's follow the play. Believe it or not this is where the saying 'Back to square one' comes from since square one was positioned over the goal areas.

Back to tonight's match where, strangely, Matt Le Tissier, worshipped by the Southampton fans, was off-form and missed three good chances in the first half. The Saints would pay for God's profligacy. Wright got the better of full-back Francis Benali and drove in a shot which Grobbelaar could only parry onto the head of Hartson. The former Luton striker gratefully nodded the ball into the empty net. It was his home league debut and he had crowned it with his second goal for the club after a winning strike at Coventry the previous Saturday.

Arsenal's goal was met by cheers from the crowd and the Jumbotron's at either corner flashed up '1-0 to the Arsenal' in yellow letters on a red background. The crowd would soon follow with a rendition of '1-0 to the Arsenal' to the tune of 'Go West' by the Pet Shop Boys. When Neil Tennant and Chris Lowe wrote the song in 1993 I'm sure they never realised it would become an anthem throughout the football grounds of Britain.

At half-time the journalists returned to the warmth of the press lounge where tea and sandwiches were waiting in the room with a bar next to the banks of telephones at each of the desks next door. Outside in the cold the Arsenal fans were watching highlights of the first half on the Jumbotron screens. It didn't last long.

The second half was better and belonged to Southampton. They should have equalised from one of a hatful of chances but eventually settled for Jim Magilton's close range drive over the stranded Seaman inside the 18 yard box after Le Tissier had threaded his way past three or four bemused Arsenal defenders. The then-Saints manager Alan Ball leapt from the dug-out, took off his checked flat cap and punched the air in triumph as his players surrounded the delighted Magilton. The Southampton fans rang out with a chorus of 'When the Saints go marching in'. The Arsenal fans rumbled in discontent.

The tabloid journalist behind me rang his office. "Are we too late to change the intro?" he asked urgently. The answer must have been no since he quickly dictated a new story incorporating the latest twist in the match for consumption at the morning breakfast table. The Arsenal fans, meanwhile, had decided to try to lift their team and sang "We're by far the greatest team...". George Graham stood beside the pitch with his hands in the pockets of his managers' touchline coat.

"A tense finish here," said the Radio Solent commentator. Then, it was all over. The final whistle was greeted with boos from the Arsenal fans. It wasn't a great game, but better than the recent match against Villa – rated by some of the reporters as the worst League game they had ever seen.

After filing their match reports the journalists gradually began to file into Arsenal's impressive press room. Built like a small theatre, there was a smart varnished pine top table decorated with the Gunners' imposing cannon crest. The managers would sit behind the table in turn to answer questions from the assembled hacks comfortably positioned in soft, cinema-style seats. Among them was Brian Glanville of The Sunday Times – one of only two journalists spoken to on first name terms by either Ball or Graham.

Ball was the first to come into the press room. He seemed reasonably pleased with the draw. "Was that a fair result?" asked one reporter. "Yes, it was two halves wasn't it? In all fairness to Arsenal they came out and worked very hard at closing us down first half; beat us up in many ways. That's what I said to my players at half-time, 'You're being intimidated here, you're being outfought, you're second on all sorts of stuff.'"

"I said 'I don't want you to be intimidated. I want to see if you're coming on as the good players I'm hoping you to be; the good little team that I'm trying to fashion you into. You must go out and compete. You must pass the ball. You must try and play through them through the middle of the pitch. Third man runs and get after them. Play your football. Bounce it off Shipperley. Runners getting after them. And I thought we were terrific second-half. Playing football all over the pitch. And we got our just rewards in the end. And it's important we did because young lads, if they don't get what they deserve, you know, they can go under very quickly. And, thank God, they got what they deserved trying to do what their manager wanted them to do."

"Seaman made a great save," noted another hack. "Both keepers made good stops today," said Ball who then remarked on Grobbelaar's outfield play. " Bruce was a bit better than Seaman out on the flanks," he said to ripples of laughter around the press room. "He drops the old left shoulder."

Graham came into the press room as Ball was leaving. They shook hands and greeted each other like old friends. Their mutual respect was obvious and Graham would refer to Ball with the utmost respect in his press briefing. Graham began by asking the reporters to tell him what 'Ballie' said first. The journalist with the droopy moustache gave him a quick summary. "He said that you stopped them playing in the first half. You dominated them and stopped them passing the ball." "I agree with him," replied a dapper looking Graham. The journalist returned to his summary. "Second half they outpassed you and they were well worth a point." "I agree with him," repeated Graham, "a good summing up."

"There's a lack of confidence", said the then-Arsenal manager. I mean a lot of the players just now are going through a period they've never known before. In the last eight years we've either been winning things or up there or nearly winning them. They know how to handle success, now they've got to handle the other situation. And this is a new experience for some of them. And I hope they don't like it." "A new experience for you as well," pointed out one hack. "Yes, but I've handled it as a player. You know I know what it's like. As a manager it's probably the worst period I've had. But I know what it's like because I've been in the situation where you do go through a bad spell."

"George, did you ever envisage a situation where you could go 13 weeks without a win at home?" Graham had a sharp answer. "No, I'll have to phone up Tottenham and ask them what it's like," he said sparking a round of laughter from the assembled hacks. "No that wasn't actually meant in cheek. You know sometimes it goes like that doesn't it. No, football's a great game for turning itself on its head. You know what I mean. You know this. Something just may happen that just sort of sparks it off again. As long as you keep doing the right things – we're not doing anything basically different.

"Never mind all the headlines about the long ball. We've never played intentionally long balls. I like the players to get out there and play and pass the ball as they see fit whether they play a short ball or whether they play a long ball. I've never instructed anybody. We do press in. We've never changed the football philosophy since I've come here. We've played the same way for eight years. Some people say that's wrong."

"How much does the criticism hurt you George, or do you try to deflect it off your players?" was the next insightful question. "I've never been under any illusions in football. I've been in football too long, since I was 15. And if you're winning, you're good, you get the points, enjoy the success. And if you're not winning you'd better take the flak that's flying. It's not becoming the best of pieces is it?

"I had plenty of problems as a player. I was an average player. I had good success as a player. But I had plenty of problems in my playing career as well, you know. But I played for a lot of good clubs, I picked up some trophies. I did OK as a player. But it wasn't all plain sailing in the way that some of the so-called experts on television now go straight from top class player into expert analysis, you know, because this life's too tough for them."

Graham had obviously been upset by former England captain Gary Lineker when he appeared on the BBC's Football Focus programme the previous Saturday lunchtime joking about allegations that Graham had received a £285,000 bung as part of the transfer deal that took John Jensen to Arsenal from Danish club Brondby.

Asked about the crisis at Highbury Lineker said, "There's a lot of pressure on George Graham at the moment. But I think the real issue is not lack of form, more what's going on off the field. Whether or not he has taken a bung, or what the inquiry is going to come up with, I don't know what George Graham's defence is. But for his sake, I hope it's better than Arsenal's against Millwall." The Gunners had just been beaten 2-0 by the South London side in the Third Round of the FA Cup in a replay at Highbury.

The impact of Lineker's remarks were shown clearly when the under-fire Arsenal manager refused to appear on Match of The Day that night following Arsenal's 1-0 win at Coventry. The former Leicester, Everton, Barcelona, Tottenham, and Grampus 8 striker had clearly touched a raw nerve and it hurt. Graham chose instead to use the post-match press conference after the 1-1 draw with Southampton to air his views on the criticism handed out by television 'experts'. He didn't name names, but it was clear who he was pointing the finger, Lineker was the target.

"There are a lot of ex-players who have taken the easy route by going into TV instead of management. They have earned a lot of money these boys, without ever having to put their head in the noose as managers do. They have never coached, never managed. But they think they can tell me how to do my job. They are entitled to their opinions on what happens on the pitch. But don't tell me how to run Arsenal when you have never been there. Who wants to go into management these days? It is far too hard for these people. They have no pedigree, yet they tell people like me what should be going on in the game."

"A man like Alan Ball I can respect. He has managed down at Exeter, he has been at the sharp end. But not these guys. Arsenal are well respected within the game and as long as I have the respect of my peers I will be satisfied. Their views are what I take on board, not those of people whose only qualification to talk is that they were once top-class players.

"I have regrets. I wish I'd been able to make the signings I wanted. I came very close with Chris Sutton. I tried for Marc Overmars and David Ginola, but those deals didn't come off because their teams were playing in the Champions' League. With hindsight, maybe I should have switched my attention and made other signings."

Graham then addressed the issue on everyone's lips. Would he be staying at Arsenal? "Some papers have called on me to resign. It's not my nature to walk away from problems. I think back to last season. We were written off after we'd lost to Bolton in the FA Cup. A few months later we were parading with the Cup Winners' Cup. Let's go for a repeat performance." On their current form Arsenal would struggle to do so.

HOLTE - WHO GOES THERE?
Aston Villa v Tottenham Hotspur - Villa Park
25 January 1995

This match was a mouth watering prospect. A revitalised Villa under new manager Brian Little against a rejuvenated Tottenham, unbeaten in 11 matches, under Gerry Francis. "It's one of those fixtures, I suspect, which neutrals would like to see because it has such promise as a spectacle," said the Villa boss. They did, it had and, most important of all, it was. This was one of the best games I'd see all season.

Unfortunately, the match at Villa Park was overshadowed by a little incident at Selhurst Park involving a certain Eric Cantona. There wasn't any kung-fu fighting here, but Villa keeper Mark Bosnich did his own version of the can-can which ended with his knee in Jürgen Klinsmann's head.

Only 20 minutes had gone when the ball was knocked over the top of the Villa defence by Spurs defender Colin Calderwood. Klinsmann ran onto it pursued by two defenders, Bosnich rushed out of his goal, the German striker knocked the ball forward with his head and felt the full force of the Villa keeper's challenge.

Klinsmann was carried off unconscious on a stretcher and took no further part in the game to the disappointment of the supporters of both teams. A black, red and yellow German flag draped over one of the exits among the Tottenham fans proclaimed: 'Klinsmann der Meister'. Tonight he had little chance to live up to the slogan.

Herr Francis was not amused. "I'm sure Jürgen got to the ball first and their keeper smacked into him after that. I'm surprised the ref didn't see that. In the end, it cost us dearly. He had a bad knock full in the face, which has left him with a terrible headache. I thought he was very brave going for the ball."

Bosnich said the collision was "unfortunate". He'd hoped to head the ball away as it swirled in the wind. "I was sorry for what happened, but I saw Jürgen at half-time and he seemed fine. In fact, he wanted to come out and play." The pictures in the following morning's papers showed the true nature of the challenge. Bosnich had his boot in Klinsmann's face with his feet almost as high as the heads of the defenders around him. The headline in The Sun was "Jürgen Horror. Klinsmann KO'd by Bosnich".

Klinsmann was carried to the Villa first aid room where he was seen by the club doctor. The diagnosis was an injured nose, a bump on the back of his head and concussion. He would later have X-rays and a scan on his face and nose as a precautionary measure.

Meanwhile, out on the pitch Bosnich was booed by the Spurs fans every time he touched the ball. But they couldn't stop Villa snatching a 1-0 win. After 18 minutes full-back Steve Staunton hit a ball down the line on the left. Dean Saunders, now at Turkish side Galatasaray with Graeme Souness, picked the ball up with his back to goal. The Holte End rose to their feet together as he turned and cut inside Calderwood. Saunders then sprinted across the edge of the box and drove a low shot beyond Spurs keeper Ian Walker into the bottom corner of the net.

Spurs stepped up the pressure in the second half of an evenly balanced match. A good old-fashioned, blood and thunder contest between two committed teams. Spurs' Romanian international Gica Popescu was put clear by Teddy Sheringham early in the second half but was caught and tackled by Villa's other full-back Earl Barrett. "Typical bloody Romanian," said the Villa fan next to me. I thought hard. "What's a typical bloody Romanian?"

I'd arrived at Villa Park early on a wet Wednesday night for a tour of the ground. I threaded my way around the infamous Spaghetti Junction and under the Aston Expressway towards the stadium. The name Holte is famous in these parts as the name of the largest Kop in the country - the Holte End. It's named after Sir Thomas Holte who built Aston Hall, a red-brick Jacobean mansion, in 1618. I could see the mansion at the top of a hill in nearby Aston Park. The Holte pub was also named after him.

I parked in the club car park and walked around the stadium past a few early arrivals from North London. I checked out the new Holte End, home of Villa's die-hard supporters, which replaced the famous huge standing terrace at the end of the 1993-94 season. The last match in front of the Holte End terracing was against Liverpool in front of 45,000 - the largest League crowd of the season.

Around the back on Trinity Road stands probably the most distinguished facade at any football ground in the country. The Italian-style architecture seems out of place at a stadium, though Soldier Field, home of the Chicago Bears American football team, looks like a Roman coliseum and is more imposing than Villa Park.

Nevertheless, with its sweeping steps leading up to the top tier of seats, the Trinity Road entrance oozes class. The red-brick walls have the authority of a local council building from the 1930s. There was a circular window on each of the twin towers either side of the stairs and the words Aston and then Villa painted on each of the towers in the team's colours. Above the stairs, between the towers, was the club crest topped with a flagpole. Only the facade of the Main Stand at Craven Cottage came close to reminding me of Villa Park, but Fulham's ground on the banks of the Thames doesn't boast such a majestic staircase.

The Trinity Road Stand was completed in 1922 and first used for a match against Blackburn. The official opening came two years later when the Duke of York, the future King George VI, made an appearance – though not in a claret and blue shirt! The stand was used as an air-raid shelter during the Second World War and was also home to a rifle company which lived in the Villa dressing room giving a whole new meaning to shouts of shoot!

I walked back towards the car park and wandered into Villa's plush reception area. The VIPs were already mingling, some drinking tea and coffee as they waited to be escorted to the various executive suites. Regular fans were also arriving for the match, many picking up their tickets at the front desk where the receptionists told telephone callers the match was a sell-out. Klinsmann was the big attraction. "Hello, Aston Villa Football Club. No, I'm sorry all tickets for tonight's match have been sold," said the blonde. It was an apology she'd give repeatedly.

I wondered if Villa's most famous fan, the violinist Nigel Kennedy, was at the match. If he was, at least he'd be sure of a ticket. Fans queuing for tickets outside the main entrance were as disappointed as those jamming the switchboard.

A group of Spurs fans kitted out in Holsten-sponsored replica shirts came to pick up their tickets. "You're in amongst the Villa supporters," said the blonde. "We can't put you there. Not wearing Spurs shirts." A quick phone call sorted out the problem. They could sing their hearts out for the lads in the corner of the new £5 million two-tier Doug Ellis Stand, formerly the Witton Lane Stand, with the rest of the colourful entourage of away fans.

I joined a group of Villa supporters for the ground tour and discovered some Spurs fans sprinkled amongst them. We were taken past the entrance to the tunnel and through to the home dressing room. The tour in front of us was just emerging from the sanctity of the Villa changing room as we arrived. It was like visiting a cathedral or stately home on a busy Sunday afternoon. Some of the Villa players had already arrived, including a smiling Andy Townsend. The players' shirts were hung around the walls ready for battle. Their shorts and socks were neatly folded underneath each peg.

Then it was down the tunnel, underneath the club's gold Lion crest with the motto 'Prepared', and out into the damp night air to see the pitch – or rather the plastic covers protecting the playing surface from the torrential rain which had engulfed the stadium. The covers are mechanically rolled out from behind the advertising boards in front of the Witton Lane Stand whenever the stadium is hit by heavy rain.

Next stop was the trophy room - a cornucopia of silverware. It contained a mini replica of the European Cup, won by Villa in 1982 under Tony Barton when they beat Bayern Munich 1-0 in Rotterdam thanks to a Peter Withe goal. Villa went on to win the Super Cup the following year, beating Barcelona. There were also replicas of the FA Cup they've lifted seven times - though not since 1920.

Villa have also won the Championship seven times, six of those successes coming between 1894 and 1910, the last occasion being 1981. They also won the elusive 'double' in 1897 – only the second team to do so after the achievement of Preston's Invincibles in the first season of League football in 1889. One week later they played their first match at what is now Villa Park, though it was then called Aston Lower Grounds, in a friendly against Blackburn.

After Villa clinched the double one journalist went along to their headquarters at the Tavistock Hotel to congratulate them. But while talking to the players, including Athersmith, a winger who once played on a rainy day with an umbrella held over his head, the reporter rashly said he was sorry they'd deprived Preston, the greatest team of all time, of their unique record. The Villa players threatened to drop him out of the window into the courtyard below! John Campbell, Villa's Scottish centre-forward, shouted: "Preston? Ha! Football was in its infancy then. They had no one to beat."

The Villa guide continued his tour by taking us through the restaurant, where supporters were tucking into a three-course meal before the match. A portrait of the club's first chairman, William McGregor, was on the wall. His place in the history of the game was secured when he founded the Football League. It's not surprising, therefore, that Villa were one of the 12 founder members.

We were then taken back outside the ground to be given a fascinating account of the history of Villa Park. Apparently, the stadium was built on what was once the Aston Lower Grounds amusement park during Victorian times. The range of activities almost rivalled those at London's Crystal Palace – the building, not the South London football club! Villa were formed in 1874 and first played in Aston Park, across the road from the amusement park. But the Lower Grounds were a logical place for a stadium and part of the park was taken over in 1895 so Villa could start to build.

Over time the amusement park was changed so that, by the time Villa Park was used as a World Cup venue in 1966, nearly all trace of the Aston Lower Grounds had disappeared. Simon Inglis outlines the changes. "The old aquarium, skating rink and restaurant became Villa's new offices and gymnasium. The ground's maintenance man took charge of the rifle range. At the rear, a practice pitch and car park was laid on the site of a theatre and concert hall, and on the far side of Witton Lane, housing was built where once had been a boating lake with ornamental island. The Witton Lane Stand covered what had been a sub-tropical garden. Another lake became, as at Crystal Palace, the site of the new pitch."

The Lower Grounds' bowling green was covered by a new social club as part of the preparations for the '66 World Cup and all links with the amusement park were lost in the mid-80's when the Victorian buildings housing Villa's offices were pulled down as part of a new development underneath the imposing North Stand, which replaced the Witton Lane Stand in the late '70s.

After the tour I was taken to an executive suite from where I could walk to my seat in the North Stand, which was as tall as the Holte End. There were hardly any supporters there yet, but a steward was in position, ready to help the thousands who would pack the stadium. He was less than happy about the recent sacking of former manager Ron Atkinson. "We couldn't believe it here," he said, shaking his head. "Big Ron shouldn't have been treated like that. He just needed more time." I asked about the new boss, Brian Little. "It's too early to say how well he'll do. We'll just have to wait and see I suppose," said the steward.

One of Little's early signings was Tommy Johnson from Derby. At least he was guaranteed a run in the first team, unlike Prime Minister John Major's son, a trialist who didn't make the grade. Johnson had joined Villa because of his respect for Little and the chance to join one of the biggest clubs in the country. Asked in the match programme who he respected most he answered Mother Theresa. Johnson must have been praying for a goal against Tottenham tonight!

As the ground began to fill up the covers were removed and the players emerged from the tunnel a good half-an-hour before the kick-off to warm up. Just before the game a fleet of cars were driven around the perimeter of the pitch as part of an advertising campaign for a local showroom. It was a world apart from the concrete cycle track used for major events until 1914. But then many things had changed at Villa Park since then. Not that Jürgen Klinsmann would remember much about it in the morning!

GOING DOWN
Chester City v Wycombe Wanderers – The Deva Stadium
31 January 1995

Archie Gemmill, Stuart Pearson, Arthur Albiston, Mike Smith, Alan Parry, Simon Garner, Cyrille Regis and Nicky Reid. It was like a who's who of football personalities past and present at Chester's Deva Stadium on a windswept night when rain had caused chaos on the roads and railways. High in the Pennines one person had died and dozens were injured after two trains collided because of flooding on the line.

The first train was believed to have been derailed by a landslide. The Chester players knew how that felt. Promotion from the Third Division one year, bottom of the Second the next. Two managers had already departed and the present incumbent, caretaker boss Derek Mann, was spending as much time trying to defend his team as they were trying to defend their goal. High-flying Wycombe were not the kind of opponents to let you off the hook.

I was originally going to Hereford on this wet Tuesday night, but that match was called off in the morning because of a waterlogged pitch. Chester's playing surface was in better condition so I travelled north in the hope of watching a match that had originally been postponed the day after New Year's because of - you guessed - a waterlogged pitch. The London Weather Centre had already reported twice the average rainfall in parts of the south in January - the highest for some seven years.

"You'll be alright in the autumn and the spring but the winter will be your problem," I was told by a number of people before my record attempt. In fact, postponements were a big help because they meant I could fit more midweek games into my already tight schedule. I had to get to places like Chester on a Tuesday night, but I'd passed my 50th match of the season and it was worth it.

Chester, the commercial centre of Cheshire, is a popular place both as a stop-off on the way to North Wales and as a tourist attraction. The town is encircled by a two-mile ring of medieval and Roman walls. Indeed, the Roman Deva or Castra Devana (the 'camp on the Dee'), founded in the middle of the first century AD, became the headquarters of the 20th legion – the Romans' largest known fortress in Britain.

The industrial revolution brought canal and railway connections making Chester the important trading centre it is today. Recent improvements in the infrastructure have created an intricate web of by-passes which are designed to relieve congestion in the town centre, though you wouldn't know it. Not that the traffic was queuing up to get to Chester's new stadium on the outskirts of town. In fact, it wasn't the best time to watch the local football team as they struggled to pick up points.

The home defence lasted just 26 minutes against Wycombe before new boy Miguel Desouza, a £100,000 buy from Birmingham, put the away side ahead. Towering Wycombe centre-half Terry Evans broke through the middle of Chester's defence and, as keeper David Felgate came out, he squared the ball for Desouza to slide it into an empty net. "Going down, going down, going down," sang the Wycombe fans. "We're already down," said a Chester fan behind me. Wycombe struck again through the same Evans-Desouza combination in first half injury time. This time Evans headed the ball down for Desouza to drive a first time shot into the bottom corner of the net.

The then-Wycombe manager, former Northern Ireland international Martin O'Neill, now in charge at Norwich, was steering his side towards a second successive promotion drive. He was without the services of former Manchester City, Blackburn and West Bromwich Albion defender Nicky Reid who was recovering from a cartilage operation. "Apart from that the manager hates my guts," he told a former QPR scout who had inquired about his position at the club in the bar before the match.

Reid played in the classic 100th FA Cup Final between Manchester City and Spurs in 1981, memorable for a five-goal replay which Spurs won 3-2 thanks to a mazy dribble from Argentinian international Ricardo Villa which ended with the ball being slotted through Joe Corrigan's legs. That was the peak of Reid's career. This was the nadir. Out of the Wycombe side through injury and unpopular with the manager.

The scout, who said he'd discovered Les Ferdinand and Andrew Impey, was now working for Charlton's managerial duo of Alan Curbishley and Steve Gritt. He'd left QPR after 10 years following a series of disputes surrounding everything from the cut he thought he deserved from the sale of the players he'd 'discovered' to the fact that they wouldn't give him a car and hadn't compensated him for a theft from his own.

The scout said Rangers former manager Jim Smith had promised him a one percent cut of the fee if Ferdinand was sold but, when Newcastle came in with a £3.8 million offer, he was told by Gerry Francis, now the boss at Spurs, that his deal had been negotiated under a different manager and he wasn't entitled to anything from the sale of players he'd brought to the attention of the club before Francis took charge.

The scout would get a cut from the sale of players he'd discovered under Francis but nothing more. The scout claimed it was all so unfair since Francis was allegedly on 20 percent of the transfer fee from the sale of Ferdinand. (An insider at Spurs later told me Francis was entitled to a percentage of any increase in a player's value at QPR between the time he'd taken over as manager and the time they were sold, but not a cut of the whole amount.)

The question of managers' receiving money from selling players – while I had no proof Francis had such a deal, Brentford manager David Webb has admitted that he gets a cut from the sale of players - seemed to me to be a conflict of interest. It meant that a manager would profit from selling the club's best players. His personal gain would therefore come at the expense of the team and the fans unless he was selling to buy other players who would improve the side – usually not the case.

Since Ferdinand wasn't sold while Francis was QPR manager I suppose all this is academic. But the scout was incensed at how unfair the system was. "I'd been there 10 years as well." "There's no loyalty in the game today," said Reid. "You don't mind people getting a slice of the cake as long as everyone is looked after," added the scout.

As he was leaving the scout gave Reid his card. "If there's anything I can do for you let me know. I'm always getting calls from people who want players." Then he left to take up his seat in the Main Stand, while I was busily totting up what a one percent cut of £3.8 million would be – £38,000, not bad if you can get it. And if you can't, there are always other players to discover.

Outside the fans were settling into their seats in the Deva stadium, named after the Roman word for Dee, the river which winds its way around this county town. The club had sold their Sealand Road Ground for about £3 million in 1990 and built a new 6,000 capacity stadium on a greenfield site a mile-and-a-half south-west of the town centre.

After ground-sharing with Macclesfield for two years, Chester moved into their new stadium in 1992 and played their first match there on 5th September, beating Burnley 3-0 in front of almost 5,000 fans. It was a very smart ground, similar to Wycombe's Adams Park, but it had no soul and was a bit like a new shopping complex: very smart, very comfortable, but ultimately sterile.

The 150 or so Wycombe fans who'd made the trip from west of London did their best to enliven the atmosphere among a crowd of only 1500. Decked out in yellow, one of them banged a drum throughout the match, much to the annoyance of the middle-aged lady behind me who at one point pleaded for him to stop. Without the drummer, however, the ground would have resembled a wake. "Come on Wycombe, Come on Wycombe" sang their fans. The Chester followers had little to cheer.

At half-time the talk in the bar was of chances missed and relegation looming. "Only 45 minutes to go," said one disgruntled supporter as we took our seats for the second half. REM's song Everybody Hurts was playing on the PA system "They ought to be playing Things Can Only Get Better shouldn't they?" I said to the young fan next to me. He'd supported Chester for seven years and this was the worst team they'd had.

It was all so different from the glory of promotion the season before, but perfectly understandable given two changes of manager and a clearout of players. "There was an Arsenal scout at the last home game watching our keeper Felgate and defender Chris Lightfoot. At half-time he said he'd wasted his time," said the young supporter. "Tranmere made a £750,000 bid for Lightfoot last season. We should have taken it when we had the chance." They'd since come back with a lower offer, but Chester had again turned it down. I told him about the former QPR scout who'd discovered Les Ferdinand. "Well, he won't discover anyone here," said the young season ticket holder.

Former Wales and Everton defender Kevin Ratcliffe was assistant manager at Chester (he's since been promoted to manager) and in the side according to my programme - the one printed for the postponed 2nd January match because it was too expensive to print another. "Why isn't Ratcliffe playing?" I asked the noisy fan next to me. "Well, he's paid so much a game, I've heard, and it's cheaper not to play him. These are minimum cost matches." Things sounded tight.

Chester's team was once graced by players of the calibre of Liverpool's Ian Rush, Arsenal's Lee Dixon and Wimbledon's Aidan Newhouse. Dixon was allowed to leave on a free, as was Gary Bennett, then at Wrexham but now with Tranmere. Bennett's transfer was particularly galling. He was the top scorer in the League with 32 goals already this season and had scored them all for Chester's arch-rivals Wrexham.

"We don't like any of the Welsh teams," a taxi driver told me on the way to the match, "but I suppose Wrexham are our main rivals." I mentioned Bennett. "Don't talk to me about it," said the cabbie, obviously still smarting from the embarrassment. I assumed he was proud of Chester winning the Welsh Cup three times – in 1908, 1933 and 1947. Not until 1975 did they achieve any success in English competition when they were promoted from the old Fourth Division and reached the League Cup semi-final.

The conditions in the second half were atrocious with rain driving across the pitch. It was a miracle the players could see, let alone play football. The weather didn't stop the home fans from complaining though. "It's like bloody ping pong out there," yelled one supporter. "Oh dear," mumbled his wife as she pondered the downside of playing in the Endsleigh League Second Division on a night like this. Fifteen minutes before the end the Chester fans began to leave. "I've got to go they're giving me a migraine," said one joining the early exodus back to town.

A photographer trying to get some close-up shots at the end of the match looked as if he was starring with Gregory Peck in Moby Dick. His fisherman's mac definitely had the wet look as he struggled to focus his camera on the celebrating Wycombe players. They stood there in triumph applauding their travelling fans before heading off for a shower and a quick pint in the warmth of the vice-presidents lounge.

A Chester official stood on the door to the lounge barring anyone without a pass. "But we're Wycombe players," said one handsome young lad as he led the injured and discarded to the bar. "That's alright then," said the official, smartly dressed in a royal blue jacket. He'd supported Chester for 40 years and said this was the worst side he'd ever seen. He enjoyed meeting all the football celebrities who visited the club though.

"Ronnie Moran showed up the other week unannounced. He didn't have a ticket and I didn't have one for him, but you've got to find somewhere for people like that haven't you. A scout showed up the other week in a tracksuit but I couldn't let him in because we have a dress code. He said no problem I've got a suit in the car. Well, then Dario Gradi (Crewe's manager) came along in a shell suit. What could I do, I had to let him into the lounge? There are certain personalities in football and you have to look after them. Suppose we want one of their players on loan?" He had a point.

He recalled the days when Chester played at Sealand Road, especially the night they knocked the mighty Leeds United out of the League Cup 3-0. "It was the only time I could remember Billy Bremner being substituted." The famous victory over the reigning League Champions took place on 13th November 1974 in front of 19,000.

The fanzine Hello Albert published a map of the old ground showing where, in relation to today's occupants at Olympus Sport, Children's World and Norweb Hairdryers, the celebrations had taken place. Little reminders like, "Centre circle Leeds kicked off from four times" and

"Where we sang our hearts out" were dotted around the map. "Pandemonium on the kop when Chester score second and third goals," was followed by, "One man loses wedding ring... another his false teeth!" What exactly were they doing on those terraces?

If you're wondering why the fanzine is called Hello Albert, here goes. Chester's Sealand Road ground was one of the first in the League to have a PA system. From as early as 1931, when Chester entered the League, the announcer would greet supporters with, "Hello Spion Kop! Hello Albert." He was apparently welcoming a long-standing supporter. The fanzine adopted the title because it "epitomises attempts at communication between Chester supporters".

As my thoughts turned to getting a taxi back to town, the official told me about the time Jack Charlton was asked to compare the current Leeds team with the one he played in. "They're pretty close in terms of ability. So what would the score be if you played them?" Big Jack was asked. "Probably 1-0." "Only one?" said the official, surprised. Jack looked at him with a sparkle in his eye, "Well, we are all over 50 now!"

SIMPLY THE BEST
Stockport County v Chester City - Edgeley Park
11 February 1995

Georgie Best once played for Stockport. Not a lot of people know that, as Michael Caine might say. (Best had a punch up with the film star in a London night club once, but that's another story). When County were struggling to survive in the mid '70s they signed a 29-year-old Best for a month - his third comeback attempt after two years out of the game. On his Fourth Division debut against Swansea he more than trebled the gate at 9,240, made two goals and scored the winner in a 3-2 victory.

Best's comeback was ironic in a way. At the height of his fame at Manchester United a much younger Georgie Boy often joined his friend and rival from Manchester City Mike Summerbee at Edgeley Park on Friday nights to watch the Third Division football on offer in the 1960's. "I usually start by watching one particular player and end up watching the referee," said Best at the time. The referee was a very important character for me today since he'd decide if my trip to Stockport was worthwhile.

Water, water, everywhere - but which game would be on. The rain hadn't stopped falling for days. All over England the heavens had opened and the match I'd planned to watch, York against Hull, was in doubt. York told me on Friday night they were 99 percent certain it would be off so I checked the fixtures on teletext. There were pitch inspections at Derby and Mansfield, as well as York. I decided to try either Bury or Stockport, but I'd have to wait until the morning, possibly even Saturday lunchtime, before I was sure either game would go ahead. It would be a close call.

On the tube platform at London's King's Cross I just had time to call Gigg Lane to see if I could arrange a ticket for Bury's match. A recorded message said there would be a pitch inspection at one o'clock. That did it. I decided to take my chances by travelling to Stockport for the game against bottom club Chester. I'd have no trouble getting a ticket and at least there was a chance it would be on. It was a wise choice.

I reached London's Euston Station 10 minutes before the next train to Manchester. The train stopped at Stockport, one station and eight minutes before its arrival at Manchester Piccadilly. There were plenty of Manchester City fans on board travelling to Maine Road for the derby match against United. Strangely, I didn't spot any Reds' supporters. Euston was always full of fans in their colours on Saturday mornings. Today I saw Liverpool and QPR supporters going to Anfield for the match between their teams. They'd share the spoils in a 1-1 draw.

The journey to Stockport highlighted the weather problem for the groundstaff in both the Endsleigh League and, to a lesser extent, the Carling Premiership. The countryside was under water. Rivers were filled to the brim and some had broken their banks; fishermen were trying their luck in what were usually green fields.

I arrived at Edgeley Park in the rain to find just one fan outside the players' entrance. I passed him as I made my way to the ticket office. "Is the game on?" I enquired. "Pitch inspection at one o'clock," said the office manager. Great. I asked the lone fan where else I could go if the game was called off. He suggested Wigan, Sheffield United, Rochdale or Liverpool. Bury had already been called off justifying my decision not to travel to Gigg Lane. Now all I could do was wait.

I talked to a couple of Stockport fans outside the Main Stand to find out more about the club. They'd reached the final of the Autoglass trophy a couple of years earlier, but their success in recent seasons was limited. They were currently just out of the running for a play-off spot but would be right back among the contenders if they could string a few wins together. The big story was the recent loss of the tallest player in the league to Birmingham – six feet seven inch Kevin Francis.

Francis had Stockport's Uruguayan-born manager Danny Bergara to thank for his success. The charismatic Bergara had a reputation as a bit of a miracle-worker – and he needed to be. "Basically, you've got to get people for £10,000 and sell them on for £100,000. You've got to work really hard with people like Kevin Francis. When he first came to the club – I love the kid and he's done brilliant for us – but I put my hands on my head and said, 'I've got it wrong this time'. But we worked on this, we worked on that, and you've got an all round deal of £800,000."

"What you've got to do is go to games and watch players and you see something in these players and the others don't. The biggest example is Kev. When I went to watch him two or three times, people were laughing. I left before the end and I'm out on the car park rubbing my hands and I'm thinking, 'This is my chance, son'. Nobody wanted big Paul Williams - bad boy this, that and the other. Get him for free from Hartlepool, he scored 14 goals in 27 games to take us to second from top in the Fourth Division and we sell him to West Brom for £250,000. You're talking about Tony Barrass – a free from Hartlepool – and Andy Preece for £15,000 from Wrexham and the rest."

"These guys don't grow on trees. You've got to take them out on the training ground and show 'em what to do – you don't tell them, you show them – and, if they're really interested in improving themselves, they'll do it. It's all a matter of getting players that desperately want to do it and, if you've got somebody who desperately wants to do it, I know that I'm one of the best at instructing them how to do it."

The Edgeley Park faithful adored Francis. Ironically, he had to play against Stockport in his second match for Birmingham. Faced with an open goal, he hit the post. "I didn't enjoy it!" he said afterwards. But he did enjoy the reception given to him by the Country fans at St Andrews. He was so overcome that he contacted the local Stockport Express newspaper to say how he felt. "I would like to thank all the County fans who gave me such a marvellous reception," he told the paper.

The Express itself highlighted how laudable it was to witness supporters cheering rather than jeering their erstwhile hero. "In an era when chants of 'Judas' are commonly hurled by fans at former favourites who have moved on, it was refreshing to hear Francis, a hero for four years at Edgeley Park, being cheered before, during and after the game." The fanzine I O County put a picture of Francis on the front cover with the tribute "Thanks for Everything Big Man. Good Luck".

The £800,000 Birmingham had paid for him would help Stockport cover some of the costs of developing their ground, including the new Cheadle End which was going up fast. The skeleton iron structure behind the goal to my right looked like something out of H G Wells War of the Worlds. Mind you, not everyone was happy. The two doddery old geezers behind me, wearing flat check caps and smoking pipes, were less than pleased. "A waste of bloody money," said one. "We need new players not a new stand," said the other.

The club were more enthusiastic about the stand. Commercial Manager John Rutter was certainly keen. "Whilst it may be true that the stand will not be full every week (a criticism echoed by the fans in the Main Stand around me), I am convinced that the facilities within the stand will reach capacity. The 250-seater restaurant will be an obvious attraction. The social club too will provide a facility that we have sadly lacked in recent years." He may be right, if the team is winning. If they're not, it won't be just the stand that isn't filled every week.

As I waited outside the ground before the match time was getting on and I was getting wet. Finally, an official emerged from the players' entrance with the news that it was on. I'd come to the right place. Stockport had spent a lot of money re-laying their pitch and improving the drainage. The expense was paying dividends. However, I was a bit concerned that a former Wigan groundsman was on the staff at Edgeley Park. Was this the same who had put sand on the pitch at Springfield Park and ruined the playing surface?

158

Stockport's game was completely overshadowed on the day by the Manchester derby. Piccadilly Gold, the Manchester radio station, was previewing the Mancunian derby with former City and Scotland defender Willie Donachie. He was asked if the weather conditions would affect the game. "If the ball skids on the pitch then it will suit Manchester United; if it doesn't skid it will suit Manchester City." I tried to work out the logic but failed.

The Stockport announcer was also aware of the big match up the road. "I hope you're all wrapped up and ready for today's action at the Theatre of Dreams," he said ironically, referring to Edgeley Park not Old Trafford. I didn't know if he'd said it with a straight face, but the Stockport defence gave a good impression of a comedy act in the first half. Defender Tony Dinning was particularly entertaining, scoring his second own goal in succession following an astute lob over his own keeper at Birmingham.

Perhaps the Stockport defenders thought bottom club Chester would be easy pickings. They certainly looked relaxed in the first half-hour. After sustained pressure the visitors went ahead in the 22nd minute through Roger Preece. Stuart Rimmer, formerly of Everton, Watford and Barnsley, broke down the left-wing before laying the ball back to the edge of the area. The cross was slightly deflected but fell perfectly for Preece who volleyed sweetly into the top left hand corner.

Worse was to follow for the home side. Two minutes later a cross from the right was headed down into the six-yard box where first Stockport's Michael Wallace and then the hapless Tony Dinning between them steered the ball over the line as they made a desperate attempt to clear. The Stockport fans behind me were livid. "You're a load of dummies," said the flat capped, pipe-smoking pensioner.

County's new signing Ian Helliwell, £20,000 from Rotherham, was anonymous and certainly not a replacement for Francis. "I don't know why we bothered to buy him," said the man whose son played for Stockport's youth team. It all looked pretty hopeless, but things would brighten up for the home fans in the second half with a goal just after half-time and an equaliser three minutes from the end. Anyway, Valentine's Day was approaching and at least the announcer didn't disappoint the home supporters. "I have a Valentine's message for you: Hilda loves Squidgy Bunny." Right!

I asked the father of the youth team member to name the best player he'd seen at County. Kevin Francis was the only one he could come up with. He'd obviously missed the silky skills of Georgie Best. Then again, don't we all.

THE BIGGEST CRIME IN FOOTBALL
Derby County v Bolton Wanderers – Baseball Ground
26 February 1995

'The biggest crime in football is to give the ball to the opposition,' said the sign on the wall above the exit from Derby's home dressing room. "Brian Clough put that sign up there," said the official showing us around the ground. It must have done the trick. Within two years of Cloughie's arrival in May 1967 the club roared into the First Division led by captain Dave Mackay, a double winner at Tottenham in 1961.

In 1972 they won the League Championship for the first time in the closest race ever seen. Derby, with Clough at the helm and Peter Taylor by his side, clinched the title by one point from Leeds, Liverpool and Manchester City. The players, including Colin Todd, Roy McFarland, Archie Gemmill, John McGovern, Bruce Rioch and Frannie Lee, found out they'd won the League in Spain where they were relaxing on holiday!

All those stars are still involved in League football with Todd and McFarland in charge at Bolton, Gemmill and McGovern managing Rotherham, Rioch guiding Arsenal and Lee installed as Chairman at Manchester City. I'm not sure what's happened to the other members of the team like Kevin Hector, Terry Hennessey and Alan Hinton.

In October 1973 Clough and Taylor sensationally resigned and moved to Brighton. Mackay returned from Nottingham Forest to restore calm after what was a major upheaval and matched Clough's achievement by steering the Rams to the title once again in 1975. The nickname comes from the county emblem of Derbyshire.

I remembered the enjoyment that Derby team gave fans all over the country when they appeared in Europe during the golden age in the club's history between 1972 and 1977. They seemed to be on Sportnight almost every Wednesday evening, along with Ipswich, taking on Europe's finest teams. Ipswich won the UEFA Cup in 1981, but Derby never reached the final stage of that competition or the European Cup. They did chalk up their record victory in the UEFA Cup though, beating Finn Harps 12-0.

Back in the dressing room the current squad's kit was neatly laid out on the wooden benches in numerical order from the goalkeeper's number one shirt to the number 14. "They never have a number 13 only a 12 and a 14," said the guide. "We're not suspicious as a club, but some of the players are. Some put their socks on the right foot first, some on the left; it doesn't always work though."

We were then led into the directors' lounge, which doubled as a trophy room. It was like a who's who of football past. The Republic of Ireland's assistant manager Maurice Setters, the former Coventry star, was in the lounge. He'd come along to watch Jason McAteer and the other Irish players. Former Coventry manager John Sillett, who led the Sky Blues to their only FA Cup triumph in the 1987 final against Spurs, was talking to Jack Taylor, the 1974 World Cup Final referee. Commentator Alan Parry had also come along and was chatting to Stoke manager Lou Macari.

Former Derby star Colin Todd, now ironically the manager at Bolton, and his colleague from the '70s, Alan Durban, were also at the match. Durban was now Derby's chief scout. The history of the club, which Todd and Durban had contributed to, was laid out in a long cabinet which ran the length of the back wall. "We won the Championship twice in the early '70s and the FA Cup in 1946, but we can't show you those because we had to hand them back," said the guide. That victory in the first post-war FA Cup was largely due to the skills of Raich Carter, Peter Doherty and Jack Stamps.

Derby Chairman Lionel Pickering was hoping to repeat that cup success. "I look back to the glory days of the 1940s when we won the FA Cup. If you speak to some of the great players of the past, they say that team was even better than our side from the 1970s," said Pickering.

Mind you, they may have had some gypsy fortune on their side. When Derby first moved to the Baseball Ground in 1895 gypsies camping on the site had to leave and as they did one of them put a curse on the ground. A local journalist was so worried about the curse that he found a gypsy camp and had it lifted before the '46 Cup Final at Wembley. It must have worked since the Rams beat Charlton 4-1.

"This trophy means a lot," said the official pointing to a silver galleon given to the club by Real Madrid. There was also a bronze ball, another gift from Madrid, and a bronze eagle from Benfica. "We have a lot of Spanish trophies for the simple reason that for over 20 years Derby used to go to Spain, mainly the Isle of Majorca." Next came the Player of the Year trophy given to the club by the family of Jack Stamps, hero of that '46 Cup victory, when he died. It was now presented every year in his memory.

Derby were one of the 12 founder members of the League in 1888, though they were formed four years earlier by members of the Derbyshire County Cricket Club who attracted attention for their amber, pale blue and chocolate coloured strip which was based on the colours worn by the cricket club. The football team quickly established itself as one of the top sides and reached 13 FA Cup semi-finals between 1895 and 1909. Unfortunately, they lost all three of the finals they contested during that time.

"And who was this gent?" said the guide pointing to a faded picture of one of Derby's greatest-ever players. "He scored 353 goals in his career, 292 of them with Derby. He still holds the individual match scoring record. We wish we could resurrect him. He died in 1938." The fans put forward a few names before settling on Steve Bloomer.

Nicknamed Paleface, Bloomer was remembered as one of the legendary stars of late-Victorian and Edwardian football. Sometimes criticised as being too selfish and relaxed, he was a brilliant goalscorer. His tally of 353 goals came in 598 League games between 1892 and 1914. The 292 he scored for Derby were chalked up in 473 appearances during two spells with the club and, in between, he put away 61 goals in 125 games for Middlesbrough His England tally of 28 goals in 23 Home Internationals was a record that stood for almost 50 years. He scored in his first 10 internationals.

Don Davies of the Manchester Guardian remembered how, as a boy, he saw a portly individual with close-cropped hair and a great white moon of a face apparently bored to death by the proceedings. "Near the end, it is true, Bloomer kicked disdainfully at a ball rolling towards him and through turning his back immediately was the only player on the field apparently who did not know he had scored." He later worked as a coach in Germany, where he was imprisoned during the First World War, and at Derby.

The official then took us over to the corner of the directors' lounge where a few more trophies were on show above the bar. "This cup was given to Derby by their very first opponents in Europe. But which country did they come from?" he asked the assembled group. Various countries were thrown at him, but nobody got the right answer. "Sarajevo of Yugoslavia, a country that doesn't exist now. That was where the First World War started," he told us, continuing the history lesson.

"When they got this trophy back here the spout was twisted on one side so the club had it repaired. When Sarajevo came over they asked us what had happened to the trophy and we explained that it got damaged in transit. Well, of course they would have noticed it since it was the only one with a straight spout! It was supposed to have been twisted all along!"

The Baseball Ground itself was developed in the 1880s as a sports ground for foundry workers. In 1889, the foundry owner, Francis Ley, went to America and was so taken with baseball that he decided to develop the game among his workers and spent £7,000 adapting the ground for what we'd probably call rounders.

Baseball was played at the stadium for years after Derby County arrived and many football clubs, including Orient and Aston Villa, sent teams to play at the ground in a national competition. Derby won the baseball title in 1897 with the legendary Steve Bloomer on second base! Nevertheless, football was still the ground's main sport.

The Main Stand in Shaftesbury Crescent was built in 1926 and the Popular Side was developed in 1932. The double-decker Osmaston End Stand was built in 1933, while the Normanton End Stand on Vulcan Street was erected in 1935. Part of the Osmaston End was known as Catcher's Corner during the baseball era.

Promotion to the First Division in 1969 encouraged Derby to build a new £250,000 stand above the East Side terracing. known as the Popular Side, on Colombo Street. It was called the Ley Stand after the sponsor, Ley's Maleable Castings Company, whose foundry ran along the entire east side of the ground and also behind the Osmaston Stand, with its Italianate chimney. Nowadays the sponsor has changed and the East Side has the words Toyota Stand along the white roof fascia.

The club spent £1 million redeveloping the Baseball ground in the two years up to 1993 with the installation of 33 executive boxes, two restaurants and a specially designed area for up to 80 disabled fans. At the same time, they decided to move to a new £15 million 30,000 all-seater purpose-built stadium at Chaddesden Sidings. But continued improvements at the Baseball Ground seem more likely. Indeed, the club had recently paid £120,000 for the freehold of the nearby Baseball Hotel. Curious indeed for a club on the move, said Nick Wheat, Editor of the fanzine C Stander.

Derby's financial position was another reason to stay at their home ground. They needed 18,000 gates to break even, compared to a recent average of 11,000, and Wheat believed the players' earnings were also draining the club's coffers with an average wage of more than £20,000 per week and some stars on much more than that.

The club had just reported a near £3 million loss for 1993/94. Chairman Lionel Pickering explained the massive deficit as the effect of having a Premier League wage bill but First Division income, in his statement to shareholders. The accounts showed that almost £3.5 million was spent on wages, while the club's turnover was only

£200,000 more than that.

The Stan The Fan feature in one of the tabloids had its own verdict on the current Baseball Ground. "Some great ideas but little chance of putting them into practice. Living on its past with little hope of a future. I'd rather take the mother-in-law out than come here. Team's lacking sparkle and so is the entire club. Shame that a once grand club now looks so tatty."

At least the ground had been much easier to get to since 1990 when British Rail opened the Ramsline Halt station a few hundred yards from the Baseball Ground, though only specials stop at the station. Not that I'd had the pleasure of travelling by train. I'd arrived at the ground by car from Harrogate, a wonderful town in North Yorkshire. Derby was easy enough to find but once I hit the city centre and the narrow roads around the ground there were few, if any, signposts.

Earlier, I'd consulted my Rough Guide to England for an idea of what Derby was like. "The proximity of the Peak District might lead you to think that Derby... could prove to be an interesting stopping-off point. Sadly, the city – a status conferred as recently as 1977 – is an uninspiring place, its predictable collection of shopping malls only slightly redeemed by the waterfront of the River Derwent, which winds its way around the northeastern corner of the centre, fringed with some pleasant parks and walks."

Derby is the county town of Derbyshire. It was called Derventio when it was a Roman station, but the Danes who took the town in 854 renamed it Deoraby. The silk mill started by John and Thomas Lombe around 1720, and which stood where the Industrial Museum is now, was not only the first to succeed in England but was also the first true factory. William Duesbury established the Royal Crown Derby works, now part of the Royal Doulton Tableware Group, in the 1750s. In the nineteenth century Derby became a centre of the Midland Railways, with large engineering workshops, and Rolls Royce moved there in 1908, two years after it was founded.

The engine of the current team was Craig Short, Derby's record signing at two-and-a-half million pounds but who now plays for Everton. He was outstanding in this match against promotion-chasing Bolton at the heart of the home side's defence. Not that he could prevent Derby going behind after less than a minute when the ball broke for Jason McAteer in the box. He turned and slotted it into the corner. The away fans in the corner of the Toyota Stand went barmy. Two Trotters supporters behind me placed incongruously among the Derby faithful also jumped up to celebrate, much to the annoyance of a sandy-haired

Rams supporter of about 20 sitting in front. "They can't stand a bit of banter," said the older Bolton fan. "He thinks we shouldn't be in this stand. It's pretty pathetic isn't it?"

However, the match was notable not for the skills of any one player but for an incident after 10 minutes which left Bolton defender Simon Coleman with a broken leg. Derby striker Marco Gabbiadini was elbowed in the face by Coleman, a former Rams player. Gabbiadini, anger etched across his face, reacted with a crunching tackle, though he did seem to go for the ball. Coleman fell to the ground writhing in agony under the weight of the challenge. The St John's Ambulancemen rushed on with a stretcher and taped Coleman's legs together. It didn't look good.

Bolton manager Bruce Rioch, the former Derby star, was absolutely furious. He leapt out of his seat in the stand and ran onto the pitch to talk to Gabbiadini, the referee and a policeman after checking on Coleman. "I just told Gabbiadini that when he puts his head on the pillow tonight and every night he will think about Simon Coleman and what happened. We should have been playing 10 men after that challenge."

Neither the referee nor the linesman took any action either for Coleman's challenge or Gabbiadini's reaction. Rioch was still fuming two hours later when he told reporters: "You all saw the incident, which I thought was a nasty one." Asked if he felt the injury resulted from a deliberate assault, he said: "It's not the sort of question I want to answer." As far as Gabbiadini was concerned he had made a fair challenge.

The whole episode overshadowed a game which Bolton desperately needed to win to keep up with Middlesbrough at the top of the First Division table. After about 25 minutes of non-stop talking and shouting by the Bolton fans behind me the Derby supporter in front of me got up out of his seat, turned around and put his fist in the air. He wanted a fight. I stood up to calm him down as his dad held onto his arm. An elderly man with thinning grey hair, plain round glasses and a grey raincoat turned around and told the Bolton fans to shut up. The atmosphere was definitely hotting up around me. I turned to my girlfriend Nicky and shrugged. Typical behaviour for agitated football fans.

"Where was the lob over the top then?" said the Bolton supporter, undaunted by the turmoil his earlier comments had caused. "That was bloody awful finishing. We should have been four up by now. That was crap. It sat up for him perfectly." He was complaining about the Trotters Dutch star Richard Sneekes who was clean through with only the keeper to beat but shot tamely into his arms. "This lot will get half a chance and score. You watch, the first chance they get they'll score."

The Bolton fans' complaints were relentless and they were even driving me mad. "This game could have been over after half-an-hour. Dead and buried. There's a lot of big boot up front." He glared at the sandy-haired lad in front. "He can come and visit me at half-time if he wants to," he said to his wife. Just then there was an announcement over the PA about forthcoming games. First the match against Grimsby on Tuesday. "We were hoping to sell the tickets after today's match, but they haven't arrived yet." Fortunately, the Millwall tickets had arrived.

Out on the pitch a girl from the RAM FM radio station, decked out in a yellow hat and a black leather jacket, was conducting the £2,000 Gold Rush draw. Her voice went through me like a knife. Piercing would have been a euphemism. She was having trouble drawing the winning number and dropped the ticket which went flying across the pitch. Meanwhile, the Rammettes did a sexy dance routine to that old classic YMCA. They were dressed in fetching white shirts and short black skirts which were perfectly colour coordinated with the black and white pom poms they waved around.

In the second half Derby tried to claw back an equaliser, but missed another chance when a header flew over the bar. "Score in a Brothel, You Couldn't Score in a Brothel," sang the Bolton fans. Very original. But also untrue. Bolton had led from that early strike by McAteer until the 82nd minute, but Derby were to snatch victory from the jaws of defeat (as they say in all the best tabloids!). Eight minutes from time there was a scramble in the box and their latest arrival Dean Yates, signed from Notts County, stubbed the ball over the line. Derby had equalised totally against the run of play.

With only three minutes left Lee Mills, on loan pending a £450,000 deal with Wolves and described by the Bolton fan as a big lad, picked up the ball midway into the Bolton half, ran unchallenged to the edge of the box and drove a flier into the top left hand corner giving the keeper no chance. The Bolton fan had been right all along.

The then-Derby manager Roy McFarland had replaced Arthur Cox and taken the club to the play-off final the previous season where they lost to local rivals Leicester through an 87th minute goal. It was their 50th win in the First Division since the inaugural 1992/93 season. But it wasn't good enough from a team which had cost £12 million of chairman Lionel Pickering's millions to assemble.

Almost £6 million was spent on five players: Short, Tommy Johnson (now at Villa), Paul Kitson (now at Newcastle), Marco Gabbiadini,

Mark Pembridge and American international John Harkes. Pickering defended the signings at the start of the season. "I have no regrets about the players we have bought. It is just unfortunate at present, when money is scarce because of clubs implementing the Taylor Report, that it is much harder to sell off some of our fringe players. We need to sell before we can buy again."

Pickering knew what he wanted and he was happy to try to emulate his peers Jack Walker and Sir John Hall. "The aim is Premier League football. I congratulate the likes of Blackburn and Newcastle for showing that money can buy success; we are the exception to the rule at present but that is not to say we cannot make it. There is no time limit and no drawing back. If we get a kick in the teeth along the way, so what?"

So was McFarland under pressure. "The number one rule in management is never to resign," he said. "I learnt that in 1973 when Brian Clough said 'Don't let the bastards grind you down'." The C-Stander fanzine clearly felt his days were numbered though. Under the headline: 'Promotion Hopes in Tatters... a beleaguered Roy Mac gets the vote of confidence' was a picture of four Romans with a glint in their eyes holding daggers! So was Roy stabbed in the back?

EMLYN HUGHES WOZ ERE
Rotherham v Cambridge United - Millmoor Ground
7 March 1995

They still talk about him in glowing terms at Millmoor. Player-manager Emlyn Hughes. The defender with the squeaky voice who also captained England, Liverpool and a variety of teams on the BBC's Question of Sport. He was the nearly man at Rotherham. After winning the old Third Division championship in 1981 they missed out on promotion to the top flight by just one point in the next campaign. The chance of glory was gone and the following season so was Emlyn.

The Merry Millers, named after the local steel mills (and not a windmill as is often incorrectly assumed), had been through it all before. In 1955 they won eight of their last nine second division games, including a final 6-1 win over Liverpool, to finish level on points with Birmingham and Luton. They'd scored more goals than the Blues but missed promotion on goal average, the measure used by the League to divide teams back then.

Arguably their greatest triumph was in 1961 when, under manager Tom Johnston, they reached the League Cup Final at Wembley against Aston Villa. The competition had only just started and didn't include all the First Division teams, but it was a great achievement for Second Division Rotherham to reach the final. They didn't win, of course, but at least they'd been to a Wembley final.

The Millers have had their fair share of famous managers, including a young Tommy Docherty in the late 1960s and former Leeds hard man Norman Hunter in the mid-1980s. Docherty tells the story of how he was in Greece with his wife having been offered the job as manager of Panathinaikos. "It could be worse" he told her. "I could be manager at Rotherham." Shortly afterwards he was! Some great players have also pulled on the red shirt over the years, such as former Manchester City and England centre-half Dave Watson, sold to Sunderland for a then club record £100,000.

Today's crop of managers and players was no less distinguished. At the helm were joint managers Archie Gemmill and John McGovern – seasoned pros who played together at Derby and Nottingham Forest and had surely learned a lot about the art of management from Brian Clough. Rotherham were struggling near the foot of the Second Division but at least they could share the burden together, like that other management double Alan Curbishley and Steve Gritt at Charlton.

The players were certainly impressed by the knowledge of the game shared by the dynamic duo. An interview with defender Nigel Johnson in the fanzine Moulin Rouge revealed their professional approach and genuine concern for the players. Johnson was asked about a cup tie at Halifax a few seasons before the duo arrived at Millmoor when he scored the winning goal but looked in considerable discomfort having just come back from injury. Was he brought back too soon?

"On occasions I was brought back into the side when I should have given it longer to recover, but when you're asked to play you just go out and play. This happens too often in football, especially in the lower divisions where squads are much smaller. Archie Gemmill and John McGovern think differently, only wanting players in for training who are 100 percent fit."

Gemmill and McGovern used their jointly signed programme notes to ask the fans to "Stick with us". But their main message was about character. "Part and parcel of a manager's job is improving his playing staff by recruiting new players. This usually entails endless telephone conversations regarding a player's ability, temperament and skill level. There is, however, one overriding factor that is less and less prevalent in the overall make up of a player and that is the ingredient of character.

"People of character will roll up their sleeves when the going gets tough and will be absolutely ruthless when they are on top. Players are always going to make mistakes but if you happen to possess this rare attribute of character you always want the ball, even if you are making mistakes, to come through a lean spell and show what you are capable of.

"In the present day you could equate this by trying to put a value on players such as Dave Mackay who was such a superb example of never-say-die spirit, and who I (Gemmill) had the absolute pleasure of playing with during my Derby County days. I could imagine Dave's value being around £10 million in today's market – at least for his left leg!"

The Gemmill/McGovern axis had passed on that character to their players judging by a narrow 1-0 win over Cambridge in a relegation dogfight at Millmoor on a cold Tuesday night. I sat in the Main Stand opposite the Millmoor Lane Stand. (The ground is also named after Millmoor Lane, the thoroughfare that runs behind the stand.) Former Derby striker Bobby Davison led the line with as much determination, if a little less speed, than in his younger days. And, when Davison began to tire, the much-travelled Imre Varadi took up the mantle.

Tommy Docherty's joke about having more clubs than Jack Nicklaus is over-used but certainly applies to Varadi. The 35-year-old striker began his career with Sheffield United before joining Everton,

Newcastle, Sheffield Wednesday, West Brom, Manchester City, Sheffield Wednesday again, Leeds, Luton, Oxford, on loan, and finally Rotherham. He applied himself with enthusiasm to the task of replacing the impressive Davison and clearly still had a zest for the game. I wondered if even he could remember all the teams he'd played for.

The local Sheffield paper, The Star, was full of praise for Rotherham's solid performance. "In pulling off a vital win last night, Rotherham United fell back on three of the major qualities which have edged them steadily through the depths of winter to where they can see light at the edge of the wood (poetic or what?). Their five-month long Millmoor invincibility, a growing reputation for being difficult to beat, and another Shaun Goater goal all combined to nudge aside visitors Cambridge United."

The win pulled Rotherham further away from the relegation zone and plunged Cambridge into deeper trouble. The away fans, less than a hundred of them, were huddled together in what used to be called the cow shed (I could see why) but was now known as The Railway End because of the railway behind that end of the ground amazingly enough! Opposite was the Tivoli End, named after the cinema that used to occupy the magnificent building on Masborough Street. It was a fine example of cinema architecture, built before the First World War, but was now a furniture store.

At half-time I walked down the steps from the Main Stand to the sponsors' lounge. Hot vegetable soup was being served and it went down a treat. I was cold and needed warming up. The Main Stand had to be demolished by the year 2000 in line with the requirements of the Taylor Report that all-wooden stands should be phased out. I doubted it would be missed.

The Chairman K. F. Booth, had announced that he was considering a plan to turn the pitch sideways and build a greyhound track as well. That would require moving a lot of scrap metal since the ground is hemmed in by the Booth family's scrap yards on three sides. On two sides of the ground the scrap yard walls are actually used as the backs of the stands. All sorts of objects can be seen jutting into the air.

Towards the end of the match the Cambridge supporters began to get behind their team by singing, to the tune of the Pet Shop Boys Go West, "We're shit and we're going down, we're shit and we're going down". That was followed by chants of "Johnson Out, Johnson Out", a reference to what they wanted Cambridge to do with manager Gary Johnson. At the end of the match the fans rushed down towards the corner of the stand where Johnson was following his players to the tunnel. "Johnson Out" they shouted again, even more vociferously. He'd been the fans' choice to replace Ian Atkins in May 1993.

There's always a team worse off than your own it seems. However, it wasn't only Rotherham's football club that was struggling. My journey to the match involved taking a train from Doncaster to Rotherham Central. The route was lined with derelict factories, scrap metal yards and tall chimneys as we passed a town called Swinton. Closer to Rotherham the factories seemed to be up and running. White smoke billowed out of enterprises with names like Finishing Banks North. Further along the line Waddington's proudly announced a 41-acre development on huge billboards beside the track.

This was clearly deep in the heart of the industrial north and pretty it ain't. There were pylons, warehouses and container yards; factory walls covered in graffiti; run-down mills and empty buildings with broken windows. Welcome to Yorkshire. The Blue Guide describes the place as "a murky town on the Don at its meeting with the Rother". I actually thought Rotherham, a town of just over 80,000 people, was actually not that bad.

The place had a cathedral and a neat and tidy central shopping area. But I was a little worried about the state of mind of the people living there. I passed a centre for Alcoholics and a private practice offering hypnotism as the answer to all problems. Maybe the locals had suffered from watching Rotherham and needed help.

I certainly did. I'd been up since 3.30 in the morning and after a very stressful day at the office caught an afternoon train to Doncaster to link up with the local service to Rotherham. By the time I arrived I was tired. I understood why Edward Wood, the previous holder of the Guinness record for visiting all the League grounds, had taken a year off to go on his travels. I was completely knackered and needed a break. I wasn't sure I could manage one more game let alone another 27.

It's strange how anything taken to excess ceases to be much fun. I'd always thought complete freedom to travel to every football ground in the country would be brilliant. In reality, long train journeys to rundown industrial towns to watch mediocre football is not the best way to use your time. It was certainly a challenge – and, after visiting 66 grounds, not one I was about to give up – but freedom for me now was not having to visit 93 football grounds in one season. Strange how your outlook on life changes with experience. Next stop Wolverhampton.

BORING, BORING, YORK
York City v Wycombe Wanderers - Bootham Crescent
14 March 1995

This was *the* most boring game I'd seen all season. Incredibly, York had gone 20 League games without a draw – 12 wins, eight defeats – until the visit of Wycombe Wanderers. Ironically, their last draw was against the Chairboys at the end of October: the result 0-0. The chance of an entertaining match was therefore remote. The Yorkshire Evening Post was full of letters criticising York for being "boring". After watching this performance I thoroughly agreed. "Utter rubbish" was one fan's reaction.

It was the sort of game where in the end you didn't want either side to score. Having watched crap football in the freezing cold, eaten a cold chicken and mushroom pie, drunk two cups of weak tea and sat on a hard wooden seat for 90 minutes I was beginning to enjoy being a martyr. A goal would have somehow compromised my suffering. The only brightness on a dour evening were the two bubbly girls from Bradford next to me. They'd come along to spy on two of the teams in contention for a play-off spot alongside their beloved Bradford City.

A sprinkling of post-match reaction provides a good idea of just how bad the Wycombe game was. Malcolm Huntington, chief sports writer at the Evening Post, wrote under the headline "Mix and match City struck by flair play loss. Snore point reward for Minstermen". His report described the evening's entertainment as "very much a match of the bread and water variety and it set up an unwanted record as far as this scribe is concerned in that it was the first time since I first watched City back in 1941 that a team has gone through a game without managing a single direct shot on target... neither side deserved to win a forgettable match in which there was little goalmouth action or excitement to keep spectators warm on a cold night."

York manager Alan Little, formerly a player at Aston Villa, gave his patched-up team a sterling tribute and was satisfied with their overall performance. "We're at the stage of the season when you get games like this, when it's dour and scrappy and teams don't want to give anything away. At times the quality was not there, the passing was not there, nor sometimes the final ball. But I cannot fault the effort put in by the team. I have to be pleased with that." No quality, no passing, no final ball equals no goals.

But what about the supporters. After all they were the ones who'd paid to watch the fare dished up by two promotion-chasing teams.

Martin Fowler, 51, a technical sales rep from Dringhouses (wherever that is) was hooked by the attractions of watching York after a 3-3 draw against Southampton in the FA Cup in January 1971. But what about tonight's match. "This was a game when not a single player seemed able to play a simple pass to feet, though the pitch and wind had to be partially responsible and this has to be the poorest playing surface at Bootham Crescent in living memory."

So there you have it: journalist, manager and fan in complete agreement that the game was crap. When asked for his man-of-the-match Fowler nominated the Wycombe fan banging his drum throughout the 90 minutes among the hundred or so Wanderers fans at the away end. Emil Grygar, drummer extraordinaire, was a local builder who followed Wycombe all over the country. Tonight he was trying to rally the travelling Wanderers supporters, while the home fans at the Shipton Street End sang, "What the fucking hell is that," and, "Who's the wanker with the drum." York manager Alan Little had criticised the home fans the previous week for a lack of exuberance. They made up for it against Wycombe, though I'm not sure Little had such chants in mind.

There have been few momentous moments at Bootham Crescent, the ground bought by York City from York Cricket Club in 1932. But it was actually one of the quaintest grounds I'd visited. Bootham Crescent, which leads to the stadium, was full of the sort of guest houses you expect to see along the seafront at a coastal resort. Handy for any away fans who feel like spending some time in the historic city.

York, with a population of almost 100,000, is actually full of B & B's serving the tourists that swarm all over the place in summer. It's one of England's most attractive old cities and, until the industrial revolution, was second only to London in population and importance. It was at the centre of the country's religious life and a key part of many of the major events that shaped the nation.

The same cannot be said of York's role in the history of English football. The best they'd ever managed was 15th place in the old Second Division in 1975. But they did cause an FA Cup upset 20 years earlier when, as a Third Division team, they beat a Blackpool side including the two Stans - Matthews and Mortensen.

In the Sixth Round they played Second Division Notts County at Meadow Lane before County's record crowd of over 47,000 and won 1-0. The winner was scored by Arthur Bottom, York's highest scorer in a season with 31 goals in 1954-55 – a feat he repeated in the 1955-56 campaign.

The Yorkshire Evening Press described the win as "York City's finest hour". Reporter Wilf Meek wrote: "Amidst scenes which I have never seen equalled before on a football ground this amazing York City team could hardly fight its way to the dressing room." Over 12,000 City fans made the journey and 14 special trains were used.

City had become only the third team from the Third Division to reach the FA Cup semi-finals (Millwall in 1937 and Port Vale in 1954 were the others, since followed by Norwich in 1959 and Plymouth in 1984). They lost 2-0 to Newcastle after a replay - the closest any Third Division team had come to a place in the Final. The Magpies went on to win the cup, while City spent their windfall extending the Main Stand.

Perhaps the team's more recent poor form - they had to apply for re-election twice between 1977 and 1981 - had something to do with the players eating too much of the chocolate produced by Terry and Rowntree-Nestle, the city's major employers along with the tourist trade.

I'd arrived on an afternoon train from London for this Tuesday night match. York Station, just outside the city walls on the south side of the River Ouse, was a 750 yard walk from the historic centre of the city and a bit further from Bootham Crescent. The city walls enclosed narrow streets, lined with overhanging rows of old buildings, that wound their way along an irregular medieval course. The city is dominated by York Minster, the largest medieval English cathedral and second in importance only to Canterbury. York's nickname, the Minstermen, comes from the monasterium.

The most interesting bit of history is that the highwayman Dick Turpin was tried and hanged at York in 1739, though his famous ride to the city was in fact made by Swift Nick (William Nevinson) in the seventeenth century and added to the Turpin legend by William Harrison Ainsworth in his novel Rookwood (1834). The only robbery I saw was the money taken from supporters by the gatemen at Bootham Crescent!

However, one tragic event that shocked everyone at the club, and led to the stand at the Shipton Street End being called The David Longhurst Stand, was the death of a player affectionately known as Longy. His dad takes up the story. "My wife and I were returning from holiday in Scotland... when we heard the shattering news on the car radio that our son David had died on the pitch at Bootham Crescent."

It was a tragedy. "Like everyone else at Bootham Crescent I will never forget the horror of seeing David suddenly collapse on the pitch, soon followed by the devastating realisation that he had died. It was a crushing blow to our club and to the city of York," said the York President at the time John Greenway.

'Longy' began his career at Nottingham Forest under the watchful eye of Brian Clough before moving to Halifax, Northampton, Peterborough and then York. "Throughout the whole of his 25 years David loved football," said his dad. "It was his whole life and he was looking forward to the new season at York. But what happened could not have been prevented."

A special memorial match between his home town team Corby and neighbours Kettering was full of glowing tributes to the young man. The most famous of his managers was Brian Clough. "Anybody who knows football club directors as well as I do will tell you that most of them would love to be in management," said Cloughie. "Most of them I've come across would regard themselves as a better judge of a player than me – and occasionally, only occasionally, I've been tempted to agree."

"I had a director at Nottingham Forest who always had a sneaking suspicion that David would make the grade with us. He was very disappointed when we let him go and has mentioned several times since then that whenever David moved clubs he always did so for sizeable transfer fees. At the time he left us we felt that David had greater prospects of furthering his career elsewhere but it's always a shame when players who grow up with you move on... I'll always remember David as a good all-round athlete."

The highlight of Longhurst's career came when he played for Peterborough in an FA Cup First Round clash at Gillingham. He scored all three POSH goals in a 3-3 thriller – including the dramatic equaliser three minutes from time. He clutched the matchball with pride that day and ended the season as the supporters Player of the Year. "David was a great favourite with our supporters," said then-President John Greenway. There could be no more fitting tribute to his memory than a stand at the home supporters end of the ground." David Longhurst's name still lives on at York on top of that stand.

Longhurst's story was tragic, but other Minstermen have had sorry tales to tell. Defender John MacPhail, a bit of a playboy, was once caught on an InterCity train with a false Young Person's Railcard during his City days, according to a soccer magazine. MacPhail was sold to Sunderland where he joined one of City's most famous managers, former Stoke centre-half Denis Smith, the man who took York to their first-ever trophy – the 1984 Fourth Division Championship. Will it be their last?

THE THEATRE OF DREAMS
Manchester United v Tottenham Hotspur - Old Trafford
15 March 1995

At last, the mecca of football. Supporters of other clubs can knock United. They can claim that manager Alex Ferguson is always whinging about referees and the media. Or that the mercurial Eric Cantona should have been banned for his kung-fu antics. They can argue that the Reds are given favourable treatment by the Football Association. And they can gloat at United's recent lack of success in the Champions League. But their stadium, Old Trafford, the Theatre of Dreams, is without parallel.

Home to legends like the Busby Babes, so tragically killed in the Munich air disaster of 1958, and to one of the greatest forward lines the world has ever seen, the trio of Best, Law and Charlton, Old Trafford is unique. For a start, no other ground in England, with the exception of Wembley, has been so perfectly designed. Most stadiums have been developed piecemeal over a number of years with no clear long-term plan. Not so United's ground, with its unbroken elliptical shape encircling the pitch. An early drawing of the ground shows that it was the same shape as it is today.

Manchester is the financial, business and cultural centre of a sprawling conurbation of three and a half million people. The city has ancient origins but is really a child of the industrial revolution which elevated it to the regional capital of the Lancashire cotton-manufacturing district. It was dubbed Cottonopolis, in the same way that Middlesbrough was known as Ironopolis.

From being just a village in 1750, Manchester grew to become the world's major cotton milling centre in only a hundred years. Its spectacular rise was based on the production of cheaper imitations of expensive Indian calicoes using machines developed from Arkwright's first steam-powered cotton mill which opened in 1783.

Waterways and railway viaducts provide the outline of the puzzle into which the city's main buildings have been placed. The first canal was cut in 1772 to connect Manchester to the coal mines at Worsley, and the world's first railway passenger line, George Stephenson's Liverpool and Manchester Railway, opened in 1830. The Castlefield area boasts the world's oldest passenger railway station. It was against this background that Manchester United were formed as the L & Y Railway Football Club.

Old Trafford lies to the south west of the city centre on the border between Manchester and Salford, the biggest town in England without a League club. England's largest canal, built by the Duke of Bridgewater in the middle of the eighteenth century to transport cotton and coal, runs behind Old Trafford. It was the first of a system of waterways which, by the early 1800s, linked Manchester with Ashton and Oldham, Bolton and Bury, and Rochdale.

A couple of hundred yards north of Old Trafford are the docks, linked to the Mersey estuary by the Manchester Ship Canal which made the city a major inland port and explains why you can see disused cranes on the horizon around the ground.

East of United's home is the huge Trafford Park industrial estate and to the south are the headquarters of Lancashire County Cricket Club – also known as Old Trafford and a good place to park on match days. When George Best first arrived in Manchester from Belfast he jumped in a taxi and asked the driver to take him to Old Trafford. "Which one?" replied the driver. Best thought he was winding him up. He didn't know there were two Old Traffords!

Mancunians, at least those on one side of the United/City divide, flock to the stadium in their thousands to cheer on the men in red. (The name for those born in the Manchester area comes from Mancunium, or Mamucium, which was a walled Roman fort on the military road from Chester to York in Castlefield at the South end of Deansgate). Visitors from all over the world also come to Old Trafford. It's more of a pilgrimage, or a visit to a holy place, than just a tour of a football ground.

United are probably the most famous club side in the world. Visitors can browse in the club shop, responsible for generating millions of pounds for United's coffers each season; they can tour the ground and museum for a fiver (three quid to see the museum only – the first to be purpose-built in British football when it opened in 1986); listen to Reds' Radio on 1413 AM; eat United's Champs own-brand meat and potato pies or drink Champs cola "available on draught in the stadium and at Tesco, Asda and all good shops". Oh, and I almost forgot, you can also watch United play football every other Saturday and sometimes in midweek too.

When the ground was opened in 1910, after United won the League in 1908 and the Cup in 1909, Old Trafford was one of the most advanced stadiums of its time and the envy of all the other League clubs. I couldn't work out why it was called Old Trafford even when it was new. I mean, it can legitimately be called Old Trafford now, since it's 85 years old, but surely it should have started out as New Trafford or just plain Trafford back in 1910!

It was designed by Archibald Leitch and could hold 80,000, though it never did. The luxurious cushioned tip-up seats were more comfortable than those used at League grounds today and attendants were even on hand to take United fans from the tea-rooms to the seats. The ground also boasted magnificent changing rooms with lavish bathing facilities, including a plunge-bath. The players were pampered in the club's own massage parlour, or they could relax in the billiards room. More serious work outs took place in the gymnasium.

Today the tip-up seats are still a feature of the ground, though they're now plastic and come without the cushioning. The changing rooms are still lavish, although any player with a cut is not allowed to use the communal spa bath because of the risk of Aids. But the billiards room, massage room and gym have all gone. They're now located at United's training ground, The Cliff.

Old Trafford was built for £60,000 on land in Trafford Park – the huge sum of money coming from a local businessman, a brewer called J.H Davies who had earlier given the club, then named Newton Heath after the L & Y Railway company's main Manchester depot, £500 to build a stand at their second ground, Bank Street in Clayton. (United's first home was at North Road, Monsall where the pitch was apparently in awful condition and the changing rooms were half a mile away at The Three Crowns pub on Oldham Road!). United's last game at Bank Street was a 5-0 win over Tottenham in January 1910, while in their first match at Old Trafford, the following month, they were beaten 4-3 by Liverpool before a crowd of more than 45,000. United won their first Championship there in 1911.

Old Trafford, then as now, attracted huge crowds. Ironically, though, United themselves were not involved in either of the games which drew the ground's largest and smallest attendances. Amazingly, Grimsby Town are responsible for the biggest-ever crowd at The Theatre of Dreams when they played Wolves before almost 77,000 in the 1939 FA Cup Semi-Final. (United's largest home League attendance was in 1920 when just under 71,000 saw the match against Aston Villa).

At the other end of the spectrum, only 13 people paid to watch a Second Division game between Stockport and Leicester at Old Trafford in 1921. Stockport's Edgeley Park ground was closed following crowd trouble and, since they were heading for relegation, their supporters stayed away. There were a lot more than 13 inside Old Trafford though, since about 2,000 watched the match for free after a United match earlier that afternoon.

Old Trafford's location near the Manchester ship canal, built in 1894 to attract ships away from the burgeoning city of United's arch-rivals Liverpool, and its closeness to the key Trafford Park industrial estate was to be a problem for the club during the war. German plans repeatedly carpet-bombed the area in a bid to destroy Manchester's industrial capacity. In March 1941 the inevitable happened when the ground suffered serious damage from two bombs after a Luftwaffe raid on Trafford Park and Salford Docks.

The Main Stand was a burned out shell, the covered terrace on United Road was damaged and the pitch was scorched from the explosions. The War Damage Commission gave United money to clear the rubble and rebuild the stands, but, in the meantime, the Reds had to share Maine Road with Manchester City. That's where the largest crowd ever to watch an English League game showed up: 82,950 for United's game against Arsenal in January 1948.

Ironic, then, that City striker Uwe Rosler should pose before press photographers during the 1994/95 season wearing a T-shirt saying: "Rosler's Grandad Bombed Old Trafford. February 21st 1941". United fans were understandably upset. The first ever United fanzine Red News summed up the feelings among the Old Trafford faithful. "We think that 'prat' is too soft a word for Uwe Rosler – someone who obviously thinks it's great fun to wear a T-shirt celebrating German bombing raids on Manchester. That City supporters could be so sick to produce the shirt is not surprising, but the fact that the Bitter Blue player in question actually wore one for the media cameras leaves a stink as fermenting as any polluted river." The fact that City allowed the press to take the pictures inside Maine Road had added insult to injury.

After the war, United were in debt and paying large amounts to City for the use of Maine Road. But after eight years at their rivals' ground, City asked United to leave. The repairs were quickly finished and United returned to Old Trafford in August 1949 for their first game at the stadium in 10 years against Bolton. This time they won 3-0. But they continued to use Maine Road for midweek European games until Old Trafford's lights were ready for a League match against Bolton in March 1957.

Since 1959, when the Stretford End was first covered, United have continually upgraded Old Trafford and are now building a third tier to accommodate the growing army of fans who want to see them play. The ground's first cantilever stand was built along United Road in 1965 in time for the World Cup the following year when three matches were played at Old Trafford. It cost £350,000 and included the first private boxes ever seen at a British football ground. Since then the cantilevers have been extended several times finishing with the Main Stand in 1985.

I'd been to Old Trafford for the first time the previous season with a former girlfriend who, after picking me up from Stafford railway station, was strangely filled with enthusiasm when I mentioned United were playing Spurs and that, if we hurried, we could just about get there in time for the kick-off. We didn't have tickets but there was no shortage of touts outside the ground willing to part with theirs for about £10 over the odds. After handing over £50 I was the proud owner of two seats for the Main Stand. Oddly, the seats weren't numbered. "Where do I sit?" I asked one of the stewards. "Well, in theory, you can sit anywhere but it's packed today. Try up there behind the press box. You can usually find a couple spare around that area."

Sure enough, just behind the press reporters and radio commentators were two seats together. Former Spurs and Liverpool keeper Ray Clemence was just in front of us commentating for Capital Gold Sport with Jonathan Pearce. Spurs lost the match 2-1 and had Teddy Sheringham carried off after a tackle by Bryan Robson – an injury that wasn't caused by Robson but would keep the Spurs' striker out of action for most of the season. For me, though, the result was secondary to watching a match at Old Trafford for the first time. It was a magical experience – a bit like your first beer or your first woman. Something that lives with you forever.

This time I'd come up by train from London for a midweek match which had been rearranged because of both sides' FA Cup commitments on the Saturday when it was originally supposed to be played. United were battling with Blackburn to secure their third title in a row – a feat that's only been achieved three times in the history of the game by Huddersfield, Arsenal and Liverpool. Tottenham were having a good run and had become a hard team to beat since Gerry Francis arrived from QPR.

The weather had taken a turn for the worse and I arrived at Manchester Piccadilly, the main railway station to the east of the city, in the pouring rain. Commuters were rushing towards the station to get out of the downpour as I made my way towards St Peter's Square which contains the largest municipal library in the world, the luxurious Midland Hotel and the town hall which divides St Peter's from Albert Square to the north.

I wandered around aimlessly looking for a hotel for the night but was having no luck. The attraction of watching Manchester United play Spurs had drawn a large following of North Londoners to the city and the hotels were fully booked. I tried one hotel along a side street off the square. It wasn't the best looking place in town but it was worth a try. The guy behind the desk had the same bad news I'd heard at a number of other hotels in town, "Sorry, but we're fully booked."

I decided to try my luck at a rather grand place called The Britannia Hotel on Portland Street. It was luxurious. A huge crystal chandelier dominated the foyer in front of a sweeping stairway. It looked expensive but they had a special midweek offer. "Do you have any rooms for tonight?" I asked. "Yes, sir. We have a room." "How much?" I asked tentatively, fearing the worse. "It's £80 a night including breakfast." For that money I wanted lunch and dinner thrown in as well. But I had little choice. "What about your special midweek rate?" I ventured. "It doesn't apply today, sir. You see there's a big football match at Old Trafford tonight." As if I didn't know. Previously, I'd booked hotels in advance, but I figured there'd be loads of hotels in Manchester. There were, but they'd been occupied already by North Londoners. At least I had somewhere to sleep tonight.

The Brittania Hotel opened in 1982 after, according to the hotel brochure, "rising out of the ashes of the Lancashire cotton industry's most famous warehouse". The S & J Watts Building, built by Samuel and John Watts, descendants of the first King of England, first opened in March 1858. They envisaged a palace, reminiscent of their heritage, and they realised their dream. This was no theatre, but it was a splendid hotel.

It was built on the site of a cottage belonging to a lady called Bridget Monks whose arm was severed at the Peterloo Massacre in 1819 when a peaceful workers' demo against the oppressive Corn Laws turned nasty resulting in the deaths of 12 people. The demo was organised by the poor who had suffered from Manchester's rapid industrialisation. They had suffered a life of misery. After failing to win in 11 derby matches Manchester City's fans could probably sympathise. At least Mrs Monks recovered!

The Watts warehouse was built in two years and cost £100,000 – an enormous sum in the 1850s. It was the largest trade building in Manchester. The building is Venetian style and each floor has been given a different theme. The granite base is Egyptian; the first floor Italian; the second floor sixteenth century Dutch; the third floor Elizabethan; and the fourth floor based on the Galerie de Glaces at Versailles. A multi-million pound conservation and development project had restored the building to its former glory. And for £80 I was staying there. All I'd wanted was a B &B for the night!

I dumped my stuff, made a quick cup of tea and rushed down to the St Peter's Square Metro to catch a sort of tram-cum-train to Old Trafford. Two young United supporters were already queuing to get to tonight's game against Tottenham. "Do you go often?" I asked them. "Whenever I can," said the taller one. "I always write off for tickets but I don't always get them. They're like gold dust." I felt privileged to have one.

The tram meandered its way through the city past busy streets lined with shops and malls before moving out towards Old Trafford. More United fans climbed aboard as we got nearer the ground. I followed the young lads from the Metro station towards the ground along Warwick Road North past fast-food takeaways and across the railway bridge to the front of Old Trafford. Stalls lined the road selling posters of the team and the players along with scarves, hats, flags and T-shirts.

The first thing you see as you reach the main entrance to the car park is a futuristic neon red Manchester United sign beckoning you to enter the Theatre of Dreams. Beneath it, to the right, is a black and white clock on the wall over the United offices dedicated to those who lost their lives in the Munich air disaster. Further to the right, on the back of the Scoreboard End, is a brass plaque listing the players and officials who died engraved on a football pitch. Even now it makes you choke up inside thinking about how sad it was for the club and the city to lose so many young players.

I walked back across the forecourt, where the United faithful came to pay their respects 37 years ago, towards the busy United shop and its pictures, mugs and replica shirts. I passed the entrance to the suite dedicated to Matt Busby, who took over as United manager just after the war in 1945, and made my way towards the museum entrance. I'd arranged for a tour and was looking forward to it so much I could almost taste it. It was like coming to the home of English football.

A smartly-dressed commissionaire in black uniform and red trimmed peaked cap stood by the door as I entered the coffee shop leading to the museum. I was taken through the shop and underneath the Main Stand, past the stewards and the police who were preparing for tonight's match. On the left was a photographer's booth where you could have your picture taken with any of United's star players. Except they're not actually there for real; you're smiling face is superimposed on a cardboard cut-out. I had mine done with Brian Mclair, who some United fans believe is a cardboard cut-out.

My guide then took me out into the magnificent stadium. The night was drawing in but the seats were empty. The kick-off was still a couple of hours away. "We've spent the equivalent to a million pounds a month on the stadium over the past nine months," said the guide. "It holds 40,000. Just think of the foresight of the engineers in the '60s when it was built. We've been able to add to it and I think it's wonderful that 30 years later we could continue to build right round. They don't get enough credit really."

We emerged from the concourse with its fast food outlets into the fading light that was enveloping the stadium. It's impossible to capture in words the majesty of the place. The magnificent Old Trafford stadium has been called "A cathedral of football" and "A tabernacle of worship". Certainly the loyal supporters who congregate inside the stadium pray for victory at every home game.

On the opposite side of the ground I could see the words MANCHESTER UNITED picked out in white seats from the red ones in the United Road Stand. I could see the tinted glass windows of the executive boxes at the back of the stand, used in Albert Finney's Charlie Bubbles - filmed the year United won the European Cup in 1968.

The film was about a boy taken to the ground to see his heroes, but who finds himself cut off inside the glass box. In those days the atmosphere inside the ground couldn't be heard in the boxes. Nowadays, speakers pipe the crowd noise into them and the volume control determines how loud the crowd is. If there's not much atmosphere you can always turn up the volume to enhance what there is. There are 95 executive boxes at Old Trafford. Those for five people cost £8,200 a season; luxury boxes seating eight people are a staggering £24,000.

Old Trafford's role in the history of the cinema is secure since the stadium has been used in more films than any other British ground. It's credits include Hell is a City starring Stanley Baker and Donald Pleasance from 1960, Billy Liar with Tom Courtenay and Julie Christie in 1963 and The Lovers starring Richard Beckinsale and Paula Wilcox from 1972.

"The security here is very strict," said the guide. "We have 13 security cameras scanning an area within a half-mile radius of the ground out as far as the railway station and the wharf canal. A policeman with a pair of binoculars, called the spotter, keeps watch over the fans. There are three holding cells beneath the stadium: one for women, one for men, and one for teenagers. We keep offenders there during the match."

I looked across to the famous Stretford End, named after the local district, where the word UMBRO and the sports company's logo were clearly visible underneath the floodlights. The Stretford End had been redeveloped and made all-seater for the start of the 1993/94 season. As the guide talked about the features of the stadium a stocky steward with a beard appeared. "He wants to leave you know. He's going," said the steward. "Who is?" said the guide. "Kanchelskis. He's told some of the lads that he wants out. He doesn't get on with Fergie and he wants to leave."

Quite why United's Russian international winger Andrei Kanchelskis wanted to leave was a mystery to me and the majority of Reds supporters. He was apparently unhappy at not being guaranteed a first team place. But, as United's manager Alex Ferguson had tried to explain, nobody had such a guarantee. "Even Cantona is not *guaranteed* a place in the first team," said my guide. At any rate, Kanchelskis was in the team for tonight's match.

The guide then took me to the old tunnel in the middle of the main stand. The players now run out from the new tunnel in the corner where the Main Stand meets the Stretford End, but United had preserved the original tunnel for posterity. "Just think of all the great players who have run out through this tunnel over the years," said the guide. "Best, Charlton, Law and all the others." He explained that the tunnel had a steep slope so they had little choice but to run out onto the pitch.

The guide also told me that nowadays the two teams walked out of the new tunnel together. "The Premier League have asked us to do this so that the away team doesn't get booed by the crowd as they would if the teams came out separately. This way you just hear the cheers from both sets of supporters."

The speakers along the roof around the ground are also used to greatest effect by making sure that any announcements for the away supporters tucked in the corner of the Main Stand and the Scoreboard End are only broadcast through the PA system directly above them. This stops the home fans from booing and whistling to drown out any instructions such as whether the away fans will be kept behind after the match or where they should go to find their coaches.

As we chatted beside the pitch the Spurs players emerged from the new tunnel in their blue and white tracksuits into a largely empty stadium. They walked slowly towards the centre circle inspecting the pitch that they would later grace with their skills. The tall blonde Norwegian international goalkeeper, Erik Thorsvedt was one of the first out, his blonde hair shining under the lights. Teddy Sheringham seemed in a good mood, smiling at Darren Anderton as he crossed the famous Old Trafford turf.

So many visitors come to look around Old Trafford from all over the world that the sign on the edge of the pitch telling people to keep off is in five languages. Unfortunately, the French word defense had been spelt incorrectly.

Next stop was the press room. Former Arsenal captain Frank McLintock and Denis Law were in the adjacent bar chatting along with former United defender Bill Foulkes. It was my lucky night. My guide whipped out his autograph book and asked McLintock and Law to sign. "I'll auction it for charity when it's full," he explained. "I've got Chris Eubank's signature in here as well as the BBC commentary team – John Motson, Des Lynam, Jimmy Hill and Barry Davies." Georgie Best and Bobby Charlton had also autographed his prize possession. "It'll fetch quite a bit of money hopefully".

The main press room was wood-panelled but, strangely, there were lots of holes around the walls where pictures ought to have been. "What happened there?" I asked. "Well, the walls used to be covered in photographs from United's history, you know, George Best, Bobby Charlton and the others. But we had some workmen in here remodelling the press room and they unscrewed them from the walls. They were fastened with spikes as well which are very difficult to remove."

Only one photograph remained above the top table where the two managers and some of the players would sit after the match to answer questions from reporters. "Denis," I called as the former United striker walked past, "any chance of a photo". He duly obliged. "You're tall," he said as I towered over him at six feet two. I wouldn't have wanted to mark him at his peak though!

My guide left me in the United coffee shop and invited me to take a walk around the museum. It was packed with caps, medals, shirts, photographs and trophies recalling United's rich history in both domestic and European campaigns. A Brian McClair Scotland shirt here; a Bobby Charlton cap there; this was nostalgia at its finest. A montage of Sir Matt being greeted with a firm handshake by a United commissionaire welcomes you to the Museum of Dreams. Once inside the place captivates the imagination as memories of great players and even greater games come flooding back.

There's a replica of the European Cup, won in a memorable Wembley final on the night of 29th May 1968 against Benfica. Who could forget that period of extra-time when Best, Charlton, Law and Kidd tore Benfica apart and inspired United to a 4-1 win that took the most prestigious European trophy to England for the first time? (Celtic were the first British winners the year before under Jock Stein.) I was eight years old at the time of the final and was allowed to stay up late, against my mum's wishes, to watch the highlights on TV after listening to the game live on the radio.

But the most poignant item in the place is something that transcends the rest of the memorabilia on show. As you climb the steps to the museum's second floor you come to a special memorial to those killed at Munich. United had started the season leading up to the disaster in devastating form. They were defending First Division champions and favourites to win the League for the third year running. They dropped only one point in their first six games, scoring 22 goals.

The team was so young that they were known as the Busby Babes – though the nickname was first used in November 1951 when Tom Jackson of the Manchester Evening News referred to United as 'The Babes' after two youngsters played against Liverpool. The gradual introduction of more youngsters over the next few seasons led to United becoming known as 'The Busby Babes'.

It was 6th February 1958 when the aircraft bringing the Busby Babes home from their European Cup tie crashed in snow on take-off. Eight players were among the 23 people killed. Among the letters and photographs commemorating that sad day is a telegram sent by the late Duncan Edwards to his landlady telling her that the plane had been delayed and he'd be home late. Edwards made his United debut at the tender age of 16 and his England debut at 18. He was 21 when he died and acknowledged as the finest player in England. Is football really more important than life or death?

It was Bobby Charlton who called Old Trafford the Theatre of Dreams. He should know. He was lucky enough to survive the Munich air disaster and live his dreams along with Best, Law and the rest of the fabulous United team which lifted the League Championship in 1967 and the European Cup in 1968. And just to prove that dreams can come true, the present United side had gone one better in the domestic game by winning the coveted League and Cup 'double' in 1993/94.

But could they have done more? As the race for a third successive title came down to the wire manager Alex Ferguson told his players: "You can win three successive titles. Do you really want it, do you have the desire to do it?... I told them I can't wait on yesterdays' heroes too long. It is not my job to be loyal. My job is to be loyal to the fans. Some of our fans spent half a lifetime – or a whole lifetime – waiting for the League title. They have spent millions of pounds coming to give us the biggest support in the land even when we were not winning."

As I walked up the steps of the Main Stand to my seat I could see a blanket of snowflakes falling in the crisp, cold Manchester night sky.

The two teams walked out onto the pitch together, like they do in the Wembley Cup Final, just as my guide said they would. A red balloon floated across the seats in front of me as I squeezed my way along a row near the front of the stand to my seat amongst the United faithful.

United dominated the opening exchanges. I grimaced every time the Reds attacked the Spurs goal, hoping Tottenham could keep them at bay. United have been known as the Reds, obviously because of the colour of their shirts, since the club was reformed in 1902 after Newton Heath, their predecessors, were put into liquidation. The black third strip used by United in the 1994/95 season was based on the kit originally worn by Newton Heath after the club was founded by railway workers in 1878 as the Newton Heath (Lancashire and Yorkshire Railway) Cricket and Football Club.

Since the 1950s United have also been known as 'The Red Devils'. The name was originally given to the Salford Rugby League Club who made an unbeaten tour of France in 1934. The French papers were so impressed by their performances that they nicknamed the team 'Les Diables Rouges', or Red Devils. Like Salford, United also played in red and thus became known as 'The Red Devils'.

A red devil was added to the club badge in the early 1970s when United, following FA advice to stamp out pirate sellers of goods bearing the club crest, decided to copyright the existing club badge. However, they found they couldn't because it was based on the City of Manchester Coat of Arms and so they replaced the part of the crest showing three diagonal stripes on a red shield with a devil. The two roses on either side were replaced with footballs, but the ship symbolising the Manchester ship canal was kept.

Meanwhile, all around me the home fans were becoming more and more frustrated as United failed to penetrate the Spurs defence. Tottenham were still clinging to hopes of a UEFA Cup place, but for United the prize was ever so slightly bigger – another Championship and a path back into the European Cup. For all their possession, the Reds could not break Spurs down.

Brian McClair was off-form, sending stray passes into no-man's land or being caught in possession, and the crowd began to get on his back. Giggs was frustratingly exciting but ultimately failed to deliver. Hughes tried a few spectacular efforts but couldn't find the back of the net. Cantona was sorely missed. There was nobody pulling the strings to undo a determined Tottenham team which was performing well under Gerry Francis. The match ended goalless.

The loss of two points against Tottenham was one of those games that would ultimately cost United a third title in a row and the chance to emulate Huddersfield, Arsenal and Liverpool. They should have wrapped up the points in the first 20 minutes, but in the end Spurs could have stolen a win in the second half.

The possibility of a second successive double, and the immortality that would go with being the only side ever to achieve the feat, was slipping away. It's hard to imagine any other team coming close to dominating the domestic game in such a fashion. Doing the 'double' once is a great achievement, perhaps doing it twice is an impossibility.

I left the ground as I had arrived, in the rain, and made my way back to The Brittania Hotel on the metro. I listened to the local Manchester radio station on my walkman as I waited for the metro to arrive. Callers, no doubt frustrated by United's failure to beat Spurs, were criticising manager Alex Ferguson's purchase of David May from Blackburn. The host was trying to defend the United boss by saying that even if May was a dud, you couldn't complain about Ferguson's activity in the transfer market since it had mostly been very astute. Besides, City fans had much more to complain about.

The following morning I walked to Manchester Piccadilly to catch the train to work in London. I left Manchester on another of those cloudy with sunny intervals days. The train passed behind back-to-back houses and then moved into a more industrial area. The first stop was Stockport and as we pulled out of the station I could see the football ground on my right. The new stand, which was just a steel frame when I saw the Chester match in early February, now had concrete terracing on the upper tier. Edgeley Park looked like Old Trafford's little brother.

Next stop was Macclesfield - home of the team that was running away with the GM Vauxhall Conference. They wouldn't be joining the elite in the Football League, however, because their ground had not been of a high enough standard the previous December - the deadline arbitrarily set by the League for clubs to meet its ground safety requirements. Macclesfield claimed the ground would be ready for the start of the 1995/96 season. But that wasn't good enough for League officials.

The irony of the situation for Macclesfield was that Chester City, now comfortably settled into their spanking new Deva Stadium on the outskirts of Chester, had shared Macclesfield's ground for two seasons whilst their new home was being built. If it was good enough for Chester to play there then why not Macclesfield? The League said they had changed the rules. There would be no League opening night at this footballing theatre.

LET'S GET BEHIND THEM
Swansea City v Shrewsbury – Vetch Field
17 March 1995

My journey to Vetch Field was delayed by a three-hour meeting with a bunch of lawyers at work. As soon as it ended I dragged my weary body into a taxi and sped off to London's Paddington station. It was a beautiful Spring evening and, apart from feeling very tired, I was looking forward to my visit to South Wales. Swansea were the Second Division form team and had just beaten Birmingham at St Andrews after stubbornly defending a one goal lead with 10 men for the best part of the second half.

One of the fascinating aspects of my travels was finding out the reasons for the various names attached to grounds, stands and teams. At Swansea I discovered that the stadium's strange name, the Vetch Field, relates to the use of the site for growing vetch, a type of bean used to feed cattle. By the time the farmer's field was converted to a football pitch it was covered in cinders and the players had to wear knee-pads to avoid injury.

I collected my ticket and went to find my seat in the main Centre Stand on Glamorgan Street, The entrance for players and officials was tucked away in between the terraced houses which obscure the stand from the road. I couldn't find it at first in the dark, but an official helped me into the ground.

Swansea were just off the play-off spots and desperately needed to beat their local rivals to climb up the table. At Birmingham they were brilliant. At home to Shrewsbury they were mediocre. "They can't play at home. They're frightened," said the supporter in front of me. He was wearing a thorn jacket and black jeans. He was the noisiest one there. "Let's get behind them," he shouted repeatedly. "Come on City," he sang, almost alone. His friends sort of joined in half-heartedly, but without any passion.

As the game drifted towards an inevitable goalless draw this particular fan became increasingly frustrated. "We've got to get behind them," he kept saying. "What's wrong with this lot," he added motioning towards the other supporters in the Centre Stand which was built in 1913 just after Swansea won their first Welsh Cup Final – they've since lifted the trophy another eight times. "You could hear a pin drop here," agreed the bulky Welsh lad next to him. Most of the hard core home fans were in the North Stand opposite. But even their sporadic chants of encouragement began to wane in the second half. "Come on," shouted the noisy fan.

As his frustration increased be began to get abusive, increasing the number of swear words and becoming more aggressive in his criticism of the sullen home fans around him. I couldn't understand why he wasn't standing on the terraces opposite with the other hard core supporters. Why sit in the Centre Stand with the older fans and the youngsters when you could sing and shout to your hearts delight in the North Bank Stand on Madoc Street?

Eventually, after Swansea had let another chance go begging, he stood up on his chair with his arms in the air. He turned to face the Centre Stand crowd and abused them for their lack of support. A big steward in a bright orange coat wearing earphones and a microphone tapped him on the shoulder. "Stop the swearing OK," he told the stroppy Swansea fan. "Well, they've got to get behind them," he answered back. "Yes, but stop the swearing," repeated the steward. "He's right," said his friend. "You've got to stop."

The noisy fan then engaged in a dispute with an older fan behind me. "We've got to get behind them," he said once again. "We'll get behind them when they start playing," said the older supporter wearing the obligatory flat cap. "We've got to get behind them now. What do you know?" "What do I know? I've been coming here for 25 years," said the older fan. "He's got a point," said the younger supporter's friend. "He has you know, if he's been coming here that long."

The impressive Swansea central defender Keith Walker drove a shot inches wide of the near post and that was the closest the home side would come to scoring with the exception of a last-gasp goalmouth scramble when one of their forwards missed an open goal when the ball bounced just over his head at the far post. "They're not good enough to go up," acknowledged the noisy home fan. He'd seen the light at last.

How distant seemed the days when former Liverpool striker John Toshack took over as player-manager and led the Swans from the Fourth Division to the First in just three seasons in the late '70s and early '80s. The late Bill Shankly said Toshack should be given a 'manager of the century' award for what he'd achieved in such a short time.

Swansea's promotion to the top flight for the first time in their history was celebrated with the opening of a new £800,000 East Stand in January 1981, incorporating the club's offices. The stand curves around the south-east corner of the ground towards the old Centre Stand, but should by now have replaced the old stand on Glamorgan Street.

However, the club simply didn't have enough money to build a new main stand.

In the gloom the East Stand looked like something out of Star Wars. The stand looks odd because it only covers three-quarters of the width of the pitch and, at the corner where it meets the Centre Stand, has a huge black floodlight pylon hanging over it like the leg of a spacecraft.

For a brief spell in March 1982 Swansea topped the First Division. I remember listening to a classic match at Anfield when the Swans took a 2-0 lead but were eventually pegged back to 2-2 in a thriller. They'd only rub shoulders with the elite for two seasons. In an effort to keep pace with their First Division rivals the club overspent in the transfer market, culminating in their record signing of Colin Irwin for £340,000 from Liverpool, but with little reward. By October 1983 they were bottom of the Second Division and, more seriously, threatened with closure.

In less than five months Toshack left the club, came back and departed again. Two years after briefly being the best team in the League, Swansea were back in the Third Division. They'd slipped down as quickly as they'd climbed up and by 1986 were in the Fourth Division. Football can be cruel sometimes, ask any Swans fan.

Of course, they'd had their moments. Apart from that brief sortie into the First Division Swansea have reached the FA Cup semi-finals twice - in 1926 and 1964, when they lost to Preston. They also beat Real Madrid 3-0 in 1927. Their most recent triumph was in the 1994 Autoglass Trophy at Wembley when they overcame Huddersfield.

Tonight's match against Shrewsbury was played in a gale-force wind which didn't help the players to put on a classic. The conditions were partly to blame for the dour performance that prevented the Swans moving within a point of a play-off spot. The home side didn't force Shrewsbury keeper Tim Clarke to make a save until the 53rd minute. That sparked Swansea's best spell. Club captain John Cornforth, hoping to win his first cap for Wales against Bulgaria in Sofia a couple of weeks later, almost broke the deadlock with a fierce angled drive that Clarke tipped over.

Shrewsbury, managed by former Cardiff keeper Fred Davies – assistant to John Bond at Swansea a decade ago – were equally lacking in invention. Swansea keeper Roger Freestone, once of Chelsea, only had one save to make in each half. That was hardly the form to enable them to record a fifth successive League win at the Vetch. And they didn't. This was my third match in a row without a goal and meant that I'd seen 270 minutes of League football without the ball hitting the back of the net. To be honest, I'd have cheered if the ball had even trickled over the line. I was cold and tired.

After the match I walked down to the seafront to find a place to stay. The hotels were spread out along the main sea road in a strip, like a mini Las Vegas. The red and green neon lights flashing HOTEL which popped up at intervals among the more low key bed and breakfasts seemed strangely out of place. I half expected to be solicited by prostitutes as I wandered along the seafront. There wasn't much I could have purchased with £12.63 if I'd had either the opportunity or the inclination. The lights were out of character with what was basically an old-fashioned seaside resort.

It was hard to imagine the local football team once hosting the likes of Manchester United and Liverpool. Tonight most of the excitement surrounded the next day's rugby international at the National Stadium between Wales and Ireland. The hordes of Irish fans who'd come over early to celebrate St Patrick's Day had filled all the hotels and B & B's along the seafront. Almost every establishment had a NO VACANCY sign. One hotel covered in neon lights said they might be able to fit me in later if the booking for their double room didn't show up. Meanwhile, my search continued.

Eventually I found a place called the Hotel Glengarrick which had a VACANCIES sign in the window. "Do you have a single?" I asked, slightly desperately. "Yes," replied the matronly lady behind the reception desk. "How come it's so hard to get a room?" "It's the rugby." "Yes, but that's in Cardiff isn't it?" "Ay, but Cardiff is packed tonight, so a lot of supporters are staying in Swansea and will travel up to the game tomorrow." It's amazing how many obstacles a record attempt has to overcome! But at least I had a bed to sleep in – and boyo did I need one.

WIZARD OF DRIBBLE
Stoke City v Reading – Victoria Ground
18 March 1995

There's nothing in the trophy cabinet at Stoke's Victoria Ground to indicate that one of the best dribblers in the game once played for the Potters. But he did, and he was there on a bright Saturday afternoon for the visit of play-off contenders Reading.

Sir Stanley Matthews CBE is today the President of Stoke City. But back in 1933 he was just a promising young winger playing alongside Freddie Steele in a team that brought First Division football back to the Potteries after a 10-year absence and took the club to a runners-up spot in 1946.

One Stoke fanatic named his baby son Stanley Frederick Steele after his heroes. The boy got his own back by growing up to play for rivals Port Vale. The original Steele had almost retired in 1939 suffering from depression, but Stoke sent him to a psychiatrist and he returned to score 10 goals in five games. If anyone knows who his psychiatrist was please let me know!

Stan left Stoke for Blackpool and the road to the highlight of his career: the Matthews Final at Wembley when his wizadry helped Blackpool to a famous 4-3 FA Cup win over Bolton (see Blackpool vs Birmingham). But he returned in 1961, aged 46. Manager Tony Waddington paid a bargain £35,000 to bring the 'Wizard of Dribble' back to the Potteries to play alongside Jimmy McIlroy and Dennis Viollet.

Matthews put 30,000 people on the gate at the Victoria Ground and helped his old club back to the First Division in 1963, playing in 36 out of their 42 League games! The star-studded team of has-beens and cast-offs had the highest average age in the Football League. But their experience was invaluable. Stan was 50 when he played his last game for the club.

Some people claim that Stoke were formed in 1863, but a more plausible date is 1868 when workers at the local railway formed Stoke Ramblers. But there's no doubt that they were one of the original twelve Football League clubs in 1888 and the second oldest League club after Notts County. Stoke have also been based at the same ground longer than any other British club – since 1878.

Until Stoke's League Cup win over Chelsea in 1972 (2-1: Eastham and Conroy) Matthews was their only claim to fame. Sure, they won the Second Division (North) title in 1927, and the Second Division

Championship in 1933 and 1963. And they'd had some great players. Gordon Banks, a key part of that League Cup winning team, had been a legend between the posts for six seasons from 1967 until a car crash resulted in eye injuries that ended his career. He was succeeded by another England great, Peter Shilton, while other stars to have worn the red and white stripes include Geoff Hurst, Adrian Heath, Garth Crooks and Mark Stein.

But the club had failed to add any silverware since the League Cup apart from the Second Division title in 1993. According to the magazine Four Four Two, "For too long, the club's rich history has been sold criminally short by the poverty of its achievements". They'd enjoyed some success under Lou Macari in his first spell at the Victoria Ground. He led Stoke to the Third Division Championship and victory in the Autoglass Trophy after a miserable spell under Mick Mills and Alan Ball which resulted in relegation to the Third Division for the first time since 1927. But Macari was now struggling to repeat the trick second time around.

The jewel in the Stoke trophy cabinet thus remains the tankard inscribed with League Cup Winners 1972. I remembered how when I was 12 years-old I'd tossed a coin with another lad in our school team to see who'd get the ticket one of our mates had for the final at Wembley. I lost and he went. I got to Wembley the following year to see Tottenham play Norwich, when Ralph Coates scored the only goal for Spurs in one of the most boring League Cup finals in history.

I remained bemused by the fact that there was nothing in the Stoke boardroom to celebrate Sir Stan's achievements. I'd seen one of his England shirts and a few caps and medals on display at a shopping centre in Stoke the year before. "Hasn't he donated one of his cap's or a medal or something?" I asked a club official. "No, I don't think so. But as President he comes to most games. He was here today." Still, I thought, there should have been something from the great man apart from the bronze bust which stands proudly inside the club's main entrance .

I'd driven to Stoke from a morning game at Hereford and arrived just in time for the kick-off. The Potteries are widely known as 'The Five Towns', but the city of Stoke-on-Trent is actually made up of six large towns which stretch for about eight miles along the A50. The joining together of the towns of the Potteries in 1925 to form the new corporation of Stoke-on-Trent persuaded Stoke to add 'City' to their name.

The two main towns are Stoke and Hanley. Stoke has suffered at the hands of its neighbour, which stands a mile to the north, since Hanley has all the main shops and the civic museum. Most people forget about Fenton, but usually remember the other three towns: Longton, Tunstall and Burslem - the home of Port Vale.

The district around Stoke-on-Trent has been Britain's main pottery centre for 400 years. A Toby Jug of Matthews, part of a series commemorating Britain's great footballers and which I was to come across in the Blackpool club shop later in the season, was made in Stoke by Wedgwood - just one of the companies, along with Royal Doulton and Spode, which gave the area its worldwide reputation.

The Potteries flourished because of the Staffordshire coal needed to fire the wares rather than because of the local marl clay. In the 1800's the area suffered from pollution and the countryside was ruined by colliery spoil heaps, marl holes and piles of broken crockery. But the main problem was the smoke from the chimneystacks and bottle kilns of the 'pot banks'. Electric firing has since replaced coal, the bottle kilns have almost gone and much of the industrial wasteland has been turned into parks.

A series of recessions have hit the pottery industry, leaving Stoke with a slightly neglected feeling - a bit like the football stadium which sits behind the motorway link road and the River Trent. Stoke City's Victoria Ground is named after the Victoria Hotel which stands opposite. During the Second World War the Butler Street Stand, built in 1935, was used as an army camp. Nowadays the only army is the red and white variety on the terraces.

The process of modernising the Main Stand on Boothen Road, a narrow street overshadowed by the Boothen Stand, began in 1960 with the first part of a three stage rebuilding plan. The final stage coincided with the club's promotion to the First Division in 1963 when the players were offered a shilling an hour over the summer to help lay the concrete for the terraces! To the right is the Boothen End, like the Boothen Stand named after the local district.

The River Trent passes by the ground a few yards behind the corner joining the Boothen End and the Butler Street Stand. The foundations of the old roof in the south-west corner of the Butler Street Stand were actually sunk deep into the river bed. The Trent is narrower here than when it passes Nottingham Forest's City Ground and Notts County's Meadow Lane stadium opposite because Stoke is closer to the river's source a few miles north of the Victoria Ground east of Vale Park in Burslem.

The two-tier Stoke End Stand on Lonsdale Street was opened in 1979, but the most recent change was the installation of 25 executive boxes in the Butler Street Stand. The problem is that the Victoria Ground has to be all-seater by August 1996 to meet the conditions of the Taylor Report. Stoke have twice failed to get planning permission for a supermarket to be built at the Victoria Ground and have even gone so far as to consider a groundshare scheme with rivals Port Vale at a new stadium. But redevelopment of their home ground is the most likely outcome.

How Stoke needed Stanley Matthews' wily skills on the wing today. Another defeat - this time by a single goal - had left City struggling near the relegation zone. Indeed, Macari would have been grateful to have any of Stoke's galaxy of stars at their peak. Freddie Steele, Stanley Matthews, Gordon Banks, George Eastham, Jimmy Greenhoff, Geoff Hurst, Peter Shilton, Jimmy Greenhoff, Sammy McIlroy, Adrian Heath, Lee Dixon, Steve Bould, Mark Stein. The list is almost endless.

The latest 'star' to appear in the famous red and white stripes was Paul Allen. I'd seen the former Spurs and Hammers midfielder sitting in the stands at Southampton when he was recovering from injury. Allen then popped up at Luton where he was making his debut on-loan. Now he was just finishing a two-month loan spell at Stoke. Current Stoke manager Lou Macari hadn't made him an offer, so the second youngest player ever to appear in an FA Cup Final was hoping another club would buy him before the transfer deadline.

"Being at Stoke has been like a breath of fresh air for me. I've played regular first team football, built up my match fitness and enjoyed being part of the action again. I don't know what the future holds. ...if I need to move to guarantee continued first-team football, then that's what I would prefer. I've no axe to grind with Southampton, but I think it's going to be difficult for me to re-establish myself there.

"Alan Ball (then the Southampton manager) came in and made it clear he wanted to lower the age of the side and, being the other side of 30, I wasn't going to fit into his plans. I had talks with Southend earlier in the season about a permanent transfer, but I felt that was not the right move for me at this stage of my career. Now, though, I am ready to listen to any offers."

"Coming to Stoke was the first time I had played my football in the north and it's opened my eyes, If the right club came in for me now, the geography would not matter." And I thought the north was places like Sunderland and Blackpool! Isn't Stoke somewhere in the Midlands? Let's hope Allen's knowledge of geography is better on the pitch. At least he should have had no trouble finding the Victoria Ground since you can't miss it from the motorway link road!

SING WHEN WE'RE FISHING
Grimsby Town v Sunderland – Blundell Park
19 March 1995

"If you want to win this division, you've got to come to places like Grimsby and win," according to Middlesborough manager Bryan Robson. "I'd rather play for Grimsby," screamed the headline on the back of The News of the World quoting Paul Gascoigne, who'd just fallen out with Spurs in a dispute over a tax bill. A young couple on The Big Breakfast, who couldn't answer five simple questions to win a holiday in Guadeloupe, were offered a luxury weekend in Grimsby as a consolation prize. They turned it down.

Stuart Holland, writing in the Leicester fanzine The Fox was terrified of relegation in the 1994/95 season, but not because his team wouldn't be playing at Old Trafford or Anfield. It was more who they would be playing that frightened him. "I just feel that a club like Leicester should have more ambition than to play Grimsby...on a regular basis...the alternative to survival is too horrible to contemplate."

And what about the Grimsby fans themselves? How do they see their town? "You can always raise a laugh at any social event by saying either, 'I was born in Grimsby' or 'I'm a Grimsby Town supporter," says Town supporter Keith Wivell. "Saying both together, however, does not give them twice the effect. You tend to get a quick smile followed by some patronising remark implying that you require some sort of treatment."

So is there anything actually wrong with Grimsby, the fishing town on the north-east coast at the mouth of the River Humber? The Mayor doesn't think so. "Grimsby's a damn sight better than the Caribbean. You can't buy fish and chips in Guadeloupe or watch Grimsby Town," he says. Whether you'd actually want to is another matter. Anyone conjuring up a mental picture of the place would definitely think of fish though.

Grimsby has been a fishing and trading port since the eleventh century and is still England's main fishing port today. The Royal Docks were constructed in the early 1850s and are dominated by the Victoria Flour Mill, built in 1906, and the Dock Tower of 1852 – modelled on the Town Hall clock tower in Sienna, Italy and the tallest brick building in Lincolnshire. The docks are mostly lined with the warehouses of the local frozen food companies. But business isn't booming anymore – the size of the catch has fallen sharply in recent years. That partly explains Grimsby Town's struggle to attract supporters. Many just don't have the money to watch football as they try to make ends meet.

Not that the club is short of ideas. On the day of the Sunderland match there was a special initiative to get more local children into the ground. Any Grimsby or Sunderland fan could take in two kids under 16 for free. The offer was also to compensate the supporters for what happened the previous year. "The corresponding fixture last season was postponed due to torrential rain after just six minutes and therefore as a gesture of goodwill to both sets of fans we wanted to introduce a special scheme for all supporters," said Grimsby spokesman Steve Wraith. "We have also extended the offer to Sunderland fans in an attempt to show our appreciation to them for making the journey to Grimsby. Hopefully the weather will be better this time."

It was, but only just. In fact, the weather was as variable as the match. Any self-respecting BBC weatherman would have put up one of those clouds with the sun peeking out from behind and described the day ahead as cloudy with sunny intervals. Outside the ground two young lads were pleading with supporters queuing for tickets to let them come in for free. One had dark hair, long on one side of his head and short on the other side. He was wearing a black and white striped Grimsby shirt down to his knees. The other lad was shorter with ginger hair and freckles. They both had a cheeky look and could easily have come straight from Fagan's band of thieves in the film Oliver.

"Please can we come in with you?" said the dark-haired one with the cheekiest grin. "We can get in free with an adult and my dad's had to go to work." Grimsby's Family Day had certainly attracted the local children along with the Yorkshire television cameras covering the game for the 'live' Sunday match. They'd brought the cameras but not good weather.

Fifteen minutes into the second half the rain came pouring down. The wind also swept across Blundell Park, making it difficult for the players and miserable for the Sunderland fans in the partly covered Osmond Stand to my left, most of whom were getting soaked. But worse was to follow. The rain gave way to snow, then sleet. Suddenly it stopped, and late in the match the sun came out again. I'd experienced the sort of weather the fishermen have to put with in Grimsby.

My seat was in the Main Stand and to get to it I'd had to walk around the ground from the front. The stand is on Harrington Street beyond which lies open land leading down to the sea. There are two parts to the stand. To my left was the newer section built in 1931, but I was sitting in the original stand which was put up in 1901, without foundations, and is the oldest surviving stand at any League ground. The roof is very uneven along the gutter and the wooden roof supports are angled like a treetop. It's a miracle the thing is still standing. But standing it is and I was grateful for the shelter it offered on a wet, blustery day.

Out on the pitch a motley group of young boys and girls were posing for photographs in front of the Family Stand before taking part in a penalty competition. One little lad looked so tiny in his almost miniature black and white striped Grimsby Town kit that his socks almost met his shorts above his knees. He wasn't having much luck with his penalties since he didn't have the strength to reach the goal with his little legs. The older lads had better fortune but even they were struggling to score many goals. The fans of both teams did their bit to support the youngsters.

The Grimsby fans behind the goal at the Pontoon End, named after the docks, cheered the loudest. They're renowned for a dance resembling the canoeists in the title sequence of the television series 'Hawaii Five-O' and for waving inflatable haddocks on the terraces. Rival fans call them 'codheads'. But these supporters don't resent their fishy connections, they revel in them – and they have a sense of humour to boot. Not for them an attempt to play down their seafaring roots. Every football town has its hallmark. Rochdale has Gracie Fields, Stoke has it's pots, and Grimsby is blessed with, well, smelly fish. Now if there was a choice maybe 'Our Gracie' would be preferable but there are some things in life you have to live with and in Grimsby it's fish.

Take Harry the Haddock for instance. He swam into the nation's consciousness during Grimsby's 1989 FA Cup run when, as a struggling Fourth Division side, they knocked out First Division Middlesborough and Reading before going down 3-1 in the Fifth Round to Wimbledon where Harry made one of his first appearances. The Grimsby fanzine Sing When We're Fishing says Harry is a forename of "deep, mystic significance" at the club. If you want to sound authentically local, by the way, you should drop the 'H'.

Grimsby's 1989 FA Cup performances were just a little better than their first appearance in the competition in 1882 when they were drawn at home to the mighty Glasgow club Queen's Park. When the Scottish team withdrew Town got a bye into the Second Round and a tie against a Rotherham Works team called Phoenix Bessemer. They lost 9-1!

The 4,000 seater Findus Stand in Grimsby Road, which towers over the rest of the ground, was built with the help of the local frozen fish company Findus. It contributed £200,000 towards the £425,000 needed to build the stand in 1982. The building work took longer than expected because every time a bore hole was drilled for the foundations it filled up with water from the sea barely a few hundred yards to the west. The stand doesn't quite run along the entire length of the pitch and there is a section of open terracing on either side. The upper tier is separated from the standing area below by executive boxes opened in 1984 and today it also includes a restaurant and offices.

The FINDUS name is picked out in white seats against a black background and can be clearly seen by ferry passengers on the Humber River when the weather is clear. The view from the Findus Stand across the roof of the Main Stand opposite is captivating. If the game is boring the fans sitting high up in the Findus Stand can watch the ships sailing up and down the Humber River. The North Humberside peninsular lies ahead, while to the right you can see Spurn Head at the tip of the Estuary. The town belonging to arch rivals Hull City is off to the left but too far away to see even on a clear day.

The fishy theme runs throughout the club. The black and white nets in each goal were originally donated by a local fishing net company. Even the chant most frequently heard on the terraces is "Sing When We're Fishing". The refrain was modified by the travelling Sunderland supporters behind the goal in the Osmond Stand after Grimsby had taken the lead in the 32nd minute. Town's number nine Steve Livingstone picked up a through ball from midfield, turned inside the 18-yard box and slotted a precise shot past Sunderland keeper Tony Norman. The home fans sang, "Down with the West Brom, you're going down with the West Brom" to which the hordes of Rokerites in their red and white shirts in the Osmond Stand away to my left responded, "Sing when you're fishing, you only sing when you're fishing".

Grimsby had only recently lost their successful manager Alan Buckley to West Brom. Despite taking the Mariners from the obscurity of the Fourth Division to mid-table respectability in the First, Buckley had not got the crowds flocking back to Blundell Park. The average home gate was still less than 6,000. Fanzine contributor Phil Ball believes this was partly because Buckley didn't really understand the town. So what is it that makes Grimsby different to similar coastal towns around Britain?

"If you want to get the crowds back, you have to understand the Grimsby area," says Ball. You have to understand that the place has a special psyche, a weird cut-off sort of identity that you only find in places like Barrow-in-Furness or Penzance. We only want characters to represent us, not pretty football."

"If you come from Grimsby, or Cleethorpes, you spend the best part of your life as a figure of fun. What is most important about being from this area is that we hate the rest of the world because it's always taking the piss out of us. We need to feel that the personnel of Grimsby Town Football Club understands this and goes out onto the field of play with the appropriate attitude. We are the most proudly parochial people on the planet. We still swoon if we get a mention on the telly, or if one of the quality papers deigns to mention us. The football at Town has to reflect how we are here, how we regard the rest of the world from out of our special shell."

Grimsby fan Phil Ball was in San Sebastian, Spain when he heard the news of Buckley's departure "I pick up the phone, only to hear my mother announce gravely across the miles. "I've got bad news." My mind races. The dog's pegged it? She's written me out of her will? Mother takes a deep breath: "Alan Buckley's resigned and gone to West Brom."

The fans wanted local heroes John Cockerill and Paul Futcher, the former Luton and Manchester City defender, to be given the job. They were put in charge temporarily, but Grimsby opted for youth and eventually chose former Nottingham Forest defender Brian Laws. Former Chelsea, Aston Villa and Nottingham Forest utility player Kenny Swain, Laws' teammate at The City Ground, was appointed as number two. The depth of feeling against the change was summed up on the front page of the fanzine which ran the headline: 'Local Haddock Resigns as Town Mascot for Several Minutes'.

Futcher's reaction was predictable. He resigned. Cockerill stayed on as youth team coach. Fanzine editor Steve Plowes explains the local reaction. "We loved Futch and Cockers; fans would applaud when Futcher bent down to lace his boots. Then Laws appeared in a suit, and in Grimsby we don't trust people in suits." If Buckley didn't understand the area is there any hope of Laws becoming more integrated into the Grimsby 'psyche'? The initial signs weren't good. One of the main changes he made in his first few weeks in charge was to take fish and chips out of the players' diet!

This is Laws first taste of football management. But the former Forest full-back is the latest in a long line of very accomplished managers to begin their careers at Blundell Park. Bill Shankly was in charge for a couple of seasons in the early 1950s before moving to Huddersfield and then Liverpool, and Lawrie McMenemy was in the hot seat from 1971-73, the last year being when Bob Stokoe steered McMenemy's beloved Sunderland to a famous victory over Leeds in the FA Cup Final. Despite the managerial talent at their disposal over the years, Grimsby Town have never won any major honours.

The fanzine included a roll call of the club's "accomplishments" inside the front cover. Relegated to Division 2: 1903, 1932, 1948. Relegated to Division 3 (South): 1920. Relegated to Division 3 (North): 1951. Relegated to Division 3: 1959, 1964, 1987. Relegated to Division 4: 1968, 1976, 1988. Thrown out of League: 1910. Applied for re-election: 1955, 1969. Ejected from Grimsby: 1898. Reappeared in Division 1 by administrative fluke: 1992. Free transferred a goalkeeper who got a star rating of 10 on his first appearance for Oxford: 1992.

In truth, Grimsby have had some, albeit modest, success. They won the Second Division Championship in 1901 and 1934, the Third Division (North) title in 1926 and 1956 and were Fourth Division Champions in 1972. (The last success was not altogether welcomed by one supporter who had promised to run naked around his firm's yard if Grimsby were promoted; he did and was presented with a special certificate by Lawrie McMenemy.) They reached the FA Cup semi-finals in 1936 (losing 1-0 to Arsenal) and 1939. In between they reached the 5th round in 1937, drawing with Wolves before a record crowd of 31,657 at Blundell Park before going out in the replay. And, last but least, won the League Group Cup (whatever that was) in 1982.

Grimsby goalkeeper George Tweedy made his first appearance for the club in that 1939 FA Cup semi-final against Wolves in front of a crowd of 76,962 at Old Trafford on 25th March. Grimsby remains the team that has attracted more fans to Old Trafford than any other. Tweedy's debut lasted only 23 minutes before he was carried off with concussion after diving at the feet of Wolves striker Dickey Dorsett.

There were no substitutes in those days so Town played most of the match with 10 men and lost 5-0. The Mariners had dominated the first 20 minutes and when Wolves scored from what many thought was an offside position in the 32nd minute it was against the run of play. Indeed, Town had played remarkably well since they were down to nine men at one stage. Wolves lost 4-0 in the final to a Portsmouth team which finished seven places below Grimsby in the League. The money earned from the cup run was used to build the Osmond Stand – named after a local family.

The Town team of the '30s and '40s was briefly among the best sides in the country with a fifth place finish in the First Division and those two cup semi-finals. It was the Golden Age for Grimsby Town Football Club. Jackie Bestall, who has a street named after him in Grimsby, and Ernest (Pat) Glover, scorer of 42 goals in the 1933/34 season, were the star players in those days. More recent discoveries include Garry Birtles and Paul Wilkinson.

Since the glory days the supporters have become so used to a diet of football mediocrity that they naturally look towards the bottom, rather than the top, of the League table. With Grimsby seventh in the First Division and battling for a play-off place, which they failed to achieve, the fans were still talking about escaping the threat of relegation. "I keep thinking another three points and we won't go down," said fanzine editor Steve Plowes.

Just before Grimsby scored a man sitting behind me with his sons called across to the woman on the other side of the gangway and shouted, "What have the kids down wrong?" She stared back looking puzzled. "I just wondered if you'd brought them here as a punishment," he explained.

The fans' natural pessimism goes back a long way. Blundell Park started out on three miles of boggy turf on the coastal approach to Grimsby. Like The City Ground in Nottingham, Blundell Park is not based in the town that bears the team's name but is actually in nearby Cleethorpes. The ground takes its name from a Peter Blundell who, in 1616, left money to Sidney Sussex College, Cambridge, The college used the funds to buy the manor of Itterby, including land which would be named Blundell Park in honour of Pete, whoever he was. As to why Sidney Sussex College, Cambridge was buying land in Cleethorpes, that's anyone's guess.

I was sure the fans behind the goal in the Pontoon Stand didn't know, or care for that matter. Their main concern was a win for Grimsby and a place in the play-offs. Five minutes into the second half Sunderland's Craig Russell had run through the middle of the Grimsby defence, twisting and turning past two, then three, defenders before laying the ball to Steve Agnew on the edge of the six-yard box. Agnew took the ball in his stride before planting it into the corner of the net. The Sunderland fans ran onto the pitch to celebrate and two of them were caught by stewards and led away by the police. "We are Sunderland, say, we are Sunderland," they sang.

After 27 minutes Grimsby took the lead again when Livingstone scored his second with a header. With the home team back in control a group of about 50 youngsters, including the cheeky chappy who had asked to accompany us into the ground, ran along the terraces in front of the Findus Stand towards the Osmond Stand containing the away supporters. They took up a position on the open terracing beside the Findus Stand and began chanting at the much bigger contingent of Rokerites to their right. The Sunderland fans looked at the rabble, most wearing their designer Grismby shirts, and sang, "What the fucking hell is that? What the fucking hell is that?"

Then the police moved in. They formed a line behind the Town fans and after a few more chants the youngsters ran back along the paddock and round into the Pontoon End where they merged with the rest of the home fans. I wondered if they were scared of the Sunderland supporters or were worried about the police presence. Whatever the reason for their retreat they obviously felt they'd achieved something in the bravery stakes by goading the away fans – albeit from the safety of the Findus Stand. I was sure they didn't do it for the exercise, though I didn't doubt after an hour and a half on the terraces they were probably as frozen as the fish fingers sold by their benefactors.

But they'd all go home happy today. Late in the match on-loan signing Jamie Forrester from Leeds capped a fine performance with his first goal for the club to make it 3-1. Here was one young man who was definitely happy to be in Grimsby. What's so great about Guadeloupe anyway?

MIKHAIL GORBACHOV'S TEAM
Wigan Athletic v Hereford United - Springfield Park
29 March 1995

Wigan Athletic. Former Soviet President Mikhail Gorbachov's team. You think I'm kidding? Gorbachov came to Springfield Park with a Russian team in his younger days when he was an official at the club. He took a liking to Wigan and has followed them ever since. His passion is such that he's said to have ordered the unscrambling of radio broadcasts from Britain so he could listen to the BBC World Service football coverage on Saturday afternoon's and track Wigan's progress.

Wigan found out about Gorbachov's interest when someone connected with the Latics saw an article in the Straits Times newspaper at a hotel in Singapore. He was so intrigued that he brought a copy of the paper back to the club's directors. They contacted the Russian Embassy in London who knew nothing about it (well, what did you expect?). But Wigan decided to invite the then Soviet President to Springfield Park. He never came back again, but the Latics have since hosted a number of Russian teams and have also played in Russia. The last team to visit was Moscow Torpedo.

There was a black and white china football in the boardroom at Springfield Park from a Russian team. It had a tap on the front for pouring out the contents. Vodka perhaps? The boardroom also contained a model of a Hereford cow, a gift from Hereford to commemorate Wigan's first match back in the Football League in 1978 - 57 years after their predecessors, Wigan Borough, became the first club ever to resign from the League. Wigan gave a miner's helmet with an engraved inscription to every League team they played that season to mark the occasion. The result of that first match against Hereford was 0-0 and it has since been long forgotten, but the cow remains.

Tonight's match against Hereford was my second attempt to see Wigan play at home. It was also my 35th birthday which meant that I'd never forget this particular game for the rest of my life – If anyone ever ask me 'Where were you on the night of your 35th birthday?' I'll remember instantly. Springfield Park; Wigan 1 Hereford 1.

Back in January I'd travelled to the ground for a game against Hartlepool but it was postponed because of a waterlogged pitch. I was given a quick look around the ground anyway, since I'd travelled all the way from London. Springfield Park was very spacious with plenty of room for development if the club decided to invest in the ground. There was talk of a move to the outskirts of town and a new leisure complex with cinemas, sports facilities and two pitches – one for rugby and one for football. So far that's all it was – talk.

The football club would just rent the ground and there would be little they could do to generate much-needed profits from other activities. For a small club like Wigan off-the-field revenue is very important and so the chances of a new ground being built under those circumstances are probably thin. More likely are steps to upgrade Springfield Park.

There's only one major sport in Wigan, as I learned from the taxi driver who picked me up from the station, and that's rugby. The rugby club regularly attracted 20,000 or more fans to their ground, while the football team struggled along on gates of about 2,000. With today's postponement Wigan had only played one home game in over a month. Since the home team now takes all the revenue from League games (but not the FA Cup where non-league clubs get a 50 percent cut of the gate receipts and League sides take 40 percent) Wigan's income had been badly hit.

"We've still got to pay the players' wages and other expenses," said one director, "but nothing has been coming in through the turnstiles in gate receipts. It's a problem for a small club like ours." My problem was where to go from Wigan to see a game of football on a very wet and windy day which had wiped out half the league fixtures, mostly in the South. "Why don't you go up to Preston, they're at home today?" said one of the directors. Another director gave me a lift back to the station in his Range Rover and I was soon on my way to Prenton Park, the home of Tom Finney (see Preston v Mansfield).

As I waited on the station platform I was asked by a Manchester University student if the Wigan game was off. "Yes," I replied. "Waterlogged pitch. Do you follow Wigan then?" "Yes, I'm from Wigan. I get back here most Saturday's to see them play." The conversation turned to Andy Lyons, their Blackpool-based winger signed from Crewe. If the game had been played Lyons would have made his 50th appearance.

He was born the year England won the World Cup, had only missed eight games since his £15,000 transfer 15 months before and was a favourite with the fans. They named him as their Player of the Year in 1993/94 after a season in which he was the club's top scorer with 11 league goals. Lyons had already notched six more in 1994/95 including his first ever hat-trick in the 4-1 win over Darlington at Springfield Park in November. The student boarded his train back to Manchester and I got back to reading the Wigan programme. Imagine my surprise when I looked up to find a freshly-showered Lyons waiting on the platform with his kit bag for a train.

He was disappointed the match had been called off. "I hate it when this happens. You know, you don't go out on Friday night and you psyche yourself up to play and then it's called off. " Wigan were struggling near the foot of the Third Division and needed all the points they could get, but a last minute goal at Mansfield the week before had cost them the match. Simon Farnworth, their keeper, was at fault with the goal.

"We came back from 3-1 down with nine men and thought we'd got the draw, but then our keeper made a mess of a save on the line and Mansfield won," said Lyons. "Simon was really upset about it afterwards in the dressing room. Still, what can you do? If you make a mistake in midfield it's nothing like as bad. Being in goal is a difficult position because if you make a mistake that's it." And so it was against Mansfield.

"Are you still in the FA Cup?" I asked. "No, Altrincham beat us," said Lyons. "I suppose it was a giant-killing," he added with a wry smile. The difference between the top non-league teams and those at the bottom of the Third Division was not that great.

"It was one of those days when we did everything but score. The ball hit the post and rolled across the line from one side of the goal to the other and then to safety. We also hit the bar. And their keeper played out of his skin. It was one of those days when we were never going to score." And they didn't, losing 1-0. "We would have played Tottenham in the next round too," said Lyons, licking his lips at the prospect of a clash with the Premier League side. "It would have been a bumper gate."

The biggest matches Lyons had played in all season were the two-legs of the Coca-Cola Cup Second Round match against Aston Villa. Wigan lost the first leg 5-0 at Villa Park and the second leg 3-0 at Springfield Park. "Anytime we looked like we might get back in it they just stepped up a gear. They were able to raise their game to a whole new level. It was frightening. Still, just to be out there with all those great players was an experience. It's a different world in the Premier League. The stadium, the facilities, everything. Their players were in the bar after the match and they all had mobile phones," said Lyons, hinting that you couldn't really afford one on Third Division wages.

Wigan had enjoyed better times in the FA Cup in January 1980 when they beat Chelsea at Stamford Bridge in the Third Round with a goal from Tommy Gore, one of the Liverpool-born members of the team. They wore a Liverpool-style all-red strip on the night described by their

Scottish manager Ian McNeill as the "greatest win in Wigan's history". They went on to play Everton at Goodison in front of the biggest crowd of the Fourth Round (51,863) and lost 3-0. It was the first time they'd got that far.

It's almost every young boy's dream to play professional football, but even when you achieve that status you can still be a million miles away from the big time. The Sky cameras just don't come to places like Springfield Park, unless there's a big cup match. If they did they'd have to negotiate a series of narrow streets to find a 14-acre site, mostly used for parking in front of the main entrance to the ground.

In the '20s the stadium was used for horse trotting, a popular sport, and there was a cement cycle track around the pitch. The terraces were covered in the '20s at the Shevington Road End and on the Popular Side in St Andrew's drive. The Main Stand, about 50 yards long and which straddles the half-way line, was rebuilt in 1954 after a fire gutted the original stand. Wigan is also one of the few clubs in the lower echelons to have installed executive boxes.

I suppose the hopefuls on the playing fields of England don't envisage turning out for a team in a place like Wigan with its reputation as a typical northern manufacturing town. It's one of the oldest Lancashire boroughs with a population of almost 80,000 and stands on high ground above the River Douglas between Manchester and Liverpool. It was once a major centre for coalmining with the first pit begun in 1450. By the late 1800s there were over 1,000 pit shafts within five miles of the town centre. The coal, some 250,000 tonnes a year, powered textile mills in Liverpool and Wigan itself. When the reigns of coal and cotton ended in the 1900s the town diversified and now includes a huge Heinz factory which produces much of the country's canned food and sauces. The company sponsors the club's family enclosure.

The town is probably best known for the old joke about Wigan Pier made popular by the Wigan-born music hall comedian George Formby Senior and recalled in George Orwell's study of industrial depression in the 1930s The Road to Wigan Pier. For over 100 years the Pier, which stands at the basin of the Leeds and Liverpool canal south of the town centre, was the hub of industrial Wigan; its sidings, warehouses, loading bays and barges were all busy with coal and cotton. After those industries declined the Pier became derelict, but in the mid-'80's was totally renovated.

A visit to Wigan Pier today enables you to "come face to face with the people from 1900 as they live and struggle to survive. See life below ground and feel the horrors of the Maypole Colliery disaster. Let us take you into an era once ruled by the twin kings of cotton and coal with an unforgettable journey into the great age of steam. Now fully restored we can show you one of the great glories of industrial Lancashire – Trencherfield Mill which provides the home for the world's largest working mill steam engine. The 2,500 horsepower engine is steamed daily."

You can still visit the seaside and see the end of the pier show, but conditions at the turn of the century didn't sound that great for most people in Wigan . "At one end of the scale there is poverty, disease and suffering caused by squalor. At the other end the rich merchants and mill owners whose wealth was provided by the workforce." It could almost have been a description of the gulf between the Endsleigh League Third Division and the Premier League!

Wigan Athletic were known as 'the finest non-League club in the North' when they were in the Northern Premier League. A non-League match against Southern League Hereford drew their largest-ever crowd of 27,500 in 1953. But they became the League's newest members in 1978 when, after a recount, they were elected in place of Southport with their 35th application for membership! For years the town was best known for its rugby league club, but now they faced competition from the Latics. They were promoted to the Third Division in 1982 and won their only cup, the Freight Rover Trophy, in 1985. But they were relegated in 1993 to the new Third Division.

Andy Lyons knew all about playing in the Third Division, though not today. I said goodbye to Lyons, a really nice bloke, and we went our separate ways. He switched platforms to get a Blackpool train; I made my way out of the station to catch a taxi to Prenton Park – one of only 17 League grounds staging any football at all on a very wet Saturday afternoon. Most of the countryside on the train ride north was water-logged so it was hardly surprising so many games were off.

ONE STANLEY MATTHEWS
Blackpool v Birmingham City – Bloomfield Road
4 April 1995

"There have been many, probably too many, who have been tagged 'great' in my time, but there is only one Stanley Matthews." These are the words of Jimmy Armfield, himself one of the 'great' players and a club colleague of Matthews during his Blackpool days. Armfield made 568 League appearances for the Seasiders and was capped 43 times at full-back for England, both club records. He knows all about Stan.

Matthews is now the President of Stoke City and the undisputed 'King of the Potteries' but his fame comes from Blackpool, where for 14 years he dominated the seaside town on the north-west coast of England almost as much as the famous Tower or the Illuminations. His finest moment in a tangerine shirt was against Bolton in the 1953 FA Cup Final, a match named after him long before a ball had been kicked at Wembley.

I travelled to Blackpool, 'famous for fresh air and fun', looking forward to seeing the Tower and the Illuminations, with its half-a-million light bulbs, that decorate the promenade. But I was more excited about delving into the legend that was Matthews.

The 500-foot Tower, built in 1894, was disappointing. An inferior copy of that other tower in Paris. The Illuminations were, well, far from illuminating. "They don't start until September and they end in November, except for a brief reapperance at Christmas," said the receptionist at the Pembroke Hotel on the seafront, (Blackpool claims to have more hotel beds than Portugal!). Apparently, the autumn is the best time to come, when the ancient, wooden trams are cleaned up and wheeled out again to carry passengers from the Tower to the South Pier. Blackpool is the only town in England which did not abandon its tram system.

Like Southend in Essex, it's a typical British seaside town. The leading resort in the north-west and one of the most popular in the country, Blackpool began to flourish when the railway arrived in 1840. The Wintergardens, with its barrel-vaulted ballroom, and the Grand Theatre were built for the first wave of tourists. The downmarket attractions came with "open air dancing for the working classes" on the Central Pier. The town became a popular venue for 'Wakes Weeks' when whole Lancashire mill towns took over the place for their annual holidays.

Blackpool is now famous for its Golden Mile of piers, fortune tellers, amusement arcades and bingo halls. The new Sealife centre, where you can see eight foot sharks circling above you as you walk through a glass tunnel, also pulls in large numbers of visitors. At the Tower World Theme Park you can ride up to the top of the famous landmark or visit the Edwardian ballroom, the aquarium or the circus between the Tower's legs. But the 40-acre Pleasure Beach theme park, which includes the world's tallest roller coaster, is the main attraction.

The Louis Tussauds Waxworks opposite the Central Pier includes an adults-only anatomy section (the mind boggles), whilst the three nineteenth century piers are jammed with amusement arcades and theatres for has-beens who are slipping down the popularity scale.

Sixteen million people come to the town every year and the football club hopes to attract many of them to its planned leisure complex, as well as pulling in new punters who perhaps wouldn't have come to the town at all. The club's swimming pool should be welcome since a dip in the sea was not recommended until the new sewage system was finished. The Sandcastle opposite the Pleasure Beach was the only place you'd really want to swim since the water was kept at a pleasant 29 degrees centigrade.

Despite my disappointment with the Tower and the lights I couldn't see, I still had Stanley Matthews to fall back on. Thankfully, Stan's legend didn't let me down. Blackpool's club shop was selling a framed pencil-drawn montage of Stan's great days, personally autographed by the 'wizard of dribble', for £99, and a limited edition (5,000) Toby Jug of Matthews in Stoke colours with his football boots skilfully moulded into a handle for £19.95. The 'unwashed' socks he wore in the '53 final were displayed in the oak-panelled chairman's room. And the quaint, old-fashioned press room was covered in black and white photos of Stan's Cup Final appearances. But his wizardry lived on most of all in the memories of almost everyone I spoke to in the town.

Blackpool were a top class team when Matthews wore the tangerine shirt which was famous all over the world. Football supporters everywhere know the names of Mortensen, Johnstone and, of course, Matthews. Everyone in Blackpool who was old enough had seen him play; to them he was simply the best

"He had this knack of pushing the ball forward to invite the full-back to make a tackle and then, as soon as the defender had committed himself, Stan was gone," said the balding middle-aged man with the beer belly sitting next to me with his son in the original Main Stand at Bloomfield Road. It was the night of Blackpool's promotion battle against Birmingham. "Stan was very quick over short distances and that's what made him great. You'd often see him on the beach running or doing exercises."

He recalled seeing Matthews in the late '50s alongside Stan Mortensen, the Blackpool Bombshell, in a testimonial match at Bolton's Burnden Park for England colleague Nat Lofthouse. Other fans I spoke to had seen Stan play at Wembley in one or other of the three FA Cup Finals the Seasiders contested between 1948 and 1953. Not one had a bad word to say about the man. "He comes back to see us every season," said a club official. "The people here welcome him with open arms. He loves the club and we love him. There will only ever be one Stanley Matthews."

The supporters speculated about how good Stan would have been if he was playing today. "The game's too quick now. It's like playing ping-pong. Stan would have got lost in the melee," said one elderly man who'd first watched Blackpool in 1908. "I'd be worried about him nowadays. They come flying in with their tackles and they're so fast that he'd have probably been injured all the time," said another life-long fan in his '60s.

But was Stan really that good? "Other football legends such as Pele, Finney, Di Stefano and Charlton really bring magical memories back as well but with Matthews there was a sort of mystique that made him different," said Armfield, now a BBC radio commentator. "...he had a ruthless streak. Once he got on top of an opponent he showed no mercy. He could taunt defenders almost like a matador with a bull. He was totally confident. It was all down to his fanatical drive for physical fitness that was superior to other footballers."

"In Blackpool he went down to the beach at eight o'clock every morning where he did light jogging, exercises and, just as important to him, deep breathing. He came to the ground and trained with the rest of us as well. His fitness level was never in doubt, even when he was past 40. He didn't smoke or drink and he experimented with health foods long before any other athlete had even considered them. Carrot juice was on the Matthews menu, although I can also recall when he would purposely go on a fast and start to build up for his next game with salads and light meals."

Matthews has never lost the will to train alone and still works out today. Armfield believes that's probably what made him better than all the rest. "Stan took great pains so as not to disappoint his public. Whenever we played we knew that Stan would be the focus of attention. We knew, as well, that there were critical eyes on him – many waiting and eager to write him off. He disappointed the cynics, as he wasn't like other footballers who start to worry about the future when they pass 30. Incredibly, even after retiring, he told me he thought he had gone out too soon."

Armfield broke into the Blackpool team as a teenager in the mid-50's and, incredibly, within a couple of seasons found himself on the same salary as the great man. Armfield had potential but it was yet to be fulfilled; Matthews was the greatest footballer in the world. There was, however, one small difference in their pay. Stan got £20 a week all through the year, while Armfield got the same during the season but £2 less in the summer. A rush of blood to the head led him to ask Blackpool's tough manager Joe Smith why he didn't get paid the same. "Because he's a better player than you," said Smith. Armfield thought for a moment and then said, "Not in the summer he's not".

Many said Matthews was too much of a loner, but it was lifestyle rather than personality that made him seem aloof. Very few people could live with his values or follow his strict fitness regime. "He was a great man to have in the dressing room," said Armfield. He lifted everybody with his presence. He was full of humility; there was never any edge on him as he realised that the next match was the one on which he would be judged – it was something I never forgot."

Stan first played for Blackpool as a guest during the War when he was stationed in the seaside town. He eventually joined the club for £11,500 and a bottle of whiskey in 1947. Joe Smith, then manager of the Seasiders, said that's what it cost to persuade the Stoke board to release him. But he'd really been stolen from under their noses at that price after failing to re-ignite his career in the potteries after six years of War. It took off again like a rocket at Blackpool and only fizzled out in the early '60s.

Stan was the first winner of the Player of the Year award in 1948, helping the Seasiders reach their first FA Cup Final. They lost 4-2 to Manchester United. In 1951 Blackpool got back to Wembley where they played a Newcastle team spearheaded by Jackie Milburn. They lost 2-0. Matthews was 38 years old. Today his chances of having another crack at winning the cup would have been almost non-existent. How many Premiership players are older than that?

But Stan was far from finished. He believed he'd get another chance. Everybody wanted him to get another chance. And in classic fairytale tradition he did. It was Coronation year and a time to celebrate. When Blackpool reached the final again everybody in the country, except the Bolton fans, wanted Matthews to pick-up a winners medal. The Post Office had to make special deliveries to Bloomfield Road to carry the huge volume of letters wishing Matthews success at last.

In a Wembley classic the Seasiders came back from 3-1 down to win 4-3. Mortensen was one hero, scoring the only ever hat-trick in an FA Cup Final. But it was Matthews who stole the headlines. Stan caused havoc down the Bolton left in the last half hour and laid on the winner for Bill Perry. That was to be his finest performance in a tangerine shirt. He came closest to a League Championship medal in 1956 when Blackpool were runners-up to Manchester United. In 1961 Stan left Bloomfield Road and returned to his roots, rejoining Stoke for £35,000.

Blackpool's flame flickered briefly after Matthews' departure when they reached the League Cup semi-final in 1962. But they were relegated from the old First Division in 1967. The Seasiders bounced back in 1970 but their comeback only lasted one season as they finished bottom – a sad ending to the career of Jimmy Armfield. The club has remained outside the top flight ever since and, after relegation again in 1978, has spent its time in the bottom two divisions. The glory years of the late 1950s are nowadays just a fading memory.

Relegation to the Fourth Division in 1981 was bad enough, but the ultimate humiliation for this once great club came in 1983 when it had to apply for re-election. Blackpool were threatened with liquidation and had to sell their best players over the summer while collection boxes were taken around the local pubs and clubs to help keep the team alive.

Blackpool's decline is reflected in the ground at Bloomfield Road. The stadium is still virtually the same as it was before the Second World War. I left the Pembroke Hotel, which lies to the north of the ground, on a sunny spring evening for the short drive along the seaside to the stadium. The Birmingham players had been driven up in their team coach that morning and had eaten a light lunch of pasta and salad at the hotel before making their way to Bloomfield Road. I asked the receptionist what she thought of the Blues players. "Arrogant," was her reply. 'Tense' may have been a kinder way to describe them since they desperately need the points tonight in their bid for the Second Division Championship and, more importantly, the automatic promotion spot.

You can't miss Bloomfield Road, and there's certainly no doubt that it's the home of Blackpool FC. The club's name is spelt out in huge tangerine letters across the front of the Main Stand. I'd written to the club the previous May and received a reply from Managing Director Gill Bridge – one of only two women in such a lofty position in the Premier or Football League. The other, of course, is Karren Brady,

Managing Director of tonight's visitors Birmingham.

Gill Bridge had been in charge of off-the-field matters for more than a year. Along with Brady, she is the most powerful woman in British football. The two had met briefly the previous New Year's Eve when Blackpool were hammered 7-1 at St Andrew's, but Brady was unable to attend tonight's game because of commitments at the office. "It was nice to meet Karren, but we did not treat each other any differently," said Bridge. "We may be the only two female managing directors but there are a lot more women who are taking a stand in football and are being appointed in top positions."

Bridge, 28, has fought for her rights in the male dominated world of British football. She's had to cope with the embarrassing situation of being shown to the ladies' room while other top executives are taken into the boardroom. "I have been ushered to the ladies room and have had to say, just a minute, I'm a director - they assume I'm a wife of a board member. But I can understand the mistake if they've never seen a woman in the boardroom before. I actually find it quite amusing."

There aren't many clubs which still have ladies' rooms, but Bridge has still come across serious rows about boardroom etiquette. "The vice-chairman at Blackpool is Vicki Oyston and she won a battle against Tranmere Rovers when they wouldn't allow her into the boardroom because she was female. They did relent eventually but it shows that prejudices are there and have to be tackled.

"Men do automatically think you don't know what you're talking about on any aspect of football. And as a woman you can be scoffed at a bit. But it's much easier now than it was 12 months ago when I first became managing director. I think Karren's paved the way for me and I am glad she was the first woman because she had a lot of barriers to break down and that's made things easier for me. She had a tremendous job to do, but, as I've found, once people get to know you and realise you know what you are talking about, they respect you.

"It's very hard work working for a football club; the hours are as required, and that includes Saturdays, and so that means a six-day week. But it's satisfying to watch the match at the end of a hard week's work, especially if we win the game. I have been married for four years and I am lucky that my husband, whose job is unrelated to football, is very understanding and accepts that I work long hours. And no, he's not jealous of me working with so many men. He's no need to be, and besides, he enjoys watching a game of football himself so he's quite often with me."

A profile of Gill and Karren in the Birmingham Evening Mail before the New Year's Eve encounter said they wouldn't be discussing "the January sales' bargains, marriage or babies". Besides, Gill had no immediate yearnings for children; she was enjoying her job too much to give it up to raise a family. And she certainly had a job on her hands at Blackpool.

One pressing need was to build a new stadium. At the moment a visit to Bloomfield Road is like stepping back in time. I felt lost without my flat cap, woolly scarf and rattle, not to mention my bicycle! A sign along the back of the West Stand reads: "Please dismount your bicycle within the ground".

My tour started in the all-wooden Main Stand where I would sit to watch the match. It was built at the turn of the century and still had the original wooden seats. The Stand was like a timber merchant's yard. There were signs everywhere warning you to stub out your cigarettes. And no wonder. A lighted match would be enough to set the whole structure ablaze as happened at Bradford's Valley Parade. Of course, there are differences – mainly the fact that rubbish hasn't been allowed to accumulate underneath the stand. But the place is still like a tinder box.

The uncovered Spion Kop was built after Blackpool's promotion to the First Division in 1930. From the South Stand at the opposite end of the ground you can see the Blackpool Tower to the left of the Kop. Thousands of seaside visitors get an aerial view of the ground every year from the top of the north-west's most famous vantage point. The tower view explains why the West Stand roof is covered in advertising.

The South Stand houses the club's offices and dressing rooms. It was very colourful with its orange seats, orange and white woodwork and orange pillars. The stand cost £131,146 when it was built in 1925. In the corner between the South and West Stands was a tiny upper tier stand, like a little directors' box, at an angle to the pitch. The view from this small box was superb. Its balcony wall was fronted by an ad for "ASHWORTH'S PIE... HERE TODAY. Pies from the very finest traditional recipes." Just the job for a half-time snack. Then again...

Next was the boardroom with its panelled walls. The oak cladding was taken from Lord Nelson's flagship Foudroyant. My guide took up the story. "Nelson sailed into Portsmouth for repairs then the Battle of Trafalgar came up and he transferred his flag to the HMS Victory, sailed and was killed. His favourite ship, the Foudroyant, lay at Portsmouth for many years. Then they decided to make it seaworthy, which they did, and in the early 1900s there was a big naval exhibition on at the Clyde shipyard. When they were toeing her along near Blackpool there was a force 10 gale, the toe path broke and she was wrecked and came ashore by the North Pier. The Blackpool chairman approached the receiver of wrecks and purchased all 15 cabins and installed them here in the boardroom. So this is real history."

Birmingham chairman David Sullivan, owner of The Daily and Sunday Sport newspapers, popped his head around the door before the match. "This is a bit of alright," he said copping a load of the historic boardroom and its trophy cabinet. Stanley Matthews' unwashed socks from the '53 final took pride of place in the cabinet. "I had them until 1987, which was the club's centenary, and I thought they had more right to them than me so I brought them back," said my guide. The cabinet also contained pennants presented by some of the famous teams Blackpool played in the '50s and '60s including Verona, Roma, Barcelona and Santos.

A larger room next to the boardroom contained a smaller trophy cabinet including a huge trophy called the Lancaster Football Association Challenge Cup. Another cabinet contained the Marsden Cup – the oldest in the world according to Blackpool – and the Manchester Football League War Cup from the 1942-43 season when Blackpool beat Arsenal 4-3.

The walls of the press room were covered in newspaper cuttings, most from the great days of Matthews and Mortensen. It was like going back in time. There were no television screens here; no faxes or mobile phones; no plug in points and modems. This was living history. I would have loved to have heard all the stories written and talked about in that room over the years. Soon it would be consigned to the past. There was talk once more of a multi-million pound project to build a new stadium.

The owner of Blackpool Football Club, Owen Oyston had recently announced plans to redevelop the ground into a sports and leisure complex to be called the International Colosseum. Like Luton's blueprint for their so-called 'Kohlerdome' stadium, Blackpool plan to use revolutionary hovercraft technology to move the pitch from a 20,000 seater main stadium to a second arena, allowing the club to maximise revenue from other events. Oyston hopes to build the 6,000 seater 'secondary' stadium to the north of the Spion Kop on the Rigby Road car park next to the new North Stand.

Luton's technology aimed to move the pitch within two to three hours. Blackpool aimed to move their playing surface within an hour to free the stadium for other events on the evening of an afternoon match. "It will also mean that, as the depth of the support structure for the pitch is three metres, there will be additional seating installed at this lower level for a whole range of events, including basketball, tennis, hockey and ice hockey," said Oyston.

The main stadium will have an all-weather sliding roof, 96 executive boxes, a glass-fronted restaurant overlooking the pitch, fast food outlets at every level, shops and kiosks around the stadium perimeter, a television and radio studio, a museum and a hall of fame. The complex will include a 200-bedroom hotel with 117 balconied suites overlooking the pitch and concert areas, conference and exhibition facilities for 1,000 delegates, a business centre, a leisure suite with a 25 metre swimming pool, a squash court, a fitness and sports injuries centre, two restaurants, a pub, themed and traditional bars, shops, kiosks, an atrium reception and landscaped car parks.

The second stadium, a top-class venue in its own right, would be used for reserve team games, exhibitions, functions, special school events, amateur football and other community events. It would also help resolve the parking problem since the pitch will be on a raised structure with room for up to 500 cars underneath. It will be a "top-class stadium in its own right" said Oyston.

The 'two stadia' concept employing hovercraft technology is already in use in Hawaii where stadium grandstands weighing 1800 tons – twice the weight of the Seasiders' pitch – are regularly moved.

According to Oyston the Colosseum will "create the necessary revenue and environment to support our aim to reach the Premier Division". It will "enhance the prospects of Blackpool Football Club becoming one of the world's leading sports and leisure complexes... It will also improve the overall infrastructure and attract large numbers of visitors to Blackpool all year round, thus having a substantial impact on the local and regional economy."

So-called 'impact' studies had shown that in the first full year an extra one million people would be attracted to Blackpool and would spend approximately £120 million. The stadium is expected to take two years to build and will create about 1,000 construction jobs and up to 1500 jobs when the development is finished. "We firmly believe this unique development will act as a catalyst for the whole of Blackpool and the region as we move into the 21st century, guaranteeing a future greatness commensurate with its past greatness," said Oyston.

One problem though. Where will Blackpool find the millions needed to build the new complex? "Owen Oyston will provide some of it and the rest will come from sponsors like those," said an official in the club shop pointing to a list of club sponsors on the wall at the back near the main office. I still couldn't believe they'd raise enough to fund such a grand development, even with help from the Football Trust.

After the tour I walked around the ground along the back of the East Stand, known locally as the 'Scratching Shed'. It was full of colourful advertisements telling visitors about the town's attractions, including the tower. The back brick wall of the Spion Kop was full of fading blue paint and was a reminder of football just after the War. The Birmingham fans arriving for the game blended in well with their blue and white scarves – unlike the last time they came to Blackpool and rioted along the seafront. Aware of the possibility of trouble, Blackpool had made the match all-ticket with none available on the night.

That seemed to do the trick since there was not a hint of trouble. The crowd were warmed up by the Tangerettes, Blackpool's answer to the Dallas Cowboys cheerleaders. Actually, they looked very smart in their orange tops, white shorts and shoes. They waved their white pom-poms in time with the music and put on a good show for the punters. One girl, in particular, was a real stunner – born to break the hearts of all the teenage guys in Blackpool. She had brown eyes and dark brown hair and a gorgeous figure. She had good rhythm, too, as she swivelled around with her pom poms. She was almost as big an attraction as tonight's opponents.

I looked up at the empty Kop, which was closed tonight, and imagined being there in the '50s when Matthews and Mortensen ran out in their baggy shorts to the cheers from supporters in flat caps and woolly scarves waving their wooden rattles. I was brought back to the '90s when the two teams came out onto the pitch.

The Tangerettes made a human tunnel with their outstretched arms for the Blackpool players to run under. "Seasiders, Seasiders," they chanted as they shook their pom poms in the air like huge snowflakes. The crowd cheered as each player's name was announced over the tannoy. The Birmingham fans sang "7-1, 7-1, 7-1," reminding the Seasiders of the score the last time they met. "Do what, Do what, Do what, Do what, Do what," responded the home fans behind the South Stand goal to my right.

It was a beautiful spring evening by the sea. All the little boys and girls were down by the brick wall at the front of the Family Stand where I was sitting. The orange and white seats in the stadium added to the colourful setting. But Birmingham ruined the carnival atmosphere when they scored after about 20 minutes. "Get in first; give 'em a good kicking," said the Blackpool fan in front of me. He looked a bit like the Toby Jugs they were selling in the club shop.

At half-time a gorilla wearing a Blackpool kit came onto the pitch and started trying to kick plastic footballs into the crowd. He failed the first few times, much to the amusement of the crowd, but eventually got the hang of it. The Birmingham fans applauded when he managed to kick a ball in their direction. Meanwhile, the cheerleaders had returned for another show in the centre circle. Suddenly, the music died on them and the away fans started booing. I felt sorry for the girls, none of whom was older than about 17. They were trying their best and deserved encouragement.

The second half began and Birmingham were soon on the attack again. Their six feet eight inch striker, Kevin Francis, recently signed from Stockport, tried a shot but miscued completely. "His legs look like they're too long for him," said one Blackpool supporter. The Seasiders equalised in the second half to the relief of their fans. But the Birmingham players weren't happy. They needed the points for their promotion drive.

As they left the pitch the Birmingham number six squared up to the Blackpool fans in the Family Stand. I thought he was about to launch himself into the supporters a la Cantona, but his team mates quickly came over to drag him away. I couldn't believe it as he stood there in front of the home fans shouting, "Come on then, come on then". He was spoiling for a fight and was clearly frustrated that the Blues hadn't secured all three points. Not the sort of end to a fine evening's football that you want to see.

Fortunately, for millions of football fans, thoughts of Blackpool turn to Stanley Matthews. What did it mean to Jimmy Armfield, who'd been reporting on tonight's match, to play with the maestro? "...the name still conjures up something magical to me and I suppose that when I look back on my career with Blackpool and England I still feel that one of my greatest honours was to play behind the great Stan for six seasons. He was to football what Fred Perry was to tennis, Len Hutton to cricket and Henry Cotton to golf. Self-taught, they were the people's champions – there was an aura about them that presented professionalism and clean living and Englishmen everywhere loved them." A shame you can't say that about too many of today's footballers!

LIFE AND DEATH
Liverpool v Southampton – Anfield
5 April 1995

"I know that I had the best dad in the whole world and I'm proud of that. Thanks Dad. Love and miss you very much. Pat."

"A true Koppite joining those so tragically killed at Hillsborough. Rest in peace Bob. Your loving wife and children."

"Terry you are so very precious to me. I will always love you. Sandra."

"Happy Birthday Grandad. All our love. Gareth and Ben."

These were just some of the dedications among the flowers laid beneath the Anfield Memorial to those who lost their lives so tragically at Hillsborough on 15th April 1989. The dead were aged between 14 and 67 years old. Tommy Anthony Howard, Eric Hankin, Paul Brown, Lee Nichol and Adam Edward Spearritt were the youngest; Gerard Baron (Snr) was the oldest. The names are listed in alphabetical order from Jack Anderson, who was 62, to Graham John Wright, 17.

The everlasting flame in the middle of the marble stone was burning brightly on a damp night in Liverpool before a home League match against Southampton. Bill Shankly used to say "Football's not a matter of life and death. It's much more important than that." Here was clear evidence, if any were needed, that his maxim was patently untrue. Nothing is more important than life itself.

It was heartwarming to see the mementoes from rival fans lying among the wreaths. A mini 'We Follow Bolton Wanderers' scarf; a copy of The Gooner fanzine signed "From all at the Arsenal". They bore testimony to the links between supporters around the country. At the end of the day it's just a game. It's as well to remember that amidst the clamour for success in modern football.

Next to the Memorial stands the famous Shankly Gate, topped with the words to the title of the famous song 'You'll Never Walk Alone', dedicated to the former Liverpool manager. It was here that supporters tied scarfs and laid flowers in the wake of Hillsborough. "The saddest and most beautiful sight I have ever seen," said then-Liverpool manager Kenny Dalglish. Supporters have to pass through the gates to reach the Main Stand.

Anfield may now be a Red fortress standing proudly on top of the hill overlooking Stanley Park and the home of arch-rivals Everton across the park at Goodison but it was once the Toffeemen who played at Anfield. Everton even won their first Championship at Anfield. But a row with their landlord, John Houlding, saw them move to Mere

Green, later Goodison, in 1892.

Houlding set up his own club and wanted to keep the Everton name, but the Football League ruled against it so he chose Liverpool FC. That name was then challenged by the local rugby union club so he settled on Liverpool AFC. Today few people even know that it was once the home of the team in blue across the park.

I drove up to Anfield with my son Lyle on a wet Wednesday night from Chester to the south of the city. The M53 took us past Ellesmere Port where there was a big Vauxhall factory and then past container ports where various goods were being unloaded along the River Mersey. Then came the Eastham oil terminal, Birkenhead – the home of Tranmere – and the Queen's Ferry.

Liverpool fans were drawn to Anfield from all around the area. I'd already seen a father and son in their red and white Liverpool scarfs getting ready to travel to the game from Chester. It was a pretty drive through farmland and rolling hills. Bright yellow daffodils also lined the route along the motorway.

I turned underneath the two-and-a-half mile long Mersey Tunnel, also known as the Queensway Tunnel, which was built between 1925 and 1934, and made my way towards the city, past the Wallasey docks with its cranes lined up along the river. "If one city in England could be said to stand as a symbol of a nation in decline it would be Liverpool," says The Rough Guide. "One of the country's main transatlantic ports and the Empire's second city, it's associated now with resilience to adversity."

"For years Liverpool has lived with poverty and mass unemployment, but nothing has broken its extraordinary spirit of community, a spirit that emerged strongly in the aftermath of Hillsborough... when the deaths of 95 Liverpool supporters seemed to unite the whole city. Acerbic wit and loyalty to one of the city's top-flight football teams are the linchpins of the Scouse culture – though Liverpool makes great play of its musical heritage... reasonable enough from the city that produced the Beatles."

Liverpool, supposedly named after the famous Liver birds, was built on trade. Until the 1700s it was just a fishing village (hard to believe, I know). But when the docks at Chester silted up and the slave trade started booming Liverpool began to take off as a port. The first dock was built in 1715. Weapons, alcohol and textiles were traded for African slaves who were then taken to the Caribbean and America. The ships returned with sugar, cotton and tobacco.

When slavery was abolished in 1807 the port continued to expand west into neighbouring Bootle, eventually becoming a chain of docks stretching for several miles either side of Pier Head along the Mersey. They not only handled freight but also emigrants leaving Europe for the Americas and Australasia. Nine million people left Europe between 1830 and 1930, but some only made it to Liverpool and the city grew five-fold in 50 years.

Immigrants from the Caribbean, China and Ireland, particularly after the potato famine of 1845, helped to create a melting pot from which Liverpool Football Club draws its support today. The urban decay which followed was partly due to the demise of the docks and Liverpool's role as an Atlantic seaport.

The docks fell into decline from the 1950s when cheap air fares hit the lucrative liner business, trade switched from the Empire to Europe and into South-Eastern ports like Tilbury, Harwich and the home of today's visitors, Southampton which also became prominent as a passenger port. And more of the goods now came in containers, which also hit the demand for dockers.

New residential, office and shop developments are gradually replacing the urban decay that followed the rise in unemployment and poverty that followed the decline in the docks. The restoration of the Albert Dock, with its shops, restaurants, offices and museums, has also sparked the rejuvenation of some of the more than three miles of idle dockland south of the city.

But the area around Anfield remains relatively run-down. Portsmouth fans claim that they penned the words to the version of 'My Liverpool Home' first heard in the early 80s which begins: In your Liverpool slums. Not that Liverpool Football Club can be accused of lagging behind in redeveloping their Anfield stadium in line with the Taylor Report. Sums of £8 million to redevelop the Centenary Stand, £9 million to rebuild the Kop and another couple of million for a second tier on the Anfield Road Stand shows the club's commitment to providing their fans with a first class ground.

Indeed, Anfield was chosen as one of the eight venues for the European Championships, to the chagrin of the Blues across Stanley Park. The club conducts tours of the stadium and the museum. "An Absolute Must for Every Football Fan or Visitor to Merseyside" says the club. "At Anfield, the image of success is a shining one, as befits one of the most famous and successful football clubs in the world... follow in the footsteps of Bill Shankly and the hundreds of legendary players over the years."

I was aiming to do just that before the match against the Saints. I began in the historic Anfield Museum and Trophy Room. The place is a cornucopia of footballing memorabilia from one of Bill Shankly's Scotland caps (he won five) to the boots worn by Billy Liddell, the Scottish-born winger known for his sportsmanship and his role in the Liverpool team of the 40s and 50s who were nicknamed Liddellpool.

There was also a telegram from Dixie Dean, the famous Everton centre-forward, the shirt worn by Ian St John in the 1965 FA Cup Final and a shield presented by the Football League to commemorate Liverpool's achievement in winning three successive League titles between 1981-82 and 1983-84 – matching Huddersfield, Bill Shankly's former team, in the '20s and the Arsenal team of the '30s.

Liverpool have never been outside the top two divisions. They have won a record 18 First Division championships, four European Cups, four FA Cups, four League Cups, the UEFA Cup and the Super Cup. They are the only team to win three major trophies in one season (the League title, Milk Cup and European Cup in 1983/84). No other British club has appeared in more European competitions. They are, quite simply, the most successful British club side ever.

The trophy room is full of their achievements and you need hours to take it all in. A more animated record can be seen in a 15-minute video on the history and "phenomenal success" of Liverpool over the years. Then you're allowed to venture behind-the-scenes to "places you'd previously imagined". A journey through the inner sanctum along backroom corridors to the players' lounge, where they relax after matches, past the treatment centre and the referee's room.

"Your imagination and senses start to go wild as the tour enters the players dressing rooms." Well, that's what the brochure says! "It's nearing kick-off and time for that final team talk before taking to the field for this all-important match. It's no time for nerves. You need to be strong. We need a good result.

"Now the time has come to walk down the tunnel to the pitch, following in the footsteps of many great reds over the years – not forgetting to touch the famous 'This is Anfield' sign on your way down for luck, as is traditional. Let your imagination take over, hear the crowd start to cheer as you emerge from the tunnel."

I took my seat in the Centenary Stand, opened by Lennart Johanssen, the President of UEFA in the summer of 1992, the club's centenary year. It used to be the Kemlyn Road Stand, but was renamed after a second tier was added. The car park behind the stand had replaced the row of houses which were demolished to make way for the new development.

It had turned into a beautiful spring night and the drizzle which had dampened the city earlier in the evening had disappeared Out in the middle of the pitch on the centre spot stood a small table. The Coca-Cola Cup sat on top. It was the perfect stage for the Liverpool team to parade the trophy they'd won the previous Saturday at Wembley by beating Bolton 2-1.

I felt like I'd been transported back to the Beatles-inspired '60s before the match as the DJ played a Mersey Beat song and then the Anfield anthem 'You'll Never Walk Alone' by Gerry and the Pacemakers. "As you walk through the storm, hold your head up high..." was reverberating around the stadium as the crowd joined in the singing. The noise was deafening as the Liverpool players came out onto the pitch.

They lined up in the middle of the park and saluted the crowd. Then the players held the cup aloft before saluting the Kop away to my left. The most famous stand in football came alive with flashes as the fans took pictures of their heroes down on the pitch. "They've brought the trophy back where it belongs," said the announcer. Liverpool's former England international defender Phil Thomson was on the pitch to lend a hand in the proceedings. The Reds' boss Roy Evans stood on the stayed on the touchline, leaving his players to take the applause of the crowd alone.

As I'd discovered on my travels, several stands around the country had taken on the name of Spion Kop. They were mostly mounds where the most fanatical fans stood to watch their team. But this was the most famous of them all – even if Arsenal claim to have had the first Kop. The name comes from Spion Kop, the hill in South Africa that was fought for by British troops, mainly from regiments in Lancashire, many of whom came from Liverpool, against Boer forces in January 1900.

More than 300 soldiers died in the attack on the hill including many of those from Liverpool. The Liverpool Kop got its name at the suggestion of journalist Ernest Edwards, sports editor of the local Post and Echo, as a tribute to those who died. Spion Kop actually means 'lookout' in Afrikaans and is therefore an appropriate name for a stand behind the goal.

The first Kop was built in 1906 when Liverpool won their second Championship. In 1928 it was extended, taking the capacity to 30,000, and had a roof put over it. The Kop wasn't as impressive as I'd imagined and nowhere near as colourful as it was on television in the days of swaying crowds, flags and scarves. The atmosphere wasn't that electric either. There were two reasons. First, it was all seated and that had definitely reduced the noise level; secondly, the fans weren't allowed to take flags into the ground because the sticks used to wave them around were considered dangerous. My son had to leave his flag outside, much to his disappointment.

The Southampton fans sat away to my right in the Anfield Road Stand with its seats of orange, ochre, violet red, green and cream – so different from the red seats around the rest of the stadium. The multi-colours were chosen deliberately when former Liverpool boss Bob Paisley complained after watching a reserve match that his players were almost invisible in their red shirts against the red seats originally installed at that end of the ground.

Bruce Grobbelaar was returning to Anfield for the first time since his free transfer the previous summer with match-fixing allegations hanging over his head. That didn't stop the Anfield faithful chanting his name as the 37 year-old keeper came out to warm up. He'd been a hero at Liverpool for 13 years, helping them win 13 major trophies.

The Saints took the lead after 14 minutes through Richard Hall after Grobbelaar's successor in the Liverpool goal, David James, could only palm out a Matt Le Tissier corner. The away fans went barmy at the Anfield Road End, singing their theme tune 'When the Saints Go Marching In'.

Liverpool were obviously still celebrating their cup win and suffering a hangover and Southampton's goal had quietened down the celebrating home fans. Rush soon revived their spirits, though, with a free header just before the half hour for his 16th goal of the season. It seemed that the players had heeded demands from Evans to keep their feet on the accelerator after their Wembley win after all.

The Kop gave Grobbelaar a rapturous reception as he took up his position between the posts for the second half. The larger-than-life keeper responded by blowing kisses and bowing to his once-adoring fans. "It was a great welcome and just what I expected," he said after the match. "It was lovely," chipped in the then-Saints manager Alan Ball.

In the second half the referee gave a decision against Southampton which the Saints fans clearly disagreed with. "Who's the Scouser in the black?" they sang accusingly. Shortly afterwards, Rush put Liverpool ahead with a 25-yard left foot shot that beat Grobbelaar after a deflection off Hall. The Zimbabwean international keeper should have saved it and the Kop saw their chance for some fun. "Who's the Scouser in the yellow?" they sang at Grobbelaar. Even he could see the funny side of it.

In the 70th minute Jason Dodd brought down Liverpool substitute Mark Walters, a replacement for defender Stig Inge Bjornebye who'd been carried off on a stretcher after breaking his left leg. Robbie Fowler put away his 29th goal of the campaign from the spot. "Evans, Evans, Evans," sang the home fans. They were clearly delighted to see the Reds canter to another win.

After the match I took the lift down to the hospitality suites beneath the Centenary Stand. The walls of the Bill Shankly Suite were lined with pictures of the great man and photos of the teams he'd steered to success. Shankly had a successful playing career with Carlisle and then Preston, with whom he picked up an FA Cup winners' medal in 1938. His first managerial job was at Carlisle but he was also in charge at Grimsby, Workington and Huddersfield before joining Liverpool.

One of the local newspaper reports on his arrival at Anfield recounted his approach to the game. "Shankly came because he thinks he can make Liverpool one of the greatest teams in the country. He will make a player kill a ball and move it all at the same time..." Shankly wanted no hard drinking and no smoking amongst his players, though they were allowed to drink herbal tea!

The Bob Paisley Suite was similarly full of photographs of his Championship winning teams and Paisley himself with Joe Fagan in the Anfield boot room. Paisley won a Championship medal with Liverpool in 1947 and first joined the coaching staff in 1954, eventually becoming Shankly's right-hand man. He inherited the manager's job in 1974 and became the most successful manager in the history of the English game before stepping down in 1983. He's now a vice-president.

I left the ground and walked along the back of the Centenary Stand past a block of flats called Anfield Court. Darkness was beginning to envelope the sky around us as we crossed Stanley Park towards my car parked in front of the Anfield Stadium. I could just make out the silhouette of Goodison on the other side of Stanley Park. I would return to get a closer look at the end of the season.

STARSHIP ENTERPRISE
Huddersfield Town v Hull City – The McAlpine Stadium
17 April 1995

"We call that the Starship Enterprise," said the steward walking along the touchline in the shadow of the Main Stand. A light rain was drizzling across the stadium on a damp spring Saturday afternoon. The steward, a short woman in her thirties, looked up at the control box supported by two of the huge concrete struts which form the base of a floodlight pylon at Huddersfield's futuristic McAlpine Kirklees ground. Science fiction meets the Endsleigh League.

I'd driven to the stadium on Easter Monday for a match against Hull. On the road I passed a car flying a Reading flag and another with a Reading scarf in the back. One car trailed a Nottingham Forest scarf from the back window, while another displayed an Arsenal sticker. I was clearly not the only football fan travelling to see a match over the Easter holidays.

I'd heard a lot about Huddersfield's super new stadium from other supporters on my travels and I was looking forward to seeing it first-hand. The ground was hard to miss. As I turned off the High Road the banana-shaped roof of the Main Stand appeared like a huge alien space-craft out of the film 'Close Encounters of the Third Kind'. I wondered if Spielberg had been called in to help design the state-of-the-art arena. I thought I might see aliens, but the only ones I came across were the away fans.

The new 51-acre site was close to the banks of the River Colne, near the club's former ground at Leeds Road. It was an emotional afternoon on 30th April 1994 when Huddersfield said goodbye to their home for the past 83 years with a League match against Blackpool. The game was billed as the 'End of an era' and many of Town's former stars turned up including Ray Wilson, England's full-back in the '66 World Cup Final.

Chris Drake explained in the club programme how it felt on the day: "The real depth of feeling for the club could almost be touched as the fans engulfed the pitch as they said farewell to the ground that had provided so much pleasure and agony for so many people down the years. As a traditionalist I felt a mixture of sadness and even resentment that it was to be replaced by the new stadium. Those feelings have now been tempered during the close season and the new plush surroundings offer fresh optimism for a club so long in football obscurity."

The land around the new McAlpine Stadium was being landscaped with small trees and shrubs as if it was set in the grounds of a hotel.

There were piles of bricks stacked up on one side where I pulled off the main road as if a building had just been demolished. I could also see an old mill nestling in the hills to the right of the stadium. Huddersfield, with a population of almost 125,000 people, was one of Yorkshire's great cloth towns. It occupies a striking position among the hills and is laid out with wide streets.

I parked in a side road and walked across a bridge over the River Colne. As I began climbing the hill up Stadium Way towards the ground I could see the tops of the floodlights, then the upper section of the South Stand and gradually the John Smiths (Kilner Bank) Stand. It was pouring with rain, but I didn't care. It was exciting to see one of the country's most advanced football grounds. When I reached the top of the hill I could see the whole of the new ground laid out before me. The sign on the front of the South Stand said simply: 'Welcome to the Alfred McAlpine Stadium'.

Huddersfield were founded in 1908 after a meeting in the Imperial Hotel two years earlier at which it was decided that a football club could be formed in what was a strong rugby area. The competition from the oval ball is still there today and Town actually share their new ground with the local Rugby League club. The football club ticket office was to the right of the main entrance, while the rugby club offices were to the left decked out in claret and gold. I walked around the stadium to the open end where the North Stand would eventually be built when the club could afford it. From the car park behind the goal I could see the whole town down below me.

The floodlights looked as if they were perched on huge concrete bunches of bananas. The lights were originally supposed to be positioned on top of the so-called banana trusses which support the roofs of the stands. The problem was that the roof on the John Smiths stand, opposite my seat in the main Riverside Stand, was too low. The lights would have shone into the eyes of fans seated on the lower tier, like me. More traditional floodlights were the 'spectator friendly' solution.

There was a light rain drizzling across the stadium as I took my seat. The Hull fans in the corner of the South Stand to my right were clearly impressed by The Alfred McAlpine Stadium, to give the ground its full name. "Shit ground, no fans. Shit ground, no fans," they sang. The irony was not lost on the home supporters who were clearly proud of their club's new premises. Hull have ambitions to put executive boxes on top of the supermarket which backs onto one end of their Boothferry Park ground; they just don't have the money. A new stadium like

Huddersfield's was just a dream for Tigers' fans.

"Where were you at Boothferry Park, where were you at Boothferry Park," they sang more realistically later in the first half followed by a quick round of "We are Hull, we are Hull, we are Hull". Strangely, the Huddersfield fans didn't respond. With the north end of the ground yet to be built, and the other end occupied by away fans, the home supporters seemed to lack a focal point. Or perhaps it was nervousness as their team struggled to grab the automatic promotion spot by becoming Division Two champions.

As I drove up to Yorkshire, through the beautiful countryside with its hills and dales, I'd heard on the radio that their promotion rivals Birmingham had lost 1-0 in a morning game at relegation-threatened Cambridge. Since the Blues would have two games in hand after Huddersfield's match against Hull, it was vital for The Terriers to win. The club was top of the Second Division and aiming to get back to the big time.

In the mid '20s Huddersfield dominated League football. They won the FA Cup in 1922 and were runners-up in the League in 1923 before becoming the first club ever to win the First Division title three seasons in a row between 1924 and 1926. They were presented with a large shield by the Football League to commemorate their achievement and visitors to the ground can see the trophy at the top of the stairs on the first floor of the executive suites. They were also runners-up in 1927 and 1928 before the glory days ended. If they'd won all six titles the record would have stood forever!

Only Arsenal (1933-35) and Liverpool (1982-84) have emulated that triple title feat. Ironically, it was the great Herbert Chapman, who later took Arsenal to three successive League Championships, who steered Town to their first two League titles. Chapman's Arsenal also ended Town's record-breaking unbeaten home run in the FA Cup from 1913 until 1932!

Town stayed in the First Division until 1952, got promoted at the first attempt, were relegated again in 1956 and then spent 14 years in the Second Division. Bill Shankly was in charge for the first three of those campaigns, before joining Liverpool in 1959, and thus managed Denis Law who played for the Terriers also in the late '50s. Other great players to grace Huddersfield's old Leeds Road ground were Ray Wilson, who went on to become a member of England's World Cup Winning team in '66 when he was playing for Everton, and Steve Kindon who also played for Burnley and Wolves.

Huddersfield regained their place in the top flight in 1970, when players like Trevor Cherry and Frank Worthington wore their colours, but lasted just two seasons in the First Division. By 1973 the Terriers had dropped into the Third Division for the first time and two years later were in the Fourth.

They began to climb back in the 1979/80 season when they won the Fourth Division Championship under Mick Buxton, later the manager of Sunderland. One hundred and one goals helped to secure the title and Huddersfield even briefly returned to the Second Division before dropping back to the Third in 1988. They were now hoping to recapture their scoring form to get out of the Second Division (the old Third Division).

Perhaps one way of boosting their striking power would be to offer their forwards the sort of incentive enjoyed by the top scorer in that Fourth Division Championship winning team Mark Lillis. He had a unique sponsorship deal from a local butcher who gave him a T-bone steak for every goal he scored. Lillis struck 20 times and didn't go hungry!

The new stadium deserved better football than that served up in the Second Division. And so did the supporters. Arthur Mellor, the Managing Director of Town-lottery sponsors Bristol Street Motors in Leeds Road, had put vinyl blue and white stripes and the shirt number of striker Andy Booth on a brand new 1.5 diesel Corsa to celebrate Town's promotion campaign. He'd even fixed up the number plates to read 'THE BEST'. "Originally we had the idea for plates saying 'GOING UP', but we didn't want to tempt fate," he said. "Basically, I'm a bit of a football nut. I've followed Town ever since I came to Huddersfield six year ago." The car was for sale at £8,485.

Booth was proving to be a hot property. He was hoping to retain his place in the England under-21 squad for the UEFA qualifier against Latvia in Riga the following week. The 20-year-old burst onto the scene the previous season with nine goals in the final 12 League games and played a big part in getting Town to the final of the Autoglass trophy at Wembley. A number of top clubs had already cast envious glances towards the young striker. The question was could Town hold onto their young star? Possibly.

"This is a great club for anyone to be at, especially with so much anticipation at the moment. But when you're from Huddersfield, like me, it's so much the better," said Booth. He had come from a well-known Huddersfield sporting family and his parents were part of Town's matchday staff. He wanted to be in the upper echelons of the League by the time his improved two-year contract, signed just before

Huddersfield went to Wembley in 1994, came to an end.

The McAlpine Stadium was certainly built for a higher level of football. When the club assessed its options for a new ground it followed a number of clubs who'd already moved into new stadiums. Paul Fletcher, Chief Executive of Kirklees Stadium Development and Huddersfield Town, and a director of Huddersfield Rugby League Club explains.

"The answer could have been very simple. We only needed to visit other stadiums recently built. Walsall's Bescot Stadium, Scunthorpe's Glanfield Park, even St. Johnstones McDiarmid Park Stadium seemed to answer the problem. But if we had followed any of these straightforward examples we would have ensured Huddersfield Town would never be a big club ever again. A basic eight, 10 or 12 thousand seater stadium would relegate the club to the lower divisions forever. We chose not to visit any of these stadiums. We had bigger plans for Huddersfield Town. We all had a dream, a vision, a mission."

On Valentines Day 1992 the project team left Manchester airport for Toronto. They decided to start by visiting probably the best stadium in the world: The Skydome. Canada's premier arena, and home of the Toronto Blue Jays baseball team, was finished in 1991 at a cost of $300 million. It's used for about 200 events a year, more than any other stadium in the world. Its features include a sliding roof, which closes in 20 minutes, and a hydraulic seating system used to create purpose-built pitches for a variety of sports and other activities including baseball, American football and soccer.

The stadium also houses a 360 bedroom Hilton Hotel in one of the stands, lounges, a leisure club and gymnasium, a nightclub and more McDonalds' sales points (80) than any other venue in the world. The hotel bedrooms overlook the pitch and can be converted to hospitality suites when events are being staged. At one Blue Jays match a television camera panned the stadium during a break in play giving three million baseball fans the perfect view of a naked couple on the bed in a hospitality suite! The project team came home inspired – well who wouldn't!

Initially, they considered an 80 bedroom hotel running parallel to the Riverside Stand, but this idea was shelved and replaced by a 450 seater banqueting suite. There were also plans for a practice pitch, but the project team decided a golf driving range would bring in vital additional revenue. A 'moat' around the pitch was also dropped as were shops, offices and a covered shopping atrium which would have linked the Riverside Stand to the hotel. The John Smiths Stand, which was to have had concessions and entrances at the back, was redesigned for a seven metre-wide concourse. The club hoped a covered area with excellent facilities and closed circuit television would pay dividends.

The term 'spectator friendly' became the theme for every decision from the quality seats to the 'knee room', toilets, concourse flooring, concessions and everything else. The project team constantly sought quality rather than quantity. The Kirklees Stadium design is based on computerised calculations of the ideal viewing distances and sightlines, resulting in an oval plan with four shell-like stands all close to the pitch.

The early plans also showed a completed 25,000 all-seater stadium with a 5,000 seater North Stand including a gymnasium and a health club. However, The Football Trust insisted that the club didn't overstretch its resources, pointing out that success on the pitch would attract enough money to build the fourth stand. The club hopes to start building within the next couple of years, keeping in mind that the foundations will have to be able to take 5-10,000 seats if Huddersfield reach the Premier League. There were also plans to include a cinema and a ski slope in the design for the new stand.

The £16 million stadium is a joint venture between the football club, Huddersfield Rugby League Club and Kirklees Metropolitan Council, who granted planning permission and put in £2 million in return for community facilities and the club's old ground at Leeds Road being made available for development. The club received £5 million from the sale of their former stadium and almost £3 million from the Football Trust. Simon Inglis writing in World Soccer magazine was amazed that the concept had turned into reality. "Who'd have believed it – a new breed of football ground, born in Huddersfield (usual associations: dour, grey, blunt). They'll be serving Bovril in the San Siro next!"

According to Town's Chief Executive Paul Fletcher: "It will become a venue for legends. It will see tears of joy and tears of sadness. Great victories by Huddersfield Town and Huddersfield Rugby League Club and also, without doubt, disastrous defeats. Fabulous memories of goals, tries, tackles, sending-offs. Memories that will be traded in bars, often distorted with age. Grandchildren will visit the stadium with their grandads... and one day bring grandchildren of their own."

And talking of disastrous defeats... Hull almost caused one when they took the lead through their big centre-back Rob Dewhurst seconds after the break. Most of the 12,000 crowd fell silent with the exception of the Hull supporters who went barmy in the South Stand. "I thought we did well in the first half against the wind and I told my players at half-time if it takes until into injury time to make it 1-0 that will be enough - but Hull scored before I sat down in the dugout," said then-Town manager

Neil Warnock. After that it was one-way traffic as Huddersfield sought the equaliser.

Twenty minutes into the second half the ball was knocked through to Booth. He controlled it and cued it up onto his right foot before shooting miles over the bar. "You fucking arsehole," shouted the Town fan behind me. The Hull keeper then delayed taking the goalkick. "Get on with it, you bastard," said the supporter next to me. Booth then got a free header which Hull keeper Alan Fettis did well to save on his line. "He shouldn't be missing those," said the Town fan.

Town had 17 goal attempts in the last 34 minutes when they won eight of their 11 corners. There were shots, headers, penalty claims, goalmouth scrambles. You name it, the Terriers threw it at Hull. But the Tigers held out gallantly to survive the second-half onslaught until centre-back Lee Sinnott grabbed his first goal for Town 17 minutes from time with a header at the far post from a fine angled cross by Mike Duxbury.

"You're not singing anymore, you're not singing anymore," rang out from the Town fans in the John Smiths Stand where most of the noise seemed to be coming from inside the stadium. "Neil Warnock's barmy army," sang the home fans. "Terry Dolan's black and gold army," responded the Hull fans to my right. The Huddersfield number four then ran onto a through ball and in his determination to reach it he clattered into the Hull keeper. "Psycho, psycho, psycho," chanted the Town fans. With a minute to go Town drove in a corner which came back off the far post and was followed by a goalmouth scramble. But still the Terriers couldn't score the winner. Then it was all over.

I'd enjoyed the electronic scoreboard almost as much as the football. In the first half Huddersfield had a shot which sailed over the bar. DEAD BALL flashed up on the screen with a picture of a gun alongside. Each time there was a corner a big white hand appeared pointing to a corner spot. The scoreboard also gave weather flashes: "IT'S GETTING WINDY" it announced towards the end of the first half, just in case I hadn't noticed as the rain swirled down across the front row of seats in the Riverside Stand – the only complaint I had about the design of the stadium.

And that wasn't all. At half-time there was an announcement over the PA system as details flashed up on the scoreboard asking for volunteers to attend an identity parade. "Six foot tall, of slim build, mousey hair, clean shaven. £5 per hour plus travelling expenses. To be held at Dews Police Station." (I wondered what would happen if one of the volunteers was picked out as the villain.) And if you were hungry at half-time the scoreboard had some suggestions. GET 'EM WHILE THEY'RE HOT flashed up after a picture of a hot dog being garnished with relish had appeared in full, delicious colour.

At the end of the match the two managers had their say at the formal press conference. "Full marks to our players for holding out and conceding only one goal," said Hull manager Terry Dolan. "Other teams might have buckled under the pressure but not Hull City. We don't give up even with five first teamers out injured."

"We feel disappointed, deflated, but my players can't give any more," said Warnock. "I think 90 points will win the title, unfortunately we can now get only 89, but it's still in the melting pot. We should have the title won by now but it's not this weekend that has cost us dearly – it's our trips to places like Wycombe, Swansea and Cardiff."

The Hull fans hadn't finished with their afternoon's entertainment though. As I left the stadium I heard a roar behind me outside the main entrance. Hull fans came charging along pushing and shoving the Huddersfield supporters and knocking a steward to the ground. "What happened?" I asked the shaken steward, a huge guy who looked as if he could look after himself. "They hit me from behind. One minute I was sorting them out and the next I was on the ground. I didn't know what had hit me." It was the first serious trouble I'd seen in 87 games of football. I suppose it had to happen sometime!

IN SEARCH OF KEVIN KEEGAN
Scunthorpe United v Scarborough – Glanford Park
22 April 1995

"Did you see Keegan play here?" I asked the St John's Ambulance man standing in the corner of the ground near the refreshment stall which served the best chips I'd had all season. "No. I'm not even interested in football. Bloody cold today isn't it." "What was Keegan like when he was here?" I asked the tall distinguished supporter with the Clark Gable moustache at half-time. "I never saw him play. I've lived in the area all my life, but I've only been coming to the football since my lad was about 10 years old. He's in his 20s now." Hadn't anyone seen King Kev play before he became rich and famous?.

Scunthorpe was an old iron and steel town of just over 65,000 people and home to one of the largest steel works in Europe. "There's 12 miles of road in there," said the taxi driver who took me to the match at the club's new purpose-built Glanford Park stadium on the outskirts of town. The history explained the club's nickname: The Iron. "The mill is about one-and-a-half to two miles square, I'd guess. I worked there once. Hard work it was. People don't like hard work these days. I always remember when they tipped the slag. There was a red glow like a sunset. It was beautiful."

It was hard to imagine beauty in a town with a name like Scunthorpe. I'd been looking forward to my visit since the name had conjured up all sorts of images in my mind and I wanted to find out if my hunch about the place was true. I thought it would be a grimy industrial town full of 1930's back-to-back houses and cobbled streets. I was completely wrong. The place was actually quite pleasant. The journey from the station to the ground took me through a suburban area of well-kept houses with neat gardens.

So this was the club where the current Newcastle manager began his career as one of the best footballers of his generation. After establishing himself as Scunthorpe's top scorer in the 1970-71 season with 11 goals, Keegan was sold to Liverpool where he joined up with former Iron's goalkeeper Ray Clemence at Anfield. In those days Scunthorpe played at the Old Showground, so-called because it was once the venue for all sorts of events including horse jumping and the Scunthorpe Show. The stadium was unique in the history of football grounds as the first to have a cantilever stand three years before Sheffield Wednesday had one built at Hillsborough.

Since Scunthorpe was an iron and steel town it should come as no surprise that the local football club should have the first stand that wasn't supported by posts to obscure the view for their fans. The United Steel Structural Company Limited, based in the town, built the stand in 1958 on favourable terms, no doubt hoping that orders for cantilever stands would come flooding in. They didn't, but at least Scunthorpe was on the map as the first club to have one. I bet their fans were over the moon!

The new cantilevered East Stand was opened for the start of Scunthorpe's first season in the Second Division after their promotion as champions of the Third Division (North). To mark the opening of the new stand, the second half of the Iron's opening game against Ipswich was covered live on BBC radio. Now that may not sound like much of an accolade, but Scunthorpe don't get live coverage on national radio every week. Twenty years later they played their last game at the Old Showground in the Fourth Division promotion play-offs in May 1988. Sadly, they lost to Torquay.

By the start of the following season they'd become the first League side of modern times to move to a new purpose-built ground when they opened their new £2.5 million Glanford Park stadium one-and-a-half miles outside the town centre on a new greenfield site just a mile away from the Old Showground. The stadium, which took 11 months to build, was paid for by the sale of the home they used for 90 years to a supermarket chain. There was enough money left over to clear the club's debts. The ground blazed the trail for those that would follow at Wycombe, Walsall and Chester.

The new stadium was opened by Princess Alexandra on 14th August 1988 for a match against a Football League X1 managed by current Wolves manager Graham Taylor. "I am delighted to be given the opportunity by the Football League to participate in this special event which has for me a special significance as it was in the Scunthorpe area that I grew up and fell in love with the game of football," said Taylor. His League team included Peter Shilton, Kevin Pressman, Peter Reid, Mark Ward and Trevor Francis.

Taylor had been a keen United fan as a youngster and often joined his dad in the press box at the Old Showground. He had fond memories of the day Scunthorpe held the mighty Liverpool to a 3-3 draw at Anfield. Before he was 16 he was training at the Old Showground with the juniors, but Taylor was allowed to drift away after a change of manager. He joined Grimsby, where he became the youngest person to gain a full FA coaching badge, and then moved to Lincoln. But the former England manager has never forgotten Scunthorpe. "It's my home town and United's results are always among the first I look for," said Taylor.

Scunthorpe could have used a couple of budding stars to help their play-off drive. They'd just been thrashed 5-0 by rivals Doncaster Rovers and were desperate to get back on the winning trail. Manager Dave Moore in his column called Young Moore's Almanac thought Scunthorpe were the better side for much of the first 45 minutes and that if they'd only lost 3-0 "people would have said we were unlucky and were on the wrong end of some diabolical refereeing decisions". I wondered how they played for the other 45 minutes! "Poor", Moore conceded, acknowledging that they had to "accept the criticism which came our way".

"No sooner do we get ourselves into a challenging position for the play-offs than we blow it. And it was particularly galling that we should reserve our worst performance of the season for a vital local derby when everyone was expecting big things of us. Last Saturday's dreadful defeat by Doncaster effectively put paid to our play-off hopes for this season. There can be no excuses, and you can't expect any sympathy after a 5-0 hiding, but I'm sure everyone who was here (all 4,366 of them) would agree that the scoreline did not tell the whole story."

Fortunately, Andy Kiwomya looked dangerous in the match against Scarborough - the first team to win at Glanford Park back in '88. He scored the third goal in a 3-1 win, but the home side still lacked ideas. Boro had more possession and were unfortunate to lose by two goals. Not that the home crowd exactly got behind their team. The freezing weather and driving rain didn't help. But it wasn't until the 90th minute when Kiwomya scored that they started singing. The travelling fans in the Yorkshire Electricity Stand were more vocal. "Come on 'Boro" was followed by "Seasiders".

The Scunthorpe fans on the Rodmill Terrace to my left even had the strangest habit of saying "Shhhhhh" whenever the scoreboard flashed up LATEST SCORES. I mean, it wasn't as if they were being announced. You could have read them and shouted your support as loud as you liked. "It just shows you how dim they are," said one elderly fan. I figured it was all tongue-in-cheek myself and actually found the whole thing rather amusing. It was certainly more entertaining than the football.

The Pleasure Island signs around the ground referred to the theme park in Cleethorpes and not, unfortunately, the thrills and spills of a Scunthorpe match. The programme advertised the attractions of the park owned by the club's official sponsors. "Only one price to pay for a fun filled day. Thrills & excitement for all the family. A Great Value Day Out. Rip-Roaring Rides. The Sensational Big Splash, The Boomerang, Razzle Dazzle, Flying Chairs, Whirler Twirl and Break Dance. Spectacular Shows. Billy Bob's Rock-a-Fire Explosion Show. Sea Lions and Parrots. Big Top Circus." There was no way The Iron could match that fun-filled extravaganza against Scarborough.

After the game the receptionist in the club office called a taxi to get me back to the station. Inside the waiting room was a lifelong Scunnies fan in his 60s. He'd braved the rain and walked the half-an-hour it takes to get to the station. "What did you think of Kevin Keegan when he played here?" I asked. "He was good. But he wasn't the best player we've ever had." I was surprised "Who was then?" I asked, thinking he might have given Ray Clemence the nod over his Liverpool and England colleague. "Barrie Thomas. We sold him to Newcastle, but they didn't use him well. He didn't get enough support and didn't fit in. Eventually he came back to Scunthorpe" I was to come across a picture of Thomas among Newcastle greats like Len Shackleton and Malcolm MacDonald on the wall of the Platinum Club Suite at St James' Park.

Thomas set a new club goalscoring record at Scunthorpe in the 1961/62 season with 31 goals in the Second Division. He was sold to Newcastle for £40,000 before the end of the season to the dismay of the Iron's fans. Many were disillusioned and refused to watch Scunthorpe anymore, saying the sale of Thomas had cost the club promotion to the First Division. United finished fourth – their best ever League placing – but not good enough to join the elite. A year later Thomas's replacement John Kaye was also transferred for £40,000, this time to West Brom, after scoring a hat-trick against Chelsea. Clemence was the next bright prospect to leave followed by Keegan.

Scunthorpe had failed to produce any more world class players, although Blackburn's Mark Atkins and Middlesbrough's Neil Cox started out at the Old Showground. The most famous sportsman to wear the Iron's shirt in more recent times was former England cricketer Ian Botham who made his debut away at Bournemouth in April 1980. His all-round ability stretched to the role of centre-forward or defender in the first team or the reserves. I wondered if anyone had seen him play for Scunthorpe?

THRILLER
Newcastle United v Tottenham Hotspur - St James' Park
3 May 1995

It was my second from last match. Newcastle against Spurs at St James' Park. Should be a great game I thought as I caught the train from Crewe. There's another St James' Park, of course, but only Exeter fans would think of it first and, given their financial plight, it may not be around for much longer. Up here there is only one St James' Park and that's the ground belonging to King Kevin and his black and white army.

So what sort of game was it between two teams fighting for a UEFA Cup place? A pretty low key affair really. Six goals, two sendings off and a penalty miss by Jürgen Klinsmann. Keegan described it as "the greatest advert for football I have seen this season." It was a true classic, probably one of the best games I've ever been fortunate enough to watch.

"I don't think we'll get anybody queuing outside asking for their money back," said Keegan afterwards. Hardly likely at a club which has some 33,000 season ticket holders out of a capacity of just over 35,000. Which made it even more remarkable that sitting next to me in the famous Gallowgate End was a bloke from Southend in Essex and his mate from Kent! Apparently, the club always holds back a couple of thousand tickets which go on sale the week before a game. He'd written in and, bingo, two seats amongst the Gallowgate die-hard home fans.

The main road outside the ground is called the Gallowgate, but the word originates from the public hangings that once took place from gallows erected where the Gallowgate End now stands. As I sat high up in a smart new executive box looking down at the Gallowgate on a tour of the ground the following morning, I wondered what the atmosphere must have been like at one of the public hangings and whether there was as much noise as there was the night of the Spurs match.

The Gallowgate End was now a brand new 11,000 seater stand built in 1994. The two guys next to me had driven for five hours to reach the ground and would head straight back after the match. "You won't get home until about 3 o'clock in the morning," I said, my brain having worked overtime to estimate their time of arrival. They nodded with a slight grin as if to say, "Yes, we know we're mad. Great isn't it" And it was in a way. One of the fascinating things about football is the lengths people go to so they can watch their team. Where would the players be without fans like these

I arrived at St James' Park from a Metro station east of the city in Chichester, South Shields, known locally as the Chi. It's more than a dozen stops from St James' but the train was already filling up with Toon Army fans. South Shields is between Newcastle and Sunderland and therefore divided between followers of the black and white stripes or the red and white stripes.

In the past the rivalry between Newcastle and Sunderland has been fierce and as far back as 1901 there was a pitched battle on the St James' Park turf. Things have changed since then, thankfully. "All the times I've been to Newcastle I've never seen any trouble," said the Toon Army fan sitting behind me with his son and daughter. That's hardly surprising. The cost of misbehaving inside St James' Park is prohibitively high. Anyone causing trouble has their season ticket taken away. For a Geordie, nothing could be worse. It's probably easier to get inside the Bank of England than to get a ticket for a Newcastle home game.

"There's been about five or six (supporters) who've lost them (season tickets) for offences like fighting, carrying a weapon and continuous bad language," said Newcastle Chief Executive Freddie Fletcher, the man partly responsible for bringing Kevin Keegan to Tyneside. "We fully recognise it's not a Sunday school picnic we're running here and football is an emotional game, but you have to ensure that people don't abuse it."

The Metro line runs along the Tyne both north and south side of the river. I was on the south side passing factory after factory, many of them covered in graffiti. Huge cranes hung their heads over the river as if trying to peek into its murky depths. "Gateshead Station next," said the driver. The Tyne was calm and the water glistened in the evening sunshine. It was the weather for cricket more than football. I got off at Monument, one stop before St James', and followed the Toon Army to the ground.

I walked past the building work that was still going on at the Gallowgate End and made my way along Leazes Terrace in St James' Street past the East Stand. The Georgian terrace must provide the classiest backdrop to any football ground in the country. I turned the corner and passed through the crowds outside the main entrance and into the main foyer of the Milburn Stand, named after the legendary 'Wor Jackie'. Milburn, who came from a famous footballing family, acquired what would now be called cult status. He was a formidable striker with a startling turn of speed but he rarely headed the ball because he suffered with fibrosis. Whenever he used his head the crowd cheered.

Milburn played his first match in 1946 and was the star of the team which won the cup three times in the 1950s, scoring the fastest ever FA

Cup Final goal after 45 seconds in 1955. Milburn scored 10 goals in 13 England appearances, after replacing Tommy Lawton as centre-forward, and 179 goals in 354 League matches. After Wor Jackie died in October 1988 thousands of fans paid their respects at his funeral. Milburn's statue stands outside the main shopping centre in Newcastle, but he would be most proud of the new stand named after him.

Originally expected to cost £4 million, the Milburn, or West, Stand had absorbed £5 million by the time it was finished in 1988. The comparison to the £8,082 14 shillings and 11d the club paid to build the old West Stand in 1906 was striking! The old stand, condemned by the local authority as unsafe, even had a swimming pool for the players which was later covered over and turned into a reservoir for the sprinkler system used to water the pitch.

As the door at the back of the main foyer opened I could see some of the Spurs players standing in line. Darren Anderton was at the front looking tense, while alongside him was Nicky Barmby, another of the young Spurs stars. I guessed Barmby wouldn't have been old enough to remember Kevin Keegan in his Liverpool and England days.

Keegan first arrived at St James' Park as a player when he left Southampton for £100,000 in August 1982. He was 31 and Newcastle's first football hero since Malcolm MacDonald. His best days were probably at Liverpool and Hamburg, but his fading talent flickered brightly for a couple of seasons on Tyneside. The crowds soared and he didn't let them down. He was made captain and scored 21 goals in his first season. Newcastle finished fifth in the Second Division, but Keegan, despite being discarded by England, banged in 27 goals in the 1983-84 season to secure promotion.

He didn't play for the Magpies in the First Division. He'd already announced that he'd retire at the end of the promotion campaign. There's a photograph of the great man wearing a black and white Newcastle cap surrounded by hordes of adoring fans on the wall of the exclusive Platinum Club at St James' Park alongside legends like Hughie Gallagher and Malcolm MacDonald.

The difference between them and Keegan is that he has returned to manage the club. "I have been a manager for not much more than a couple of years and it really seems like ten," said Keegan. "So much has happened at St James' Park, which is the only place I wanted to manage anyway. When United asked me to succeed Ossie Ardiles there was no prospect of me turning it down. Having finished my playing career on Tyneside with promotion to the top flight in 1984, I knew that if I could turn a losing team into a winning one then it would be the most special place in the game to be manager."

"My gut feeling was that I could be that winning manager and, close as we came to relegation to the old Third Division in these first few months, I had the same gut feeling that we would stay up. Once we had, and I had been given the opportunity to strengthen the squad, we enjoyed a wonderful season to finish as First Division champions. Very early in the campaign we were locking thousands of fans out. That did not surprise me in the slightest.

"The one thing I knew for certain when I took this job in February 1992 was that if I could give the Geordies just a glimpse of a brighter future, something worthy of their support, then they would back me to the hilt. That's how it was when I was here as a player and when you have supported failure for more years than you care to remember the prospect of something better – and lasting – is very appealing."

A lot of the credit for the transformation of St James' Park must go to Sir John Hall, whose millions have helped finance the redevelopment of the ground. Surprisingly, he was initially reluctant to get involved. "I never wanted to become chairman of Newcastle United. They can write that on my gravestone because it's the rock solid truth. I wanted the club to change, of course, because without change and investment it was never going to be the club the most loyal supporters in the game deserved."

Sir John may have once been reluctant but there was no escaping his influence now. The terracing at the Leazes Park End of the ground had been replaced by the £5.6 million Sir John Hall Stand, with seats for just over 11,000. Whatever they put on his gravestone, the stand will ensure that Sir John's name lives on.

Hall started to get really involved when Newcastle faced relegation to the old Third Division for the first time in their history. "To have gone down would have been catastrophic." The rest is history, as they say. Under Hall turnover has soared from £5 million a couple of years ago to three times that amount. Newcastle have spent almost £20 million on ground improvements to comply with the Taylor Report.

The ground has been chosen as a venue for the 1996 European Championships. Its selection is belated compensation because St James' Park was not used to stage games in the 1966 World Cup following a dispute with the city planners over a lease. Newcastle were so incensed that they threatened to leave the city - the use of Sunderland's Roker Park to stage some of the matches didn't help.

"My ambition is to turn Newcastle United into one of the finest clubs in Europe," says Sir John. "We are some way from that, but we have come a long way in the last two years and as long as our fans understand that if they want us to be genuinely ambitious they cannot have their soccer on the cheap then we can look ahead to an even better future. But I know how much this club means to Geordies everywhere. And that's why I'm the chairman when I never wanted to be."

The chairman's stand was as packed as the rest of the stadium when the Newcastle and Spurs players came out onto the pitch. An awful song with the refrain 'Howay the Lads' was being played by the club DJ. I'm sure the home fans were as relieved as me when it was time for the game to start – and the song to end! As the teams prepared for the kick-off the noise inside the ground was deafening.

After 10 minutes Newcastle were two goals ahead through Gillespie and Peacock, their first for the club, and the atmosphere had risen to new heights. A wall of noise swirled around the stadium as the Toon Army celebrated. Their joy was short-lived. Tottenham hit a purple patch which saw first Barmby, then Klinsmann and, finally, Anderton put Spurs ahead in a six minute spell midway through the half. Anderton's goal was copybook stuff – a 25 yard curler into the top left-hand corner of Srnicek's goal. It was unbelievable. The home fans were stunned. It took them a long time to find their voice again but when they did they got behind their team. "Sing your hearts out for the lads, sing your hearts out for the lads," sang the faithful.

The second half also began brightly with both sides playing entertaining, attacking football. Then Barmby broke clear, rounded Srnicek and was brought down. Penalty. But worse was to follow for Newcastle. The referee held up the red card and their popular keeper was off. The crowd were in uproar. Boos rang around the ground as the fans reacted angrily to the decision. Former Liverpool keeper Mike Hooper was brought on to replace Ruel Fox and his first job was to face the penalty from Klinsmann. The tall blonde German striker ran up and drove the ball towards the centre of the goal. Hooper dived to his left but managed to save the ball with his feet. The home fans went wild, the noisiest they'd been all night. It was the turning point in a match of turning points.

In the 65th minute Spurs central defender Colin Calderwood received his second booking for a foul on Malcolm Allen and joined Srnicek in the showers. Hooper then saved brilliantly to keep out another Anderton blockbuster. But the last word was left to the inimitable Peter Beardsley. Spurs defender Sol Campbell failed to cut out a through ball and Beardsley got in behind him like lightening to drive the ball past Ian Walker in the Spurs goal from 15 yards.

Soon afterwards Beardsley collected the ball and walked across to the corner of the Gallowgate and Milburn Stand to take a corner while Keith Gillespie was receiving treatment nearby. The fans applauded and Beardsley clapped them and put up his right thumb. The show of mutual respect and warmth of feeling was genuine. They appreciated his genius, he was grateful for their support. Newcastle pressed for a winner. It was not to be and a draw was probably a fair result.

After the match I stood in the Gallowgate just taking in the feeling of being inside such a magnificent stadium. As I soaked up the last bit of atmosphere, I was starting to get nostalgic. My record attempt nearly over, I realised I'd been living in a fantasy world.

Most people do not watch a league match every two to three days. They don't drive or take trains all over the country to football grounds all week, every week. They live normal lives with jobs and wives and kids. They go down the pub with their mates, or to the cinema or take the missus out for a meal. Me, I'd had little time for anything but football over the past nine months. It would soon be time to return to the real world. As I made my way out into the streets surrounding St James' Park I felt I was leaving behind more than just another football stadium. I was leaving behind a way of life.

After spending the night in South Shields I returned to St James' Park the following morning for a ground tour. The other tourists included a Norwich fan taking a course in Newcastle (the place not the language!). We were taken down some steps towards the tunnel first of all. A black and white sign with the words 'Howay The Lads' stands proudly over the exit like the one at Liverpool which proclaims 'This is Anfield'.

Next it was the dressing rooms. Each player's number was painted on the wall above his peg with a marker pen. "We used to have proper numbers, but the kids would peel them off on these tours so we decided to use a pen. All the first team numbers were there with the exception of number nine. "When Andy Cole was here the kids rubbed their fingers over his number just to take something of his home with them," said the guide.

I wasn't sure if I'd ever make it back to St James' Park, but I knew I'd probably never see Klinsmann play there again. When he announced at the end of the season that he would be leaving Spurs for Bayern Munich I knew I was right. Being there to see the German star score in front of the Gallowgate was worth the journey all on its own. He would be missed.

GLADWYS SINGS THE BLUES
Everton v Southampton – Goodison Park
6 May 1995

I'd made it at last. Goodison Park was my 93rd football ground. I'd journeyed almost 20,000 thousand miles, seen 372 stands and terraces, more than two thousand players, two broken legs, countless goals, near-misses, ricochets, headers, corners, shots, tackles, penalties, fans and more taxis, buses, planes and trains than some people travel on in a lifetime. And it seemed like a lifetime since I began back in September. But now I'd reached my final game: Everton, about to win the FA Cup, against Premier League survivors Southampton.

Like a relegation-haunted manager I too felt as if I'd only just survived the season. I'd probably seen as many games as the most peripatetic bosses in football. I hadn't taken on the viewing workload of most scouts, but they tend to stick to one area whereas I'd been to every town and city in the country that boasted a League team.

It was a fitting finale to finish at Everton's Goodison Park on a glorious sunny afternoon in early May for what would be the club's last home match. It had been a season of highs and lows which saw them battling relegation as they progressed to the FA Cup Final against Manchester United. Today the crowd was more preoccupied with League points than Cup glory. Most supporters would rather their team stayed in the Premiership than tasted cup success.

I parked my car in Stanley Park which separates Goodison from Anfield. I could see Liverpool's ground ahead of me on top of the hill which drops down to Everton's home on the other side of the park. It's ironic that Everton – the name comes from the district to the west of Stanley Park – originally played at Anfield for eight years from 1884 to 1892. They even won their first Championship at the ground in 1891. It was only when Everton left after a dispute with their landlord that Liverpool were formed.

The Toffees, named after a shop called Ye Ancient Toffee House close to the club's Sandon Hotel headquarters, moved to Mere Green, later renamed Goodison Park, on the north side of Stanley Park. They paid just over £8,000 for the new ground - a large sum even in those days. Goodison was to became the country's first major football stadium. In September 1892 Everton beat Bolton 4-2 in the first match played at what was described as "one of the finest and most complete grounds in the kingdom".

I couldn't see Goodison as I left my car and walked through Stanley Park towards the ground, but it wouldn't be hard to find. Hundreds of Evertonians in their royal blue replica shirts and blue and white scarves and hats were descending on the stadium as if it were a temple. I glanced back at Anfield standing proudly on the horizon. It seemed to be keeping an eye on the proceedings below so it could report back to Liverpool boss Roy Evans.

I could hear the shouts of youngsters playing football behind the car park. One team in royal blue, the other in red. You wouldn't expect anything else in this part of Merseyside. It was a beautiful spring afternoon. The daffodils in Stanley Park's Marie Curie Field of Hope were past their best, but bluebells had popped up to take their place. At the other side of the park I could see the top of Goodison's impressive new Park End stand ahead of me, partially hidden behind a used car lot.

I made my way towards the Main Stand in Goodison Road. The streets were packed with Everton fans desperate to join the queue for the lower tier of the Gladwys Street End. The rest of the ground was sold out. Relegation fears and cup fever had attracted the fans to Goodison.

The main entrance stands opposite a row of terraced houses. Above the various entrances in Goodison Road is a large board with instructions on how to get to each part of the ground – very useful for away fans. I collected my tickets for the Family Area and was taken down the tunnel and out onto the pitch before the match by an official.

The official ran through some of Everton's history, including the fact that they once played at Anfield. Interviews with the players and manager Joe Royle were being played out over the PA along with background on the two teams. "It can be a nightmare trying to announce the players names," she told me. "Our announcer has just been told it's not Amokaachi but Amokatchi, so he's got that wrong all season." The big Nigerian forward had wandered past us just ahead of David Unsworth as we walked towards the tunnel. "It's a good job he doesn't have to announce the name of the Portsmouth winger who everyone calls Precki," I said. "Well, he used to play for us, you know, so he's already had practice at getting that one wrong."

After the tour I walked back along Goodison Road to take my seat in the Family Area amidst a sea of blue and white. Two teenage boys were standing by the refreshment stand dressed up with royal blue and white painted faces and blue curly wigs. Royal blue balloons drifted across the heads of the supporters. Flags were being waved. Along with the red and white of the Southampton fans opposite, the ground was a colourful spectacle.

The noise began to pick up as the kick-off approached. Joe Royle was fully aware of the importance of their support. "Make no mistake, the vocal support, especially at home, has been comparable with anything in the country and it is no coincidence that our home form in particular has been so encouraging with the fans behind us roaring us on."

I looked across at the Southampton supporters sitting opposite in the corner of the Bullens Road Stand. They were taunting the Evertonians with chants of "Down with the Villa. You're going down with the Villa". The white wooden boards running along the balcony wall which divides the upper and lower tiers of the stand were decorated with a blue criss-cross pattern in steel. It was the hallmark of one of football's unsung heroes, architect Archibald Leitch. He was responsible for the building of many famous grounds including White Hart Lane, Fratton Park, Craven Cottage, Bramall Lane, Villa Park, Roker Park, Old Trafford – the list is almost endless.

I guessed none of the Everton supporters had ever heard of Leitch, still less realised he'd designed the Bullens Road Stand. But his work was still there for all to see, even if they don't take much notice of it in these days of cantilever stands and removable pitches. Leitch's double-decker stand was built in 1926 for £30,000. EVERTON is picked out in white from among the blue seats.

Leitch also designed the original Main Stand at Goodison, built in 1909 and replaced in 1971 by the present three-tiered stand on Goodison Road. The old stand cost £28,000, while the new one, albeit nearly twice as big, and the largest in Britain until Chelsea built their East Stand, cost £1 million. It is divided into three sections. The front part, where I was sitting, had a line of executive boxes behind it, though they weren't part of the original design. The middle section is for VIPs like the directors, match sponsors and other visitors. There's a lift to the upper tier - only the second I'd come across at any League ground along with the one in the Milburn Stand at St James' Park. "I haven't been up there though," said the official pointing to the upper tier, "I'm scared of heights." I could see why, as I looked up at the seats near the top. They were far above ground level, offering a superb view.

The Main Stand contains a portrait of the legendary William Ralph 'Dixie' Dean, Everton's record goalscorer with 349 goals between 1925 and 1937, including the Football League record of 60 in the 1927-28 season when he was just 21-years-old. Next to the picture is a commemorative inscription saying he died in March 1980 after the Merseyside derby at the age of 73. The Guardian's Stephen Bierley quoted a friend's daughter who, on her first visit to Goodison read the plaque and said, "No wonder. He shouldn't have been playing at that age." His ashes were scattered at Goodison, scene of his most fruitful years when he was often described as the best centre forward England has ever produced.

Dean was born in Birkenhead and joined Tranmere Rovers in 1924 before being sold to Everton the following year. His career was threatened in 1926 after he fractured his skull in a motorbike accident. However, he soon recovered to score 18 goals in 16 appearances for England and to help Everton win the title in 1928 and 1932 as well as the FA Cup in 1932. Herbert Chapman offered Everton "anything they wanted" for Dean's services but they wouldn't sell. In 1936 Dean broke Steve Bloomer's record of 352 League goals and when he left Notts County in 1939 for Sligo Rovers he'd scored a career total of 473 goals (including 37 hat tricks) in 502 League, FA Cup, representative and international matches between 1923 and 1939.

Dean lived in one of the club's terraced houses next to Goodison and was therefore very familiar with the Church of St Luke the Evangelist which cuts into the ground in the corner between the Main Stand and the Gladwys Street End. The church is only a few feet from the stands and is a well-known landmark in the area. I hadn't noticed it from my seat in the Main Stand but I had a good look after the match. Everton once tried to have the church removed to acquire extra land but they failed. It's not always progress to remove long-standing oddities. They're what gives a ground character and distinguishes it from the other 91 League venues around the country.

The Gladwys Street Stand was rebuilt and covered in 1992 to provide the home fans with more modern facilities. The fanzine Gladwys Sings the Blues takes its name from the traditional end for home fans which cost £50,000 when it was built in 1938. George V1 and the Queen Mum came to visit the ground to see the stand just after it was completed.

The most recent Royle visitor was, of course, manager Joe who I'd met at Oldham's Boundary Park earlier in the season before he replaced Mike Walker at Goodison. He had turned things around since his arrival, but had so far failed to secure Everton's Premiership future following the club's abysmal start under Walker. But Big Joe, the club's star centre-forward in the 1960s and '70s, had been given royal treatment by the fans. They could see he'd made progress – Everton had lost only once in nine games and their form since November was top six stuff. The fans were firmly behind him and his efforts to restore the team to former glories.

"The Chairman and Board of Directors are committed to restoring the glory years to Goodison Park," said Royle. "Everything about the club is geared to that success, and it simply must be achieved. New faces will appear to supplement those players who have given their all to the club this season. Take it from me, a more genuine or honest bunch of lads you could not wish to meet. They have all been proud to pull on that blue and white shirt, as I was in my playing days."

Speaking of royalty, Goodison Park was the first League ground to be visited by royals when George V and Queen Mary came to inspect local schoolchildren in 1913. Goodison was also used by the Territorial Army for drill practice in the First World War and, shortly afterwards, the Chicago White Sox and New York Giants baseball teams played an exhibition match at the ground.

These days it's only used for football, though problems with the drainage had left the pitch in less than perfect condition. It seemed to have been heavily watered, one of Joe Royle's tactical innovations, but Everton still couldn't keep the ball on it. Southampton manager Alan Ball complained about the playing surface after the match. "Not like in your day," one reporter noted. "We used to pass the ball," said the Saints' flame-haired boss, a fiery member of Everton's 1970 Championship winning team. The pitch would be dug up and returfed after the match to get it ready for the Japan Brazil match played at Goodison as part of the International Challenge Tournament also involving England and Sweden. That game would see the return of World Champions Brazil for the first time since the 1966 World Cup and was billed as 'A Summer Samba Special'.

Goodison was the venue for five games in the '66 World Cup including a wonderful quarter-final between Portugal and North Korea, which the Portuguese won 5-3, and the semi-final between West Germany and Russia. Only Wembley was chosen to host more games in the competition than Goodison. Some of the terraced houses originally built by the club for their players were demolished before the World Cup to improve access to the ground from Stanley Park. There would be no such preparations for the 1996 European Championships, however, since Goodison was overlooked in favour of Anfield.

The rivalry with Liverpool is known throughout the football world. It also explains some of the landmarks chalked up over the years involving Everton's arch rivals. For instance, the record crowd at Goodison was on 18 September 1948 for the First Division match between the two teams. The first floodlights at the ground were used for a friendly against Liverpool on 9th October 1957. And nobody needs reminding of the recent Wembley matches between the two sides starting with the first all-Merseyside final in the Milk (League) Cup of 1984, which Everton lost in a replay at Maine Road, and the two FA Cup Finals, in 1986 and 1989, which they also lost. Despite nine Championships, four FA Cups (five including the imminent victory over Manchester United) and a Cup Winners' Cup Everton always seem to have been in the shadow of their neighbours across Stanley Park. Those recent Cup Final defeats hadn't helped.

Today's game against Southampton was disappointing and didn't hold out much hope that Everton were about to come out of the shadows. The teams did, however, emerge from the tunnel into bright sunshine. As the players ran onto the pitch to the sound of the theme tune from the old Z-Cars television series they received a rapturous welcome from both sets of supporters. Like the girl who flirts all night before saying no, the afternoon promised much but failed to deliver. There was nothing for Southampton to play for since they had already secured their place in the Premiership after a season in which they had flirted with relegation in time-honoured fashion. For Everton Premiership safety was still to be confirmed and the stakes were therefore much higher.

Le Tissier was missing from the Saints teamsheet with a sore heel prompting Derick Allsop in The Sunday Telegraph to consider that, "Southampton without Le Tissier are like the VE celebrations without Vera Lynn". Well it's true that he makes the Saints midfield sing! Alan Ball was disappointed that his star player was missing. "I am sorry because I wanted him to play. I wanted the people here to see him." Even without the man Ball calls genius Southampton still played neat, tidy football and created more than enough chances in the second half to have won. According to Bill Borrows in The Sunday Times, "As Southampton's fluid, hard-working formation went comfortably about its business the Everton midfield, the self-styled Dogs of War, set about imposing themselves on the game and disrupting the rhythm of their opponents."

From where I was sitting Everton were crap. They struggled to control the ball; couldn't pass it accurately; and generally looked a very poor side. I could see why they were near the bottom of the Premiership and, on this form, they had no chance of overturning the form book against United in the FA Cup Final to be played a week on Saturday. The only two Everton players with any flair and skill were on the bench. The biggest cheer of the first half came when one of them, former Spurs star Vinny Samways, out-of-favour since Royle's arrival, was brought on to replace the ineffective John Ebbrell. Anders Limpar, the Swedish international who was to play such an influential role at Wembley, also appeared in the second half to give Everton some width down the right.

Why Samways and Limpar weren't in the team from the start only Joe Royle knows. "Why doesn't he play your two most skilful players?" I asked the Everton fan next to me, a bald man in his forties with a moustache. I felt he would have the answer since his comments throughout the match were unbiased and fair. "I don't know. We just can't understand it," he told me in a broad Liverpool accent, or should that be a broad Everton accent? Rory O'Keeffe, a Gladwys Sings The Blues editor, couldn't understand it either. In an article addressed to Royle he wrote: "No Everton fan could have any doubts as to your ability as a manager, but this conundrum still gnaws at my brain. Why play John (Ebrell)? Why for so long have you left out players such as Stuart, Grant, Amo (admittedly untried as yet in a midfield role), and Samways for a being surely sent by Satan to torture us all?"

Stephen Bierley's match report in The Guardian the following Monday was instructive. His earlier reference to Dixie Dean prompted him to conclude that "there were moments on Saturday when the whole of the Everton side seemed to be performing like septuagenarians on speed. Apart from a few notable teams and a few notable performances, the Premiership continues to represent the unending Sky-high triumph of mediocrity. And they do not come much more mediocre than this current Everton team... The one certainty is that Joe Royle must start spending some of (Chairman) Peter Johnson's money on players who are capable of a little more than scuffling about in the undergrowth... a ball-player must be found from somewhere and provided with a surface to match his skills. Everton remain in trouble because they are an extremely ordinary team."

Johnson, writing in the match programme, said Everton were at "the beginning of a new successful era" and that "the buzz is positively tangible". But there was certainly no chance of this Everton side repeating the amazing run of the 1931 team which scored 33 goals in just four games against Sheffield Wednesday, Newcastle, Chelsea and Leicester. Nigerian international Daniel Amokachi belied his recent good form, which had seen him hit five goals in four games, and was guilty of one particularly glaring miss in which he scooped the ball over the bar from inside the six-yard box. "Out of Amo" ran the headline in The Sunday Mirror. "He only scores the difficult ones," said Royle. Still, a point was better than nothing and as it turned out was more than enough to preserve Everton's Premier League status.

The last word on the match has to go to Martin Palmer of The Observer, obviously a frustrated poet. His first paragraph read: "Under burnished blue skies of Iberian intensity, the awful realisation of impending doom stole up on Everton like an afternoon hangover on a Spanish beach." Not quite how I would have described the match. And what was all that about impending doom? Try telling that to next year's Cup Winners' Cup entrants as they continue to battle in the Premiership.

After the match I drove to the Dolby Hotel, a new building on the refurbished Albert Dock, scene of my previous visit to see 'The Beatles Story' the morning of the Tranmere Oldham match at Prenton Park back in late January. The weather was considerably warmer now and the water from the Mersey lapped gently against the walls of the dock as I sipped a lager on the hotel terrace. I was feeling quite content now. I had set a new record which would be recorded for posterity in the 1996 Guinness Book of Records. Life was sweet.

That night I went with my girlfriend to find a restaurant down by the docks to celebrate. The first place we tried was Thai and it had just been filled by a party of 28. There aren't that many restaurants on the Albert Dock but eventually I queued for a table at an Italian called Est Est Est. There was a desk near the front door where diners were received by an authentic Italian owner, complete with stylish moustache. It was covered in pictures of past and present Liverpool and Everton players sitting at candlelit tables smiling alongside the owner and his waiters. Steve McManaman, Neil Ruddock, Ray Houghton, Graham Souness and David Burrows were just some of the star names. And the food that attracted them? Just like mama used to make and absolutely delicious.

The next morning I wandered back to the docks and walked along the Mersey. The famous Ferries were carrying passengers backwards and forwards and I could hear distant strains of Gerry Marsden's "Ferry Across the Mersey". I knew the song, of course, but hadn't realised they actually played it on every ferry crossing. It must drive the captain mad. The docks were also hosting an exhibition on the Liverpool industries of the past complete with pictures of factories turning out all sorts of useful gadgets. Footballers were still the most prized assets on Merseyside though.

As I looked out across the Mersey I felt it was fitting that my record attempt should end there. Liverpool Football Club and The Beatles were probably the most famous institutions the city had created. The best players Britain had produced arguably played for Manchester

United, but the best team we've ever put together was probably the Liverpool side of the 1970s and '80s which conquered Europe so often and collected the games' domestic honours almost at will. Merseyside was the heartbeat of football.

The rivalry between the two big Merseyside clubs is thankfully pretty friendly. But victory in those hard-fought derby games means a whole lot to the fans. A few weeks after Everton's cup success at Wembley I was returning home from work when I heard the faint strains of the song 'Singing the Blues' drifting along a London platform. As I approached the singer his words became clear. "I never felt more like Singing the Blues when Liverpool win and Everton lose, Oh Everton, You've got me singing the Blues." The Toffees fan was pretty drunk, but good-natured. He had reason to sing. His team had won the Cup and Europe beckoned. As the venue for my last match Goodison would always have a special place in my heart too. How does it go. "I never felt more like..."

PROFILE OF A RECORD

1) Carlisle United v Exeter City – Brunton Park – 10 Sept, 1–0, 6,213
2) Middlesbrough v Sunderland – Ayresome Park – 11 Sept, 2–2, 19,578
3) Wycombe Wanderers v Hull City – Adams Park – 13 Sept, 1–2, 4,626
4) Millwall v Burnley – The New Den – 14 Sept, 2–3, 7,375
5) Doncaster Rovers v Hereford – Belle Vue Ground – 16 Sept, 3–0, 1,938
6) Leicester City v Tottenham Hotspur – Filbert Street – 17 Sept, 3–1, 21,300
7) Ipswich Town v Norwich City – Portman Road – 19 Sept, 1–2, 17,405
8) Southend United v Bolton Wanderers – Roots Hall – 24 Sept, 2–1, 4,507
9) West Ham United v Arsenal Upton Park – 25 Sept, 0–2, 18,495
10) West Brom v Portsmouth – The Hawthorns – 28 Sept, 0–2, 13,545
11) Colchester United v Bury – Layer Road – 31 Sept, 1–0, 3,286
12) Chelsea v West Ham United – Stamford Bridge – 2 Oct, 1–2, 18,696
13) Southampton v Everton – The Dell – 8 Oct, 2–0, 15,163
14) Coventry City v Ipswich Town – Highfield Road – 10 Oct, 2–0, 9,509
15) Northampton Town v Mansfield – County Ground – 11 Oct, 0–1, 4,993
16) Leeds United v Tottenham Hotspur – Elland Road – 15 Oct, 1–1, 39,362
17) Bolton Wanderers v Oldham Athletic – Burnden Park – 16 Oct, 2–2, 11,106
18) Nottingham Forest v Wimbledon – The City Ground – 17 Oct, 3–1, 20,287
19) Manchester City v Tottenham Hotspur – Maine Road – 22 Oct, 5–2, 25,473
20) Portsmouth v Middlesbrough – Fratton Park – 23 Oct, 0–0, 7,281
21) Fulham v Carlisle United – Craven Cottage – 29 Oct, 1–3, 5,563
22) Wimbledon v Norwich City – Selhurst Park – 30 Oct, 1–0, 8,242
23) Oxford United v Blackpool – The Manor Ground – 1 Nov, 3–2, 5,610
24) Brighton v Bournemouth – Goldstone Ground – 2 Nov, 0–0, 5,631
25) Blackburn Rovers v Tottenham Hotspur – Ewood Park – 5 Nov, 2–0, 26,933
26) Oldham Athletic v Tranmere Rovers – Boundary Park – 6 Nov, 0–0, 6,475
27) Watford v Southend United – Vicarage Road – 12 Nov, 1–0, 8,551
28) Charlton v West Bromwich Albion – The Valley – 13 Nov, 1–1, 10,876
29) Sheffield United v Southend United Bramall Lane – 26 Nov, 2–0, 13,405
30) Bristol City v Grimsby Town – Ashton Gate – 3 Dec, 1–2, 6,030
31) Queen's Park Rangers v West Ham – Loftus Road – 4 Dec, 2–1, 12,780
32) Reading v Middlesbrough – Elm Park – 6 Dec, 1–1, 10,301
33) Barnsley v Bristol City – Oakwell – 7 Dec, 2–1, 4,305
34) Gillingham v Wigan Athletic – Priestfield Stadium – 10 Dec, 0–1, 2,257
35) Luton Town v Derby County – Kenilworth Road – 11 Dec, 0–0, 6,400
36) Bournemouth v Wrexham – Dean Court – 16 Dec, 1–3, 2,505
37) Notts County v Portsmouth – The County Ground – 17 Dec, 0–1, 6,382
38) Exeter City v Torquay United – St James's Park – 26 Dec (11am), 1–2, 5,538
39) Bristol Rovers v Bournemouth – Twerton Park – 26 Dec (3pm), 2–1, 6,913
40) Torquay United v Hartlepool United – Plainmoor – 27 Dec, 2–2, 3,172
41) Cambridge United v York City – Abbey Stadium – 28 Dec, 1–0, 3,285
42) Peterborough v Cambridge – London Road – 31 Dec (12.30pm), 2–2, 7,412
43) Brentford v Oxford United – Griffin Park – 31 Dec (3pm), 2–0 7,125
44) Sheffield Wednesday v Southampton – Hillsborough –2 Jan (3pm), 1–1, 28,424
45) Tottenham Hotspur v Arsenal – White Hart Lane – 2 Jan (8pm), 1–0, 28,747

46) Wrexham v Leyton Orient – The Racecourse Ground – 14 Jan, 4–1, 6,616
47) Port Vale v Tranmere Rovers – Vale Park – 15 Jan, 2–0, 7,944
48) Preston North End v Mansfield Town – Deepdale – 21 Jan, 2–1, 8,448
49) Tranmere Rovers v Oldham Athletic – Prenton Park – 22 Jan, 3–1, 5,581
50) Arsenal v Southampton – Highbury – 24 Jan, 1–1, 27,213
51) Aston Villa v Tottenham Hotspur – Villa Park –25 Jan, 1–0, 40,017
52) Lincoln City v Hereford United – Sincil Bank – 28 Jan, 2–1, 2,545
53) Chester City v Wycombe Wanderers – The Deva Stadium – 31 Jan, 0–2, 1,524
54) Plymouth Argyle v York City – Home Park – 5 Feb, 1–2, 5,572
55) Shrewsbury Town v Plymouth Argyle – Gay Meadow – 7 Feb, 3–2, 3,029
56) Stockport County v Chester City – Edgeley Park – 11 Feb, 2–2, 4,405
57) Chesterfield v Barnet – The Recreation Ground– 14 Feb, 2–0, 2,978
58) Swindon Town v Bristol City – The County Ground – 15 Feb, 0–3, 9,881
59) Hull City v Stockport County – Boothferry Park – 18 Feb, 0–0, 4,576
60) Darlington v Gillingham – Feethams – 21 Feb, 2–0, 1,548
61 Hartlepool United v Exeter City – The Victoria Ground – 25 Feb, 2–2, 1,440
62) Derby County v Bolton Wanderers – Baseball Ground – 26 Feb, 2–1, 11,003
63) Barnet v Exeter City – Underhill – 28 Feb, 1–1, 1,325
64) Berwick Rangers v Meadowbank – Shielfield Park – 4 Mar, 1–0, 455
65) Sunderland v Tranmere Rovers –Roker Park – 5 Mar, 0–1, 12,043
66) Rotherham United v Cambridge United – Millmoor – 7 Mar, 1–0, 2,208
67) Wolverhampton Wanderers v Sunderland – Molineux – 8 Mar, 1–0, 25,926
68) Birmingham City v Swansea City – St Andrew's – 11 Mar, 0–1, 16,191
69) York City v Wycombe Wanderers – Bootham Crescent – 14 Mar, 0–0, 2,800
70) Manchester United v Tottenham Hotspur – Old Trafford – 15 Mar, 0–0, 43,802
71) Swansea City v Shrewsbury Town – The Vetch Field – 17 Mar, 0–0, 4,130
72) Hereford United v Scarborough – Edgar Street – 18 Mar (12am), 2–1, 1,479
73) Stoke City v Reading – The Victoria Ground –18 Mar (3pm), 0–1, 10,006
74) Grimsby Town v Sunderland – Blundell Park – 19 Mar, 3–1, 5,697
75) Norwich City v Ipswich Town – Carrow Road – 20 Mar, 3–0, 17,510
76) Bradford City v Swansea City – Valley Parade – 21 Mar, 1–3, 4,417
77) Bury v Mansfield Town – Gigg Lane – 25 Mar, 2–2, 4,188
78) Burnley v Port Vale – Turf Moor – 28 Mar, 4–3, 10,058
79) Wigan Athletic v Hereford United – Springfield Park – 29 Mar, 1–1, 1,492
80) Rochdale v Barnet – Spotland – 1 Apr, 2–2, 1,834
81) Blackpool v Birmingham City – Bloomfield Road – 4 Apr, 1–1, 4,494
82) Liverpool v Southampton – Anfield – 5 Apr, 3–1, 29,881
83) Cardiff City v Rotherham United – Ninian Park – 8 Apr, 1–1, 6,412
84) Leyton Orient v Bristol Rovers – Brisbane Road – 11 Apr, 1–2, 2,338
85) Crystal Palace v Tottenham Hotspur – Selhurst Park – 14 Apr, 1–1, 18,068
86) Walsall v Rochdale – The Bescot Stadium – 15 Apr, 0–0, 3,766
87) Huddersfield Town v Hull – Alfred McAlpine Stadium – 17 Apr, 1–1, 12,402
88) Scarborough v Darlington – McCain Stadium – 18 Apr, 3–1, 2,182
89) Scunthorpe United v Scarborough – Glanford Park – 22 Apr, 3–1, 2,079
90) Mansfield Town v Torquay United – Field Mill – 29 Apr, 2–2, 3,216
91) Crewe Alexandra v Hull City – Gresty Road – 2 May, 3–2, 3,870
92) Newcastle United v Tottenham Hotspur – St James's Park – 3 May, 3–3, 35,603
93) Everton v Southampton – Goodison Park – 6 May, 0–0, 36,851